LOCOMOTI
AT THE
GROUPI

London Midland and Scottish Railway

LOCOMOTIVES AT THE GROUPING

London Midland and Scottish Railway

H. C. CASSERLEY

and

STUART W. JOHNSON

LONDON

IAN ALLAN LTD

First published 1966
This edition 1974

ISBN 07110 0554 0

Published by Ian Allan Ltd, Shepperton, Surrey
and printed in the United Kingdom by
Biddles Ltd, Guildford, Surrey

Acknowledgements

Grateful acknowledgement is due to the L.M.R. Publicity Department, Euston House, for a number of dimensional details, to Mr. G. H. Daventry, expert in Midland locomotive history, for kindly checking and making sundry minor corrections with regard to the M.R. section, and to Mr. G. M. Dunn for supplying certain particulars regarding locomotives taken over from the S.M.J.R.

Photographs are by H. C. Casserley unless otherwise stated.

Foreword

In presenting this series of four volumes dealing with locomotives inherited at the 1923 Grouping by each of the newly constituted Companies, it has not been found practicable to adopt a uniform lay-out throughout, owing to the widely varying differences of enumeration and classification inevitably adopted on each of the four railways, arising from the many hundreds of types of locomotives acquired from nearly fifty previously independent Companies each with its own individual stock of engines.

In the case of the London, Midland and Scottish Railway, notwithstanding that this was by far the largest of the four groups, inheriting approximately 10,400 locomotives (as against 7700 by the L.N.E.R., 4050 G.W.R., and 2400 S.R.) the position is comparatively simple in that this Company quickly evolved a comprehensive renumbering scheme whereby all classes were brought together in one series, thus providing an obvious method of presentation by enumerating the various types involved in simple numerical order.

A brief account of the numbering schemes previously adopted by the principal constituents will at this stage be appropriate.

Midland Railway

Previous to 1907 the numbering scheme on this line had been extremely haphazard; sometimes new engines had been constructed in consecutive series, and at others given scattered numbers. The position was complicated by an extensive 'duplicate' list, under which the older engines were given the suffix 'A' and new ones took the same number in what was known as 'Capital stock'. Further, a great deal of renumbering took place amongst older engines, some engines carrying as many as four or five different numbers during their career, often without any apparent reason, whilst again it was not uncommon for a certain number to be carried successively by more than one engine of the same class. In 1907 it was decided to renumber the whole stock on a logical basis, doing away with the duplicate list entirely and grouping each class in one continuous series. This very sensible arrangement was used by the L.M.S. as a whole on its formation, and many years later was copied, with some modification, by the L.N.E.R., and eventually adopted by British Railways for its standard types.

The Midland arrangement provided for four sub-groups: (a) Passenger tender engines (b) Passenger tank engines (c) Freight and shunting tank engines and (d) Freight tender engines, in each case the oldest engines coming first, with suitable gaps allowed for new construction, although eventually these were found insufficient in some cases and a certain amount of deviation from the methodical pattern had to take place.

London and North Western Railway

On this line no sort of established order prevailed, new engines being given the first vacant number which occurred, owing either to scrapping or placing of an older engine on which at that time constituted the 'duplicate list, not in this case by the addition of a suffix, but by renumbering above 3000. This process had gone on throughout the whole history of the L.N.W.R., with the result that by 1923 the only continuous runs of any sort occurred with the numbers 1801–1980 and a few smaller batches in the 2000's; this happened when the locomotive stock was increasing so rapidly that new blocks of numbers previously unused had to be appropriated to provide sufficient numbers.*

Lancashire and Yorkshire Railway

Much the same system prevailed as on the L.N.W.R., but in this case there was no duplicate list and there was a greater tendency to keep individual classes together to some extent, especially in later years.

Caledonian Railway

Classes found very often in continuous runs, although different batches of the same class would probably not run consecutively. The C.R. had a duplicate list system similar to the L.N.W.R., in this case by renumbering their engines over 1000.

Glasgow and South Western Railway

Previous to 1919 somewhat haphazard, with a quantity of engines on the duplicate list distinguished by the suffix 'A'. In that year Mr. Whitelegg renumbered the stock on an orderly basis bringing all classes together.

Highland, North Stafford and Furness Railways

These three of the smaller lines had much in common in this particular respect. With locomotive stocks totalling 173, 192 and 138 respectively, there was no great need under independent ownership

---

* This statement has to be qualified with regard to the numbers 1801–1980 insofar as that previous to 1897, the 1800's and 1900's had been used for the 'duplicate list', which was then transferred to the range 3000 upwards.

for any co-ordinated plan. Nevertheless, several of the classes on the Highland, were in fact numbered in one small consecutive sequence. All had duplicate lists formed by the addition of the suffix 'A' (sometimes 'B' on the Highland) to the number.

London, Midland and Scottish Railways

The highest number in the Midland list at the grouping was 4026, and with one or two very minor adjustments to make room for engines taken over from the North Stafford and Stratford on Avon and Midland Junction Railways, which were incorporated into the M.R. in the appropriate places consistent with their status as passenger, tank, or goods engines, the M.R. retained their old numbers in the new L.M.S. list, the range 1–4999 being the complete allotment.

L.N.W.R. engines were renumbered in the block 5000–9999* on strict Midland pattern, the small stock from the Wirral Railway also being included in this bracket.

The L. & Y.R. were given the range 10000–12999,* 10000's for passenger tender engines, 11000's for tanks, and 12000 for freight tender engines. The Furness, Maryport and Carlisle, Cleator and Workington, and Knott End were also incorporated.

It should be mentioned here that for a year before the Grouping the L.N.W.R. and L. & Y.R. companies had been amalgamated, but so far as the locomotive stock was concerned this made no difference and the stocks of the two lines retained their separate identities.

Finally the three Scottish lines were treated homogenously, the engines of each being renumbered respectively in the 14000's (passenger tender engines), 15000's (passenger tanks), 16000's (shunting engines) and 17000's (freight tender engines).* The highest number in the L.M.S. stock remained at 17997 for a number of years (a C.R. 0–8–0) until 1934, when the L.N.W.R. idea of a duplicate list was revived, again caused by the necessity of providing for new construction. As it was desired to give all new engines 4-figure numbers, the method was adopted of renumbering some of the older classes by the addition of 20000. After Nationalisation on 1st January, 1948 the B.R. renumbering scheme provided for all L.M.S. engines to be increased by 40000, thus bringing all L. & Y.R. and Scottish engines into the 50000's. A few exceptions to the general rule were made to certain classes, which were completely renumbered into a 58000 series, particulars of which are given in the appropriate places.

* It should be mentioned that some of the older engines never actually carried the new number allocated to them, being scrapped before due for repainting. This is referred to in the tabular lists of the smaller railways, where the information is known, but not the larger Companies, L.N.W.R., L. & Y.R., C.R. and G. & S.W.R.

This record deals in the main only with engines which actually came under the new ownership on 1st January, 1923† or already on order at that date, but reference is made to further construction of pre-grouping designs which took place subsequently.

These mainly concerned M.R. types, several of which were adopted in standard classes for several years and built in large numbers, in the case of the Fowler class 4 0–6–0's even as late as 1940. The only other pre-grouping designs perpetuated were twenty 4–6–0's and ten 0–4–4T's of C.R. origin, which came out in 1925–6.

A number of additional engines came into the fold in 1930, when the locomotives of the hitherto independent Somerset and Dorset Joint Railway were absorbed into the L.M.S. and these definitely need to be included, as although not actually becoming L.M.S. property until seven years after the amalgamation they must obviously be ranked as pre-grouping engines, most of them being of standard M.R. design in any case.

The livery first adopted as standard for the L.M.S.R. was Midland red for all passenger engines, tanks included, and black for the remainder. The M.R. style of large tender numerals and smokebox door number plate (both inherited originally from the U.S.A.) was also adopted as standard.

This was not at all popular in some of the other divisions, the C.R. people in particular were sorry to lose the distinctive Caledonian blue, but on the other absorbed lines at least, with the possible exception of the Furness and G. & S.W.R., the new magnificent livery could not be regarded as anything but a great improvement. The H.R. at Inverness adopted the new livery enthusiastically, and around 1927/8 could boast some of the best kept engines in the British Isles.

Unfortunately Crewe took very unkindly to the new regime, and after a certain number of desultory applications of red paint, it decided to follow its own course, and revert to repainting its engines out in funereal black. It even objected to the renumbering scheme, and for a time engines contrived to appear from Crewe works still with their L.N.W.R. numbers. The basic truth is of course that the L.N.W.R. were unable to stomach the emergence of their old rival the Midland as the senior partner in the new set-up.

In 1928 for economy reasons it was decided to reduce drastically the number of engines to be painted in the splendid, but unfortunately, expensive, M.R. red, and henceforth the standard livery was to be black, with a single red lining-out in the case of passenger engines. Only the largest express types, which included the Midland Compounds, continued to qualify for the red livery. It is perhaps

† Excluding Irish. See note on page 11.

some consolation to reflect that as the last of the Johnson single wheelers was withdrawn in the same year, none of these handsome engines ever suffered the indignity of acquiring black livery.

It may be pure coincidence, but at the same time seems fairly significant, that the general rot in the standard of maintenance which has reached such appalling standards in these days, seems to have originated about this period, when the outside appearance of a locomotive first began to be considered of secondary importance.

At the same time the practice of placing the engine numbers in large figures on the tenders ceased and the more usual cabside position adopted. This was another way in which Crewe had refused to conform to hitherto standard policy, very few of their engines ran with tender numerals. They also did not like the smokebox door number plates, eventually removing them even when they had been already fitted. St. Rollox also did the same, and they disappeared from most Scottish engines until the practice was again eventually revived by B.R.

About 1937 a new style of lettering and numerals was adopted in the form of block figures, but this was found unsatisfactory, and a reversion was made to the more handsome serif type which remained until the end of the L.M.S. regime.

At the time of writing (February 1966) pregrouping engines of the L.M.S. are almost extinct in ordinary service, although a few fortunately remain preserved. The survivors embrace five of Johnson's earlier 0–6–0T's, of which No. 41708, built in 1879, is the oldest engine on B.R. Whilst still nominally on the stock list they have not worked for some while, and by the time this book appears they will probably have been officially withdrawn.

There still at this time remain three of his later 1899 series, Nos. 47201, 47202, and 47231, forerunners of the 'Jinty' design adopted by the L.M.S. as a standard type, of which a good many are still in service.

There are also two small M.R. 0–4–0T's, Nos. 41528 and 41533, and the restored C.R. single and H.R. 4-6-0, both restored to working order, but scheduled to be placed in Glasgow Museum after which they will run no more. The last of the M.R.-built class 4 goods went late in 1965, but a few of the more numerous L.M.S.-constructed ones still remain, although scheduled for early extinction. None of the other constituents of the L.M.S.R. has now any representative locos at work on B.R., although mention might perhaps be made of a North Stafford 0–6–2T sold out of service still at work at a Colliery near Manchester in its old N.S.R. colours, in which it was repainted for exhibition purposes at Stoke a few years ago. This in itself is somewhat bizarre, in that the N.S.R. was the first of the railways which came into the L.M.S. (apart from a very few small lines) to become extinct as far as locomotives were concerned, the last of which was withdrawn from L.M.S. stock as long ago as 1939.

Of pre-grouping designs still remaining at the time of writing, the next few months will see the withdrawal of the last of the standard Fowler class 4 goods, leaving only a certain number of the 'Jinty' 0-6-0T design, direct descendents of the M.R. Johnson type, a few of which may well last into the fast approaching final era of steam on British Railways.

Irish Lines

For reasons of space it has not been found possible to include in this volume the two railways in Ireland which at the time were under the ownership of the Midland and L.N.W.R. respectively. The former Belfast and Northern Counties Railway was amalgamated with the English M.R. in 1903, and thereafter worked as part of that company's system, whose tentacles eventually stretched from Shoeburyness in the south east, Bournemouth in the south, through joint ownership of the Somerset and Dorset Joint Railway, Yarmouth on the east coast, reached by the Midland and Great Northern Joint Railway, Swansea in South Wales, Carlisle, Stranraer in south west Scotland, through part ownership of the Portpatrick and Wigtown, and over the Irish Sea, Belfast and Londonderry, reaching eventually Killybegs and Ballyshannon, on the County Donegal Railway, jointly owned by the Midland Railway and the Great Northern of Ireland.

The engines of the Northern Counties Committee, which the old B. & N.C.R. became known as, were latterly painted in Midland red, and after the grouping carried the new L.M.S. crest for many years until the L.M.S. interests in Northern Ireland were eventually sold out to the newly formed Ulster Transport Authority.

The L.N.W.R. also had a small system on the other side of the Irish Channel, the Dundalk Newry and Greenore Railway, worked by six Webb saddle tanks of pure Crewe design, which retained all their typical L.N.W.R. features until the line was eventually taken over by the G.N.R. and subsequently closed entirely.

2-4-0 Kirtley double framed Midland IP

Built 1866-1874

Weight:
41 tons 5 cwt.

Driving Wheel Diameter:
6′ 3″

Boiler Pressure:
140 lbs.

Tractive Effort:
12,338 lbs.

Cylinders:
18″×24″

Valve Gear:
Stephenson

Number built: 29.

First loco withdrawn 1895; last loco withdrawn 1947.
No. in service (1/1/23) 21; (1/1/48) 0.

1	5	9	13	17	22*
2*	6	10	14	18	
3	7	11	15	19	
4	8*	12*	16	21	

*Surviving engines in 1934 had 20000 added to their numbers, becoming 20002, etc. These are indicated by an asterisk.

In 1930 No. 1 was restored to its former M.R. state as No. 156A for preservation, but was subsequently broken up.

No. 20002 was given the same treatment in 1948, becoming M.R. 158A, and in this condition still survives as a museum piece.

2-4-0 Kirtley double framed Midland IP

Built 1870-1871

Usually referred to as the 800 class, the original numbers of the first engines being 800-829.

Weight:
40 tons 10 cwt.

Driving Wheel Diameter:
6′ 8″

Boiler Pressure:
140 lbs. (some engines 160 lbs.)*

Tractive Effort:
*Varied between 11424 lbs. and 14144 lbs. owing to differences in boiler pressure and cylinder dimensions.

Cylinders
18″×24″ (some engines 18″×26″)

Valve Gear:
Stephenson

Original number in class: 48.

First loco withdrawn 1905; last loco withdrawn 1936.
No. in service (1/1/23) 24; (1/1/48) 0.

24	31	36	40	49	60*
25	32	37	41	50	62
28	33	38	46	53	64
29	35	39	47	54	67

*No. 60, the only surviving engine in 1934, became 20060 in that year.

2-4-0 Kirtley Rebuilt Johnson single framed
Midland IP
Built 1871-1875

Weight:
36 tons 13 cwt.

Boiler Pressure:
140 lbs.

Cylinders:
18″×24″

Driving Wheel Diameter:
6′ 8½″

Tractive Effort:
11,424 lbs.

Valve Gear:
Stephenson

Number built: 60.

First loco withdrawn 1905; last loco withdrawn 1938.
No. in service (1/1/23) 50; (1/1/48) 0.

68	78	90	99	108	118
69	80	92*	100	109	119
70	81	93	101	110	120
71	82	94	102	112	121
72	83	95	103	113	122
74	84	96	104	115*	123
75	85	97	105	116	124
76	87*	98	107	117	126
77	89				

*Three surviving engines in 1934 became Nos. 20087, 20092, and 20115 in that year.

2-4-0 Kirtley Rebuilt Johnson single framed
Midland IP
Built 1874—1875

Weight:
36 tons 13 cwt.

Boiler Pressure:
140 lbs.

Cylinders:
18″×24″

Driving Wheel Diameter:
6′ 3″

Tractive Effort:
12,338 lbs.

Valve Gear:
Stephenson

Number built: 20.

First loco withdrawn 1921; last loco withdrawn 1933.
No. in service (1/1/23) 19; (1/1/48) 0.

127	131	134	137	140	144
128	132	135	138	142	145
129	133	136	139	143	146
130					

2-4-0 Johnson Midland IP

Built 1876

Some engines rebuilt with Belpaire firebox from 1926 onwards

Weight:
40 tons 10 cwt.

Boiler Pressure:
140 lbs.

Cylinders:
18″×24″

Driving Wheel Diameter:
6′ 3″

Tractive Effort:
12,338 lbs.

Valve Gear:
Stephenson

Number built: 10.

First loco withdrawn 1912; last loco withdrawn 1950.
No. in service (1/1/23) 8; (1/1/48) 1.

147 149	150 152	153*	154	155*	156

*Two surviving engines in 1934 became Nos. 20153 and 20155 in that year. The last mentioned engine was transferred to the Service Dept. from 1933-1936 and carried plates "Engineer South Wales" being stationed at Abergavenny. It was allocated B.R. No. 58020 in 1948 but never carried it.

2-4-0 Johnson Midand IP

Built 1876—1880

Some engines rebuilt with Belpaire firebox from 1926 onwards

Weight:
40 tons 16 cwt.

Boiler Pressure:
140 lbs.

Cylinders:
18″×26″

Driving Wheel Diameter:
6′ 6″

Tractive Effort:
12,770 lbs.

Valve Gear:
Stephenson

Number built: 40.

First loco withdrawn 1922; last loco withdrawn 1948.
No. in service (1/1/23) 39; (1/1/48) 1.

157* 158 159 161 162 163 164	165 166 167 168 169 170 171	172 173 174 175 176 177 178	179 180 181 182 183* 184	185* 186 187 188* 189 190	191 217 218 219* 220 221

*Surviving engines in 1934, indicated by an asterisk, had 20000 added to their number. No. 20185 was allocated B.R. No. 58021 in 1948 but never carried it

2-4-0 Johnson Midland IP

Built 1877-1881

Some engines rebuilt with Belpaire firebox from 1926 onwards

Weight:
40 tons 16 cwt.

Boiler Pressure:
140 lbs.

Cylinders:
18″×26″

Driving Wheel Diameter:
7′ 0″

Tractive Effoert:
11,863 lbs.

Valve Gear:
Stephenson

Number built: 20.

First loco withdrawn 1919; last loco withdrawn 1941.
No. in service (1/1/23) 20; (1/1/48) 0.

197 198	200 201	202 203	204*	205	206

No. 204, the only engine surviving in 1934, was renumbered 20204 in that year.

Class continued below (272-81)

2-4-0 Johnson Midland IP

Built 1876-1881

Most of the class rebuilt with Belpaire firebox from 1926 onwards

Weight:
40 tons 16 cwt.

Boiler Pressure:
140 lbs.

Cylinders:
18″×26″

Driving Wheel Diameter:
6′ 9″

Tractive Effort:
12,376 lbs.

Valve Gear:
Stephenson

Number built: 65.

First loco withdrawn 1925; last loco withdrawn 1949.
No. in service (1/1/23) 65; (1/1/48) 1.

192	213	229	240	251*	262
193	214	230	241	252	263
194*	215	231	242*	253	264
195	216*	232	243	254*	265
196	222	233	244	255	266*
207	223	234	245	256	267*
208	224	235	246	257	268
209	225*	236	247	258	269
210	226	237	248	259	270
211	227	238*	249	260	271
212	228	239	250	261	

*Engines surviving in 1934, indicated by an asterisk, had 20000 added to their number. No. 20216 was allocated B.R. No. 58022 in 1948, but never carried it.

Note: Engines 217-221 see Nos. 157-191.

Kirtley 0-6-0 No. 22822 as rebuilt with Belpaire boiler.

Standard Johnson 0-6-0 in approximately original condition (but with modified chimney and other details) as renumbered by B.R. One of the last to retain the Johnson boiler.

Later development of the Johnson 0-6-0, class 3. One of the only two to receive a superheater and extended smokebox.

Final development of the Johnson 0-6-0, the large class 4 superheated variety introduced by Fowler in 1911 and subsequently built in large numbers by the L.M.S. This view shows one of five engines constructed for the S. & D.J.R. in 1921, which did not come into L.M.S. stock until 1930.

'Cornwall' working a directors' special about 1920. L.P.C.

One of the 6′ 3″ variety of Webb 2-4-0's, all of which did yeoman service on the L.N.W.R. main line for many years.

'Precursor' No. 25188 'Marquis', rebuilt with superheater and Belpaire firebox.

'Experiment' No. 5457, 'City of Dublin', one of the not very numerous L.N.W.R. engines which aquired a smokebox door number plate, later removed. [L.P.C.

Small standard gauge works shunter at Crewe. [L.P.C.

L.N.W.R. Crane engine for service at Crewe works.

L.N.W.R. 'Box tank' No. 6407. These engines were at first incorrectly numbered in the passenger series, but were later altered to run from 7850 onwards with the freight tanks to conform to the standard pattern. [W. H. Whitworth

Webb 'Special Tank' allocated to Earlestown carriage and wagon works Unnumbered in the L.N.W.R. or L.M.S. lists, but eventually known as 'Carriage Dept. No. 8' Finished up at Wolverton in 1957. [L.P.C.

Ramsbottom DX goods, of which several hundred were built between 1858 and 1872, the earliest example of standardisation on a large scale. This view shows the engine running with its L.N.W.R. No. 3085 on the cabside and new L.M.S. No. 8072 on the tender [*W. H. Whitworth*

Webb 0-8-0, originally 3-cylinder compound, rebuilt as simple engine with small boiler.

One of the 4-cylinder compounds as running with large boiler and leading pony truck. This engine was scrapped in this form in 1928 and never converted to 0-8-0 simple, as were most of the class. [*W. H. Whitworth*

One of Robinson's 2-8-0 type for the Great Central Railway, constructed for the War Dept. and eventually disposed of after the first World War, fifty being aquired by L.N.W.R.

2-4-0 As 197-206

272 273	274 275	276 277	278 279	280	281

2-4-0 Stratford-on-Avon & Midland Junction 1P

Built 1903

Weight:
39 tons 5 cwt.

Boiler Pressure:
160 lbs.

Cylinders:
17″×24″

Driving Wheel Diameter:
6′ 1″

Tractive Effort:
12,922 lbs.

Valve Gear:
Stephenson

Number built: 1.

No. in service (1/1/23) 1. Withdrawn 1924.

Number 290 (S.M.J. 13). The engine never actually carried its allocated L.M.S. number.

Notes on the Midland Johnson 4-4-0s

Mr. S. W. Johnson built altogether 350 4-4-0s for express passenger working between 1876 and 1903. All but the last 85 were generally speaking of the same original basic design, but with driving wheels varying in diameter between 6′ 6″ and 7′ 0″ and the dimensions progressively enlarged with various batches up to the year 1901. Unfortunately most of them suffered from a common defect in being considerably underboilered, and from 1904 onwards the whole class—with the exception of the original thirty engines, which were never rebuilt, were completely renewed by Mr. R. M. Deeley, with much larger boilers pressed at 175 lbs per sq inch, and at the same time the decorative splashers which were one of the distinctive features of Mr. Johnson's engines, both of the 2-4-0 and 4-4-0 variety, were done away with, considerably altering the general appearance of the engines. Some of the series were provided in lieu with a handsome combined sweeping splasher covering each pair of driving wheels, whilst others had two separate splashers, the rear one of course combined with the cabside. Later modifications included in some cases the provision of Belpaire fireboxes, or extended smokeboxes, or both, with the result that by the 1920's there were many individual varieties amongst the still saturated engines. However, in 1912 Fowler, who had replaced Deeley, undertook a further complete rebuild, commencing with engine 483, with the provision of a superheater, raised framing over the coupling rods, and other modern (for that period) refinements, and the complete series ranging from 483 to 562 were speedily dealt with in this manner, the last conversion being in 1914. Attention was then given to the engines of the earlier series many of which were likewise reconstructed, and this involved in many cases a very complete reconstruction, as some of these engines had 6′ 6″ or 6′ 9″ wheels, but they emerged identical with the '483' class, which were 7-footers. Some authorities indeed regard them as completely new engines, but this is not very satisfactory, as some parts, probably the bogie wheels, cabs, tenders, and so on, would undoubtedly have been used, and the engines retained their old identities. This '483' class was of course adopted by the LMSR, with slight modifications, principally the substitution of 6′ 9″ wheels in lieu of 7′ 0″, as a standard class in 1928 and a further 138 engines, Nos. 563-700 were built to the design, but they do not come into the present picture. Of the original Johnson engines just described, a total of 265 all told, all but a few of the original 30, which as stated were never rebuilt, were still in service at the time of the grouping in 1923. The earliest engines remained in practically their original condition to the end, apart from such minor differences as change in chimney design, and one of them received an extended smokebox. Mr. Johnson's final designs of 4-4-0 were the large class 3 Belpaires, of 1900, again making a distinct breakaway from his well known traditional appearance, and the first five of the famous 3-cylinder compounds, the design of which was developed by Deeley in 1905. Both of these last classes proved to be a great improvement on their predecessors, and the eighty Class 3 Belpaires, later known as the '700's' together with the eventual forty-five Deeley compounds, were destined to bear the brunt of the express working for the remainder of the Midland Company's independent existence. This line, together with the S.E. & C.R. was unique amongst the principal British railways in never employing anything larger than a 4-4-0 for its top link main line duties.

4-4-0 Johnson Midland 1P

Built 1876

Weight:
40 tons 7 cwt.

Driving Wheel Diameter:
6′ 6″

Boiler Pressure:
140 lbs.

Tractive Effort:
12,770 lbs.

Cylinders:
18″×26″

Valve Gear:
Stephenson

Number built: 10.

First loco withdrawn 1911; last loco withdrawn 1930.
No. in service (1/1/23) 6; (1/1/48) 0.

300	303	304	305	306	308

4-4-0 Johnson Midland 1P

Built 1877

Weight:
43 tons 14 cwt.

Boiler Pressure:
140 lbs.*

Cylinders:
18″×26″

Driving Wheel Diameter:
7′ 0″

Tractive Effort:
11,863 lbs.*

Valve Gear:
Stephenson

Number built: 20.

No. 323 rebuilt 1909 with extended smokebox.
*Some engines had 160 lbs. pressure with 13,558 lbs. tractive effort.

First loco withdrawn 1904; last loco withdrawn 1934.
No. in service (1/1/23) 10; (1/1/48) 0.

310 311	314 317	319 320	323 325	326	327

4-4-0 Johnson Somerset & Dorset Joint 2P

Built 1891

Rebuilt 1907 onwards

(Taken into L.M.S. stock 1930)

Weight:
46 tons 8 cwt.

Boiler Pressure:
160 lbs.

Cylinder:
18″×26″

Driving Wheel Diameter:
5′ 9″

Tractive Effort:
13,523 lbs.

Valve Gear:
Stephenson

Nos. 302 and 303 latterly carried Belpaire boilers.

Original number in class: 6.

First loco withdrawn 1928; last loco withdrawn 1931.
No. in service (1930) 4; (1/1/48) nil.

(former S. & D.J.R. number in brackets)

300 (14)	301 (15)	302 (17)	303 (18)

No. 300 never carried its L.M.S. number.

4-4-0 Deeley Somerset & Dorset Joint 2P

Built 1908
Rebuilt Belpaire firebox 1921

(Taken into L.M.S. stock 1930)

Weight:
47 tons 8 cwt.

Boiler Pressure:
175 lbs.

Cylinders:
18″×26″

Driving Wheel Diameter:
6′ 0″

Tractive Effort:
15,795 lbs.

Valve Gear:
Stephenson

Number built: 2.

First loco withdrawn 1931; last loco withdrawn 1938.
No. in service (1930) 2; (1/1/48) nil.

320 (77)	321 (78)

4-4-0 Johnson/Deeley Somerset & Dorset Joint 2P

Built 1903-1914
Rebuilt Fowler 1921 similar to Midland Railway '483' class

(Taken into L.M.S. stock 1930)

See M.R. '483' class for dimensions.

Number built: 5.

First loco withdrawn 1951; last loco withdrawn 1956.
No. in service (1930) 5; (1/1/48) 5.

322 (39)	323 (40)	324 (41)	325 (42)	326 (43)

4-4-0 Johnson Midland 2P

Built 1882-1883
Rebuilt Deeley 1906 onwards
Some again rebuilt Fowler 1923

Weight:
48 tons 12 cwt.†

Boiler Pressure:
175 lbs.

Cylinders:
18″×26″

Driving wheel Diameter:
6′ 9″

Tractive Effort:
15,470 lbs.

Valve Gear:
Stephenson

Number built: 30.

†Engines with extended smokeboxes weighed 51 tons 2 cwt.

First loco withdrawn 1925; last unrebuilt loco withdrawn 1937.
No. in service (1/1/23) 30; No. in service (Rebuilds) (1/1/48) 5.

328	333	338	343	348	353*
329	334	339	344	349	354
330	335	340	345	350	355
331	336	341	346	351*	356*
332*	337*	342	347	352	357

*Rebuilt to '483' class during 1923.

4-4-0 Johnson Midland 2P
Built 1885-1886
Rebuilt Deeley 1904 onwards
Some again rebuilt Fowler 1923-1924

Weight:
48 tons 12 cwt.†

Boiler Pressure:
175 lbs.

Cylinders:
18″×26″

Driving Wheel Diameter:
7′ 0″

Tractive Effort:
14,829 lbs.

Valve Gear:
Stephenson

Number built: 20.

†Engines with extended smokeboxes weighed 51 tons 2 cwt.

First loco withdrawn 1925; last unrebuilt loco withdrawn 1940.
No. in service (unrebuilt) (1/1/23) 19; No. in service (rebuilds) (1/1/48) 5.

358	362*	365	368	372	375
359*	363	366	369	373	376
360	364*	367	371	374	377*
361					

*Rebuilt to '483' class 1923 (No. 370 already so rebuilt in 1922).

4-4-0 Johnson Midland 2P
Built 1888
Rebuilt Deeley 1909-1912

Weight:
51 tons 2 cwt.

Boiler Pressure:
175 lbs.

Cylinders:
18½″×26″

Driving Wheel Diameter:
6′ 6″

Tractive Effort:
16,862 lbs.

Valve Gear:
Stephenson

Number built: 15.

None of this batch received a third rebuild or was ever superheated.

First loco withdrawn 1925; last loco withdrawn 1952.
No. in service (1/1/23) 15; No. in Service (1/1/48) 3.

378 379 380	381 382 383	384 385 386	387 388	389 390	391 392

4-4-0 Johnson Midland 2P

Built 1891
Rebuilt Deeley 1904 onwards
Some again rebuilt Fowler 1922-1923

Weight:
48 tons 12 cwt.

Boiler Pressure:
175 lbs.

Cylinders:
18″×26″

Driving Wheel Diameter:
6′ 6″

Tractive Effort:
15,962 lbs.

Valve Gear:
Stephenson

Number built: 10.

First loco withdrawn 1925; last unrebuilt loco withdrawn 1928.
No. in service (unrebuilt) (1/1/23) 5; No. in service (rebuilds) (1/1/48) 7.

393	394*	396*	398	399	

*Rebuilt to '483' class, 1923. (Nos. 395, 397, 400, 401 and 402 already so rebuilt in 1922.)

4-4-0 Johnson Midland 2P

Built 1893-1900
Rebuilt Deeley 1905 onwards
Some again rebuilt Fowler 1914 onwards

Weight:
48 tons 12 cwt.

Boiler Pressure:
175 lbs.

Cylinders:
$18\frac{1}{2}$″×26″

Driving Wheel Diameter:
6′ 6″

Tractive Effort:
16,862 lbs.

Valve Gear:
Stephenson

Number built: 55.

First loco withdrawn 1925.
Last unrebuilt loco withdrawn 1927 (except Nos. 460 and 465 which lasted until 1930-31.)
No. in service (unrebuilt) (1/1/23) 24. No. in service (rebuilds) (1/1/48) 35.

428	438*	442	451	467	474
429	439*	445	457	469	475
431	440	449	460†	472*	476
435	441	450*	465†	473	481

*Rebuilt to '483' class, 1923. The remaining engines between 428 and 482 not tabulated above had already been rebuilt to 483 class.

†The last two engines of this series to receive the intermediate Deeley rebuilding, were not dealt with until 1910. and these assumed the appearance of the 378-392 series, with Belpaire firebox, extended smokebox, and separate splashers.

4-4-0 Johnson Midland 2P '483' class

Built 1882-1901
Rebuilt Deeley 1904 onwards
Rebuilt superheater etc., by Fowler 1912-1923

Weight:
53 tons 7 cwt.

Boiler Pressure:
160 lbs.

Cylinders:
20½″×26″

Driving Wheel Diameter:
7′ 0″

Tractive Effort:
17,585 lbs.

Valve Gear:
Stephenson

First loco withdrawn 1948; last loco withdrawn 1963. No. in service (1/1/23) 142; No. in service (1/1/48) 298. (Including 15 further rebuilds in 1923 from earlier series†, 8 acquisitions from the Somerset & Dorset Joint Railway* and 138 new engines built 1928-1932.)

*Five of these engines were given the numbers 322-326, (q.v.) the Johnson class 1 engines having by then been scrapped.

332†	407	430	461	490	511
337†	408	432	462	491	512
351†	409	433	463	492	513
353†	410	434	464	493	514
356†	411	436	466	494	515
359†	412	437	468	495	516
362†	413	438†	470	496	517
364†	414	439†	471	497	518
370	415	443	472†	498	519
377†	416	444	477	499	520
394†	417	446	478	500	521
395	418	447	479	501	522
396†	419	448	480	502	523
397	420	450†	482	503	524
400	421	452	483	504	525
401	422	453	484	505	526
402	423	454	485	506	527
403	424	455	486	507	528
404	425	456	487	508	529
405	426	458	488	509	530
406	427	459	489	510	531

532	538	543	548	553	558
533	539	544	549	554	559
534	540	545	550	555	560
535	541	546	551	556	561
536	542	547	552	557	562
537					

†Rebuilt 1923

Further locos of this class constructed subsequent to the grouping were as follows:—

563—612 Built 1928.
613—632 Built 1929.
633—635 (At first ran as S. & D.J.R. 44—46). Built 1929. Taken into L.M.S. stock 1930.
636—660 Built 1931.
661—700 Built 1932.

4-4-0 Adams North Stafford 2P (N.S.R. classes G and KT)

Built 1910-1912

Weight:
47 tons 11 cwt.†

Boiler Pressure:
175 lbs.†

Cylinders:
$18\frac{1}{2}'' \times 26''$†

Driving Wheel Diameter:
6′ 0″

Tractive Effort:
18,708 lbs.†

Valve Gear:
Stephenson

†Engine 38 (class KT) had $20'' \times 26''$ cylinders; boiler pressure 170 lbs.; weight 50 tons 14 cwt. and tractive effort 20,872 lbs.

Number built: 5.

First loco withdrawn 1928; last loco withdrawn 1933.
No. in service (1/1/23) 5; (1/1/48) 0.

Former N.S.R. numbers shown in brackets.

595 (86)	596 (87)	597 (170)	598 (171)	599 (38)

Renumbered 5410-5414 in 1928 on construction of new standard class 2 4-4-0's.

4-2-2 Johnson Midland 1P

Built 1887-1899

Engines	Weight:	Boiler Pressure:	Cylinders:	Driving Wheels	Tractive Effort:
600-607, 610-619		160 lbs.	$18'' \times 26''$	$7'\,4\frac{1}{2}''$	12,945 lbs.
608, 609, 620-659		160 lbs.	$18\frac{1}{2}'' \times 26''$	$7'\,6\frac{1}{2}''$	13,372 lbs.
660-669		160 lbs.	$19'' \times 26''$	7′ 6″	14,104 lbs.
670-684		170 lbs.	$19'' \times 26''$	$7'\,9\frac{1}{2}''$	15,279 lbs.

(*Note:* The final batch of Johnson singles, Nos. 685-694, class 2P built 1899-1900, were all scrapped by 1922.)

Number built: 85.
(excluding the above mentioned class 2P series.)

First loco withdrawn 1919; last loco withdrawn 1928*.
No. in service (1/1/23) 43.

*The last engine in service, No. 673, has been preserved in M.R. colours with its original number 118.

No. 600 was latterly fitted with a Deeley cab and worked the Directors' saloon from Derby.

600	639	651	661	668	676
614	640	652	662	669	677
627	641	654	663	670	678
628	643	655	664	671	679
632	644	657	665	672	680
633	645	659	666	673	682
635	649	660	667	674	683
638					

4-4-0 Johnson Midland 3P

Built 1900-1905

Most rebuilt by Fowler with superheater 1913 onwards

Weight:
55 tons 7 cwt.†

Boiler Pressure:
175 lbs.†

Cylinders:
$20\frac{1}{2}'' \times 26''$†

Driving Wheel Diameter:
6′ 9″

Tractive Effort:
20,065 lbs.†

Valve Gear:
Stephenson

†Unrebuilt engines: 180 lbs. pressure; $19\frac{1}{2}'' \times 26''$; 18,674 lbs. tractive effort; 54 tons 5 cwt. weight.

Number built: 80.

First loco withdrawn 1925. Last unrebuilt loco withdrawn 1926.
Last rebuilt loco withdrawn 1953.

No. in service (1/1/23) 80; (1/1/48) 22.

700	714	728	741	754	767
701	715	729	742*	755	768
702	716§	730	743	756§	769
703	717	731	744	757	770
704	718	732	745	758§	771§
705	719	733	746	759§	772*
706	720§	734§	747§	760	773
707§	721	735	748	761	774§
708	722	736	749*	762§	775§
709	723	737*	750§	763§	776
710	724	738	751*	764§	777§
711	725	739	752	765	778*
712§	726	740	753§	766	779*
713	727				

§ Superheated between 1923 and 1925, after which no more were rebuilt and the remainder, indicated*, were withdrawn in 1925-1926.

4-4-0 Deeley Midland 4P

Built 1909

Weight:
58 tons 5 cwt.

Boiler Pressure:
200 lbs.

Cylinders:
$20\frac{1}{2}'' \times 26''$

Driving Wheel Diameter:
$6' 6\frac{1}{2}''$

Tractive Effort:
23,662 lbs.

Valve Gear:
Deeley

Number built: 10.

First loco withdrawn 1925; last loco withdrawn 1928.
No. in service (1/1/23) 10.

990 991	992 993	994 995	996 997	998	999

Nos. 991-999 were allocated 801-809 in 1926 (No. 990 had by then already been withdrawn and 992 was scrapped without carrying its new number).

4-4-0 Johnson/Deeley Midland 4P 3 cylinder compound

Built 1901-1909

Weight:
61 tons 14 cwt.

Boiler Pressure:
200 lbs.

Cylinders:
1 HP $19'' \times 26''$
2 LP $21'' \times 26''$

Driving Wheel Diameter:
$7' 0''$

Tractive Effort:
21,840 lbs.

Valve Gear:
Stephenson

Original Number in class: 5 (Johnson built). Plus 40 of Deeley's modified design. (A further 195 built by the L.M.S. subsequent to the grouping.)

The original five engines were rebuilt between 1914 and 1919 to conform with the later Deeley design of 1905.

No. 1040 was superheated in 1913, Nos. 1000-1004 between 1914-19, and the remainder between 1919-27.

First loco withdrawn 1948; last M.R. built loco withdrawn 1953*.
No. in service (1/1/23) 45; (1/1/48) 240.

*The original engine No. 1000 has been preserved; but in its modified Deeley form and not in its original condition.

1000 1001 1002 1003 1004 1005 1006 1007	1008 1009 1010 1011 1012 1013 1014 1015	1016 1017 1018 1019 1020 1021 1022 1023	1024 1025 1026 1027 1028 1029 1030	1031 1032 1033 1034 1035 1036 1037	1038 1039 1040 1041 1042 1043 1044

Further locos of this class constructed subsequent to the grouping were as follows:—

1045—1084	Built 1924.	1185—1199	Built 1927.
1085—1129	Built 1925.	900—924	Built 1927.
1130—1134	Built 1926.	935—939	Built 1932.
1135—1184	Built 1925.		

(A further 20, Nos. 940-959 were to have been built but the order was cancelled.)
Last L.M.S.-built loco withdrawn 1961.

0-4-4WT Kirtley Midland double framed IP
Built 1869-1870

Weight:
43 tons 10 cwt.

Boiler Pressure:
140 lbs.

Cylinders:
18″×24″

Driving Wheel Diameter:
5′ 2″

Tractive Effort:
14.925 lbs.

Valve Gear:
Stephenson

Number built: 26.

First loco withdrawn 1921; last loco withdrawn 1935.
No. in service (1/1/23) 26; (1/1/48) 0.

1200	1205	1209	1214	1218	1222
1201*	1206	1210	1215	1219	1223
1202	1207	1211	1216	1220	1224
1203*	1208	1213	1217	1221	1225
1204					

*Nos. 1201 and 1203 were renumbered 1212 and 1213 in 1930 to make way for 0-4-4T's acquired from the Somerset & Dorset Joint Railway which it was desired to incorporate in the L.M.S. list at the beginning of the 0-4-4T series. The numbers 1200, 1202, 1204-1207, 1212 and 1213 were already vacant by that time owing to the Kirtley engines having been scrapped.

0-4-4T Johnson Midland IP
Built 1875-1900
Many rebuilt 1925 onwards with Belpaire Firebox

Number	Weight:	Boiler Pressure:	Cylinders:	Driving Wheel Diameter:	Tractive Effort:
1226-1235	53 tons 4 cwt.	140 lbs.	18″×24″	5′ 4″	14,460 lbs.
1236-1265	53 tons 4 cwt.	140 lbs.	17″×24″	5′ 7″	13,810 lbs.
1266-1350	53 tons 4 cwt.	140 lbs.	18″×24″	5′ 4″	14,460 lbs.
1351-1430	53 tons 4 cwt.	150 lbs.	18″×24″	5′ 4″	15,490 lbs.

Valve Gear:
Stephenson

Number built:
205

Nos. 1311-1321 and 1371-1385 were fitted with condensing apparatus for working through the Metropolitan tunnels in the London area.

First loco withdrawn 1919; last loco withdrawn 1960.

No. in service (1/1/23) 201; (1/1/48) 65.

1226†	1261*	1297	1332	1366*	1400
1227	1262	1298*	1333	1367*	1401
1228	1263	1299	1334	1368*	1402*
1229	1264	1300	1335	1369	1403
1230	1265	1301	1336	1370*	1404
1231	1266	1302	1337*	1371*	1405
1232	1267	1303*	1338	1372	1406*
1233	1268	1304	1339	1373*	1407
1234	1269	1306	1340*	1374	1408
1235	1270	1307§	1341*	1375*	1409
1236	1271	1308	1342*	1376	1410
1237	1272*	1309	1343	1377*	1411*
1238	1273*	1310	1344*	1378	1412
1239*	1274	1311	1345	1379*	1413*
1240	1275*	1312	1346	1380	1414
1241	1276	1313	1347	1381	1415
1242	1277	1314	1348*	1382*	1416*
1243	1278*	1315*	1349	1383	1417
1244	1279	1316	1350*	1384	1418
1246*	1280	1317	1351	1385§	1419
1247*	1283	1318	1352	1386	1420*
1248	1284	1319	1353*	1387	1421*
1249*	1285	1320	1354	1388	1422*
1250	1286	1321	1355	1389*	1423*
1251*	1287*	1322*	1356	1390*	1424*
1252*	1288	1323	1357*	1391	1425*
1253	1289	1324*	1358*	1392	1426*
1254	1290*	1325	1359	1393	1427
1255*	1291	1326	1360*	1394	1428
1256	1292	1327	1361§	1395	1429*
1257	1293	1328	1362	1396*	1430*
1258	1294	1329	1363	1397*	
1259	1295*	1330*	1364	1398	
1260*	1296	1331	1365*	1399	

†The original engine No. 1226 when withdrawn in 1930 was repainted in M.R. colours with its old number 6 for preservation, but was broken up in 1932.

Engine 1305, which does not appear in the above table as it had been sold to the S. & D.J.R. in 1921, becoming No. 54 on that line, was restored to the L.M.S. list in 1930 when the S. & D.J.R. engines were absorbed, and given its old number 1305. For a time it ran as such still painted in S. & D.J.R. blue livery. The only instance of a true Midland engine (i.e. excluding M.R. types built for the M. & G.N.J. and S. & D.J.R.) ever being painted other than red or black (or before 1881 green).

* Engines surviving Nationalisation on 1st Jan., 1948, were allocated Nos. 58030-58091 in the British Railway list but in a few cases did not last long enough to carry their new numbers.

§ Withdrawn early in 1948 with no B.R. number allocated.

0-4-4T Johnson Somerset & Dorset Joint IP

Built 1877-1885

(Taken into L.M.S. stock 1930)

Weight:
43 tons 10 cwt.*

Driving Wheel Diameter:
5′ 4″

Boiler Pressure:
160 lbs.

Tractive Effort:
14,811 lbs.

Cylinders:
18″×24″

Valve Gear:
Stephenson

*Except No. 1305, which was standard with M.R. 1266-1350. Nos. 1230-1232 latterly carried Belpaire boilers.

Original number in class: 13.

First loco withdrawn 1921; last loco withdrawn 1946.
No. in service (1930) 12; (1/1/48) nil.

1200 (10)	1202 (12)	1204 (14A)	1206 (30A)	1230 (52)	1232 (55)
1201 (11)	1203(13)	1205 (29A)	1207 (31A)	1231 (53)	1305 (54)

No. 1305 was originally a M.R. engine, purchased by the S. & D.J.R. in 1921. On being re-absorbed in the L.M.S. it reverted to its former M.R. No. 1305.

Nos. 1200 and 1204 never carried their L.M.S. numbers.

0-4-4T Adams North Stafford (N.S.R. class M)

Built 1907-1920

Weight:
57 tons 16 cwt.

Driving Wheel Diameter:
5′ 6″

Boiler Pressure:
175 lbs.

Tractive Effort:
20,055 lbs.

Cylinders:
18½″×26″

Valve Gear:
Stephenson

Number built: 9.

First loco withdrawn 1931; last loco withdrawn 1939.
No. in service (1/1/23) 9; (1/1/48) 0.

Former N.S.R. numbers in brackets:

1431 (9)	1433 (12)	1435 (42)	1437 (17)	1438 (19)	1439 (54)
1432 (11)	1434 (41)	1436 (15)			

2-4-0T Longbottom North Stafford IP (N.S.R. class B)

Built 1882-1895

Weight:
43 tons 18 cwt.

Boiler Pressure:
150 lbs.

Cylinders:
17″×24″

Driving Wheel Diameter:
5′ 6″

Tractive Effort:
13,400 lbs.

Number built: 21.

First loco withdrawn before 1923; last loco withdrawn 1933.
No. in service (1/1/23) 12; (1/1/48) 0.

Former N.S.R. numbers in brackets:

1440 (17A)	1443 (27A)	1446 (48A)	1449 (10A)
1441 (18A)	1444 (29A)	1447 (2A)	1450 (71)
1442 (22A)	1445 (23A)	1448 (1A)	1451 (7)

2-4-2T Clare North Stafford IP (N.S.R. class A and B)

Built 1878-1882 as 2-4-0T

Rebuilt by Longbottom as 2-4-2T

Weight:
56 tons 8 cwt.

Boiler Pressure:
150 lbs.

Cylinders:
17″×24″

Driving Wheel Diameter:
5′ 6″

Tractive Effort:
13,400 lbs.

Original number in class: 8.

First loco withdrawn before 1923; last loco withdrawn 1934.
No. in service (1/1/23) 6; (1/1/48) 0.

Former N.S.R. numbers in brackets:

1454 (52)	1455 (35)	1456 (40)	1457 (21)	1458 (24)	1459 (61)

0-4-0ST Johnson Midland Unclassified

Built 1883-1903

Weight:
23 tons 3 cwt. (1500-1517)
32 tons 3 cwt. (1518-1527)

Driving Wheel Diameter:
3′ 10″

Boiler Pressure:
140 lbs. (1500-1517)
150 lbs. (1518-1527)

Tractive Effort:
8,744 lbs. (1500-1517)
11,641 lbs. and 12,471 lbs. (1518-1527)

Cylinders:
13″×20″ (1500-1517)
15″×20″ (1518-1527)

Valve Gear
Stephenson

Number built: 28.

First loco withdrawn 1920; last loco withdrawn 1958.
No. in service (1/1/23) 23; (1/1/48) 4.

1500	1505	1509	1514	1518	1523
1502	1506*	1510	1515	1519	1524
1503	1507	1511	1516	1520	1525
1504	1508	1513	1517	1522	

*No. 1506 renumbered 1509 in 1930 to make way for engines acquired from the S. & D.J.R., which became 1500-1507. The remaining M.R. engines below 1510 had by that time all been scrapped.

0-6-0ST Fox-Walker Somerset & Dorset Joint 2F

Built 1874-1876

(Taken into L.M.S. stock 1930)

Weight:
43 tons 17 cwt.

Driving Wheel Diameter:
4′ 0″

Boiler Pressure:
160 lbs.

Tractive Effort:
19,652 lbs.

Cylinders:
17″×24″

Valve Gear:
Stephenson

Number built: 9.

First loco withdrawn 1928; last loco withdrawn 1934.
No. in service (1930) 8; (1/1/48) 0.

1500 (1)	1502 (3)	1504 (5)	1505 (6)	1506 (7)	1507 (9)
1501 (2)	1503 (4)				

Nos. 1501 and 1503 never carried their L.M.S. numbers.

0-4-0T Deeley Midland Unclassified

Built 1907-1922

Weight:
32 tons 16 cwt.

Driving Wheel Diameter:
3′ 9¾″

Boiler Pressure:
160 lbs.

Tractive Effort:
14,635 lbs.

Cylinders:
15″×22″

Valve Gear
Walschaerts

Number built: 10.

First loco withdrawn 1957; two locos still in service 1965 (Nos. 41528 and 41533).
No. in service (1/1/23 and 1/1/48) 10.

1528 1529	1530 1531	1532 1533	1534 1535	1536	1537

0-6-0T Longbottom North Stafford 2F N.S.R. class D

Built 1882-1899

Weight:
45 tons

Driving Wheel Diameter:
4′ 6″

Boiler Pressure:
150 lbs.

Tractive Effort:
16,376 lbs.

Cylinders:
17″×24″

Valve Gear:
Stephenson

Number built: 49.

First loco withdrawn 1928; last loco withdrawn 1937.
No. in service (1/1/23) 49; (1/1/48) 0.

Former N.S.R. number in brackets:

1550 (3)	1560 (60)	1570 (57)	1580 (135)	1590 (145)
1551 (20)	1561 (63)	1571 (73)	1581 (136)	1591 (146)
1552 (33)	1562 (49)	1572 (50)	1582 (137)	1592 (147)
1553 (36)	1563 (62)	1573 (56)	1583 (138)	1593 (148)
1554 (37)	1564 (124A)	1574 (47)	1584 (139)	1594 (149)
1555 (43)	1565 (125A)	1575 (130)	1585 (140)	1595 (150)
1556 (44)	1566 (126)	1576 (131)	1586 (141)	1596 (151)
1557* (16)	1567 (127)	1577 (132)	1587 (142)	1597 (152)
1558 (32)	1568 (128)	1578 (133)	1588 (143)	1598 (153)
1559 (34)	1569 (129)	1579 (134)	1589 (144)	

*Owing to a misunderstanding No. 1557 carried the number 21557 for a short time in April 1934.

Webb 2-4-2T No. 6665. [*W. Leslie Good*

Bowen-Cooke 4-6-2T No. 6978, turned out in early L.M.S. style. Not a great number of engines, apart from the Claughtons - ever aquired the red livery. [*W. H. Whitworth*

One of Whale's 4-4-2T's still in L.N.W.R. colours at Willesden in 1926.

Beame's large 0-8-4T's did not appear until 1923 after the amalgamation, and the first fifteen were turned out with L.N.W.R. numbers but the initials L.M.S. on the side tanks. [*L.P.C.*

North London steam crane loco, originally built in 1858 and rebuilt in its final form in 1872, thereafter becoming permanent shunter at Bow works.

North London 0-6-0T No. 2877 (L.N.W.R. numbering).

North London inside cylinder 4-4-0T No. 2648 (L.N.W.R. numbering).

Standard N.L.R. 4-4-0T No. 6445 at Derby in 1929, being retained for preservation but later broken up.

Hookhams' 4-cylinder 0-6-0T, built for the N.S.R. just before the grouping The valves were set to give 8 exhausts per revolution of the driving wheels, thus anticipating the S.R. 'Lord Nelsons'. [L.P.C.

One of several varieties of N.S.R. 0-6-0. At first numbered 2326 in the L.M.S. list, it became No. 8653 when this block of numbers was required for new Fowler 2-6-4T's. [L.P.C.

This engine was not a success on the quick starting and stopping passenger services for which it was designed, and it was rebuilt as a tender engine in 1924. Although allocated L.M.S. No. 1599 in the tank series it never carried it, and on conversion was renumbered in the 0-6-0 tender series. [W. H. Whitworth

One of the S. & D.J.R. 2-8-0's acquired in 1930. Although a Derby design, none of the type was ever built for the parent company. At first numbered 9670-9680, they later became 13800-13810, and this view, taken in 1932, shows the engine bearing both numbers on the smokebox door.

S. &. D.J.R. 4′ 6″ 0-6-0 No. 2887, taken over in 1930.

One of the only two tender engines formerly owned by the L.T. & S.R., which became L.M.S. 2898 and 2899.

One of the miscellaneous collection of 0-6-0's acquired from the Stratford on Avon and Midland Junction Railway.

One of the earliest series of Kirtley 0-6-0's with straight frames. The later engines had curved frames as in the illustration of No. 22822. No. 2385 was formerly M.R. No. 2320, and dated back to 1856. [*L. R. Tomsett*

0-6-0T Hookham North Stafford 3F

Built 1922

Weight:
56 tons 15 cwt.

Boiler Pressure:
160 lbs.

Cylinders (4):
14″×24″

Driving Wheel Diameter:
4′ 6″

Tractive Effort:
30,948 lbs.

Valve Gear:
Walschaerts

Number built: 1.

Number in service (1/1/23) 1; (1/1/48) 0.

This was an experimental engine constructed with crank axles set at 135° resulting in eight exhausts to each revolution of the driving wheels (thus anticipating the 'Lord Nelson' of the Southern Railway). It was not a success as first built and was converted to a tender engine in 1924. It never actually bore its allocated number of 1599 in the 0-6-0T list but went directly to 2367 in the tender series on rebuilding.

1599 (23). Later 2367 (q.v.)

0-6-0ST Hudswell Clarke North Stafford 1F

Built 1866

Rebuilt 1880-1

Weight:
39 tons 3 cwt.

Boiler Pressure:
150 lbs.

Cylinders:
17″×24″

Driving Wheel Diameter:
4′ 0″

Tractive Effort:
18,424 lbs.

Number built: 2.

First loco withdrawn 1927; Last loco withdrawn 1933.
Number in service (1/1/23) 2; (1/1/48) 0.

1600 (58A)	1601 (59A)

0-6-0T Kerr Stuart North Stafford 1F

Built 1919

Weight:
34 tons 3 cwt.

Driving Wheel Diameter:
3′ 9″

Boiler Pressure:
160 lbs.

Tractive Effort:
16,622 lbs.

Cylinders (outside):
15″×20″

Number built: 2.

First loco withdrawn 1932; last loco withdrawn 1933.
No. in service (1/1/23) 2; (1/1/48) 0.

1602 (74)	1603 (75)

0-6-0WT Midland 1F

Built E. B. Wilson & Co. 1848 (1605), Derby 1862 (1607)

Rebuilt by Kirtley and Johnson

Weight:
Not available

Driving Wheel Diameter:
4′ 2″

Boiler Pressure:
140 lbs.

Tractive Effort:
11,550 lbs. (1605)
16,184 lbs. (1607)

Cylinders:
15″×22″ (No. 1605)
17″×24″ (No. 1607)

Valve Gear:
Stephenson

Number in existance 1907: 5.

1605 withdrawn 1924; 1607 withdrawn 1928.
Number in service (1/1/23) 2; (1/1/48) 0.

1605 (late M.R. 1601)	1607 (late M.R. 1604)

The renumbering of 1601 was necessitated by the N.S.R. 0-6-0T's having overspilled into the 1600's, but there was no apparent reason for the alteration of 1604.

0-6-0T Midland 1F

Built 1880 (1606), 1886 (1608)

Acquired 1895 from Severn & Wye Railway*.

Weight:
39 tons 11 cwt.

Boiler Pressure:
140 lbs.

Cylinders:
17″×24″

Driving Wheel Diameter:
4′ 3″

Tractive Effort:
16,184 lbs.

Number built: 3.

First loco withdrawn 1920; last loco withdrawn 1924.
Number in service (1/1/23) 2; (1/1/48) 0.

1606	1608

* Six locomotives in all were acquired by the Midland Railway (the others going to the Great Western) of which four were still in existence in 1907, becoming Nos. 1605-1608. No. 1605 was withdrawn in 1911 and 1607 (which was similar to 1606 and 1608) in 1920.

0-6-0T Kirtley Midland 1F

Built 1871
Rebuilt Johnson

Weight:
38 tons

Boiler Pressure:
140 lbs.

Cylinders:
17″×24″

Driving Wheel Diameter:
4′ 3″

Tractive Effort:
16,184 lbs.

Number built: 10.

First loco withdrawn 1923; last loco withdrawn 1927.
Number in service (1/1/23) 10; (1/1/48) 0.

1610 1611	1612 1613	1614 1615	1616 1617	1618	1619

0-6-0T Johnson Midland 1F

Built 1874-1900
Many rebuilt 1919 onwards with Belpaire firebox

Weight:
39 tons 11 cwt.

Boiler Pressure:
140 lbs.*

Cylinders:
17″×24″

Driving Wheel Diameter:
4′ 7″

Tractive Effort:
15,005 lbs.*

*Some engines had 150 lb. boilers and 16,080 lb. tractive effort.

No. 1831 was completely reconstructed in 1932 as a diesel unit, and as such was the direct forerunner of the standard 0-6-0 diesel shunter since constructed in large numbers by the L.M.S. and B.R.

Number built: 280.

First loco withdrawn 1920; five locomotives still officially in stock 1/1/66 although stored out of use (Nos. 41708, 41734, 41763, 41804 and 41835).

Number in service (1/1/23) 279; (1/1/48) 95.

1620	1668	1715	1762	1809	1856
1621	1669	1716	1763	1810	1857
1622	1670	1717	1764	1811	1858
1623	1671	1718	1765	1812	1859
1624	1672	1719	1766	1813	1860
1625	1673	1720	1767	1814	1861
1626	1674	1721	1768	1815	1862
1627	1675	1722	1769	1816	1863
1629	1676	1723	1770	1817	1864
1630	1677	1724	1771	1818	1865
1631	1678	1725	1772	1819	1866
1632	1679	1726	1773	1820	1867
1633	1680	1727	1774	1821	1868
1634	1681	1728	1775	1822	1869
1635	1682	1729	1776	1823	1870
1636	1683	1730	1777	1824	1871
1637	1684	1731	1778	1825	1872
1638	1685	1732	1779	1826	1873
1639	1686	1733	1780	1827	1874
1640	1687	1734	1781	1828	1875
1641	1688	1735	1782	1829	1876
1642	1689	1736	1783	1830	1877
1643	1690	1737	1784	1831	1878
1644	1691	1738	1785	1832	1879
1645	1692	1739	1786	1833	1880
1646	1693	1740	1787	1834	1881
1647	1694	1741	1788	1835	1882
1648	1695	1742	1789	1836	1883
1649	1696	1743	1790	1837	1884
1650	1697	1744	1791	1838	1885
1651	1698	1745	1792	1839	1886
1652	1699	1746	1793	1840	1887
1653	1700	1747	1794	1841	1888
1654	1701	1748	1795	1842	1889
1655	1702	1749	1796	1843	1890
1656	1703	1750	1797	1844	1891
1657	1704	1751	1798	1845	1892
1658	1705	1752	1799	1846	1893
1659	1706	1753	1800	1847	1894
1660	1707	1754	1801	1848	1895
1661	1708	1755	1802	1849	1896
1662	1709	1756	1803	1850	1897
1663	1710	1757	1804	1851	1898
1664	1711	1758	1805	1852	1899
1665	1712	1759	1806	1853	
1666	1713	1760	1807	1854	
1667	1714	1761	1808	1855	

0-6-0T Johnson Midland 3F

Built 1899-1902

All rebuilt between 1919 and 1942 with Belpaire firebox

Weight:
48 tons 15 cwt.

Driving Wheel Diameter:
4′ 7″

Boiler Pressure:
160 lbs.

Tractive Effort:
20,836 lbs.

Cylinders:
18″×26″

Valve Gear:
Stephenson

Number built: 60.

Nos. 1900-1929 and 1940-1949 were fitted with condensing apparatus for working through the Metropolitan tunnels in the London area.

First loco withdrawn 1954; 3 engines still in service, 1/1/66 (Nos. 47201, 47202 and 47231).

Number in service (1/1/23 and 1/1/48) 60.

1900	1910	1920	1930	1940	1950
1901	1911	1921	1931	1941	1951
1902	1912	1922	1932	1942	1952
1903	1913	1923	1933	1943	1953
1904	1914	1924	1934	1944	1954
1905	1915	1925	1935	1945	1955
1906	1916	1926	1936	1946	1956
1907	1917	1927	1937	1947	1957
1908	1918	1928	1938	1948	1958
1909	1919	1929	1939	1949	1959

All renumbered 7200-7259 in 1934-7.

Further locos of this class, the design being slightly modified, were constructed as follows:—

7100-7149	(later renumbered 7260-7309)	Built 1924-5
7150-7156*	(later renumbered 7310-7316)	Built 1929 (taken into L.M.S. stock 1930.)
16400-16519	(later renumbered 7317-7436)	Built 1926
16520-16599	(later renumbered 7437-7516)	Built 1927
16600-16749	(later renumbered 7517-7666)	Built 1928
16750-16764	(later renumbered 7667-7681)	Built 1931

*At first ran as S. & D.J.R. Nos. 19-25.

A number of the above engines were still in service during 1966.

0-6-4T Deeley Midland 3P

Built 1907

All rebuilt with Belpaire firebox and superheaters between 1920 and 1926

Weight:
72 tons 8 cwt.

Boiler Pressure:
175 lbs.

Cylinders:
$18\frac{1}{2}'' \times 26''$

Driving Wheel Diameter:
5′ 7″

Tractive Effort:
19,756 lbs.

Valve Gear:
Stephenson

Number built: 40.

First loco withdrawn 1935; last loco withdrawn 1938.
No. in service (1/1/23) 40; (1/1/48) 0.

2000	2007	2014	2021	2028	2035
2001	2008	2015	2022	2029	2036
2002	2009	2016	2023	2030	2037
2003	2010	2017	2024	2031	2038
2004	2011	2018	2025	2032	2039
2005	2012	2019	2026	2033	
2006	2013	2020	2027	2034	

0-6-4T Adams North Stafford 5F N.S.R. class C

Built 1914-1915

Weight:
72 tons

Boiler Pressure:
160 lbs.

Cylinders:
$20'' \times 26''$

Driving Wheel Diameter:
5′ 0″

Tractive Effort:
23,573 lbs.

Valve Gear:
Stephenson

Number built: 8.

First loco withdrawn 1934; last loco withdrawn 1937.
No. in service (1/1/23) 8; (1/1/48) 0.

Former N.S.R. numbers in brackets:

2040 (30)	2042 (53)	2044 (173)	2045 (174)	2046 (4)	2047 (5)
2041 (31)	2043 (70)				

0-6-4T Adams and Hookham North Stafford 4P N.S.R. class F

Built 1916-1919

Weight:
77 tons 7 cwt.

Boiler Pressure:
170 lbs.

Cylinders:
20″×26″

Driving Wheel Diameter:
5′ 6″

Tractive Effort:
22,769 lbs.

Valve Gear:
Stephenson

Number built: 8.

First loco withdrawn 1934; last loco withdrawn 1936.
No. in service (1/1/23) 8; (1/1/48) 0.

Former N.S.R. numbers in brackets:

2048 (114) 2049 (115)	2050 (116) 2051 (117)	2052 (118)	2053 (119)	2054 (120)	2055 (121)

4-6-4T Whitelegg London, Tilbury & Southend 3P

Built 1912

Weight:
94 tons 12 cwt.

Boiler Pressure:
160 lbs.

Cylinders:
20″×26″

Driving Wheel Diameter:
6′ 3″

Tractive Effort:
18,859 lbs.

Valve Gear:
Stephenson

Number built: 8.

First loco withdrawn 1929: last loco withdrawn 1934.
No. in service (1/1/23) 8; (1/1/48) 0.

No L.T.S.R. numbers carried.

2100 2101	2102 2103	2104	2105	2106	2107

Nos. 2101-2106 were allocated Nos. 2193-2198 in 1930, but 2101 and 2102 were withdrawn without carrying their new numbers.

4-4-2T Whitelegg London, Tilbury & Southend 1P

Built 1880-1892

Weight:
58 tons 12 cwt.

Driving Wheel Diameter:
6′ 0″

Boiler Pressure:
160 lbs.

Tractive Effort:
13,998 lbs.

Cylinders:
17″×26″

Valve Gear:
Stephenson

Number built: 36.

First loco withdrawn 1929; last loco withdrawn 1936.
No. in service (1/1/23) 36; (1/1/48) 0.

L.T.S.R. Numbers and Names removed c. 1912 (shown in brackets):

2110 (1 Southend)	2122 (13 Black Horse Rd)	2134 (25 Stifford)
2111 (2 Gravesend)	2123 (14 Leigh)	2135 (26 West Thurrock)
2112*(3 Tilbury)	2124 (15 East Ham)	2136 (27 Whitechapel)
2113 (4 Bromley)	2125 (16 Low Street)	2137 (28 Romford)
2114 (5 Plaistow)	2126 (17 Thames Haven)	2138*(29 Stepney)
2115 (6 Upton Park)	2127 (18 Burdett Road)	2139 (30 Fenchurch)
2116*(7 Barking)	2128 (19 Dagenham)	2140 (31 St. Pancras)
2117 (8 Rainham)	2129 (20 Hornchurch	2141 (32 Leyton)
2118 (9 Tilbury Docks)	2130 (21 Upminster)	2142 (33 Wanstead)
2119 (10 Grays)	2131 (22 Commercial Rd)	2143 (34 Tottenham)
2120 (11 Stanford)	2132*(23 Laindon)	2144 (35 West Ham)
2121 (12 Pitsea)	2133 (24 Ockendon)	2145 (36 Walthamstow)

*Fitted with round cab (and at one time also condensing apparatus) for working over the District Railway lines.

Nos. 2110-2119 became 2200-2209 in 1923 and were again renumbered 2077-2086 in 1930.
Nos. 2120-2124 became 2210-2214 in 1925 and were again renumbered 2087-2091 in 1930.
Nos. 2125-2134 became 2190-2199 in 1927 and were again renumbered 2067-2076 in 1930.
Nos. 2135-2145 became 2056-2066 in 1930.

4-4-2T Whitelegg London, Tilbury & Southend 3P

Built 1897/8 (later rebuilt) and 1909

Weight:
71 tons 10 cwt.*

Driving Wheel Diameter:
6′ 6″

Boiler Pressure:
170 lbs.

Tractive Effort:
17,390 lbs.

Cylinders:
19″×26″

Valve Gear:
Stephenson

*Nos. 2146-2157, 70 tons 15 cwt.

Original Number in class: 16 (35 further engines constructed by L.M.S. between 1923 and 1930).

First loco withdrawn 1951; last L.T. & S. built loco withdrawn 1952*.
*No. 2177 has been preserved in old L.T. & S.R. colours as 80 'Thundersley'.
No. in service (1/1/23) 16; (1/1/48) 51.

L.T.S.R. numbers and names removed c. 1912 (shown in brackets):

2146 (37 Woodgrange)	2152 (43 Great Ilford)	2176 (79 Rippleside)
2147 (38 Westcliff)	2153 (44 Prittlewell)	2177 (80 Thundersley)
2148 (39 Forest Gate)	2154 (45 Shoeburyness)	2178 (81 Aveley)
2149 (40 Benfleet)	2155 (46 Southchurch)	2179 (82 Crowstone)
2150 (41 Leytonstone)	2156 (47 Stratford)	
2151 (42 East Horndon)	2157 (48 Little Ilford)	

Nos. 2146-2157 became 2135-2146 in 1930 and were again renumbered B.R. 41953-41964 in 1948.

Nos. 2176-2179 became 2147-2150 in 1930 and were again renumbered B.R. 41965-41968 in 1948.

Further locos of the class constructed subsequent to the grouping were as follows:—

2110-2119 built 1923. Renumbered B.R. 41928 41937 in 1948/9.
2120-2124 built 1925. Renumbered B.R. 41938-41942 in 1948/9.
2125-2134 built 1927. Renumbered B.R. 41943-41952 in 1948/9.
2151-2160 built 1930. Rebumbered B.R. 41969-41978 in 1948/9.

Last L.M.S. built loco withdrawn 1960.

4-4-2T Whitelegg London, Tilbury & Southend 2P
Built 1900-1903

Weight:
67 tons 16 cwt.

Boiler Pressure:
170 lbs.

Cylinders:
19"×26'" (some engines 18"×26")†

Driving Wheel Diameter:
6' 6"

Tractive Effort:
15,606 and 17,388 lbs.†

Valve Gear:
Stephenson

Number built: 18.

First loco withdrawn 1947; last loco withdrawn 1953.
No. in service (1/1/23) 18; (1/1/48) 17.

L.T.S.R. Numbers and Names removed c. 1912 (shown in brackets).

2158 (51 Purfleet)	2164 (57 Crouch Hill)	2170 (63 Mansion House)
2159 (52 Wennington)	2165 (58 Hornsey)	2171 (64 Charing Cross)
2160 (53 Stepney Green)	2166 (59 Holloway)	2172 (65 Victoria)
2161 (54 Mile End)	2167 (60 Highgate)	2173 (66 Earl's Court)
2162 (55 Bow Road)	2168 (61 Kentish Town)	2174 (67 Westminster)
2163 (56 Harringay)	2169 (62 Camden)	2175 (68 Mark Lane)

These engines became Nos. 2092-2109 in 1930. In 1948 they were allocated B.R. Nos. 41910-41926 (omitting No. 2105, already scrapped), but only Nos. 41922, 41923 and 41925 survived to carry their new numbers.

4-4-2T Adams North Stafford 3P (N.S.R. class K)

Built 1911-2

Weight:
70 tons 10 cwt.

Boiler Pressure:
160 lbs.

Cylinders:
20″ × 26″

Driving Wheel Diameter:
6′ 0″

Tractive Effort:
23,573 lbs.

Valve Gear:
Stephenson

Number built: 7.

First loco withdrawn 1933; last loco withdrawn 1935.
No. in service (1/1/23) 7; (1/1/48) 0.

N.S.R. numbers shown in brackets:

2180 (8) 2181 (45)	2182 (46)	2183 (55)	2184 (13)	2185 (14)	2186 (39)

0-6-2T Whitelegg London, Tilbury & Southend 2F

Built 1903-1912

Weight:
64 tons 13 cwt.

Boiler Pressure:
170 lbs.

Cylinders:
18″ × 26″

Driving Wheel Diameter:
5′ 3″

Tractive Effort:
19,320 lbs.

Valve Gear:
Stephenson

Number built: 14.

First loco withdrawn 1958; last loco withdrawn 1962.
No. in service (1/1/23) and (1/1/48) 14.

L.T.S.R. Numbers and Names removed c. 1912; Midland Numbers first number in brackets:

2220 (2180 69 Corringham)	2227 (2187 76 Dunton)
2221 (2181 70 Basildon)	2228 (2188 77 Fobbing)
2222 (2182 71 Wakering)	2229 (2189 78 Dagenham Dock)
2223 (2183 72 Hadleigh)	2230 (2190)*
2224 (2184 73 Cranham)	2231 (2191)* *Taken direct into
2225 (2185 74 Orsett)	2232 (2192)* Midland Railway stock
2226 (2186 75 Canvey Island)	2233 (2193)* in 1912.

These engines reverted to their former M.R. numbers, 2180-2193, in 1939. In 1947 they were again renumbered 1980-1993 (subsequently becoming B.R. 41980-41993).

0-6-2T Longbottom North Stafford 2F (N.S.R. class DX)

Built 1899-1902

Weight:
55 tons 5 cwt.

Boiler Pressure:
150 lbs.

Cylinders:
18″ × 24″

Driving Wheel Diameter:
4′ 6″

Tractive Effort:
18,360 lbs.

Valve Gear:
Stephenson

Number built: 6.

First loco withdrawn 1927; last loco withdrawn 1931.
No. in service (1/1/23) 6; (1/1/48) 0.

Former N.S.R. numbers in brackets:

2234 (58)	2235 (154)	2236 (155)	2237 (59)	2238 (76)	2239 (77)

0-6-2T Adams North Stafford 3F (N.S.R. class L)

Built 1903-1923

Weight:
59 tons 12 cwt.*

Boiler Pressure:
175 lbs.

Cylinders:
$18\frac{1}{2}$″ × 26″

Driving Wheel Diameter:
5′ 0″

Tractive Effort:
22,070 lbs.

Valve Gear:
Stephenson

*Later engines from 2254 onwards had weights varying between 63 tons 17 cwt. and 64 tons 19 cwt.

Number built: 34.

First loco withdrawn 1928; last loco withdrawn 1937.
No. in service (1/1/23) 30; (1/1/48) 0.

Former N.S.R. numbers in brackets:

2240 (124)	2247 (99)	2254 (51)	2261 (172)	2268 (27)
2241 (125)	2248 (156)	2255 (64)	2262 (72)	2269 (28)
2242 (165)	2249 (157)	2256 (65)	2263 (18)	2270§ (1)
2243 (166)	2250 (93)	2257 (69)	2264 (22)	2271§ (2)
2244 (167)	2251 (94)	2258 (89)	2265 (25)	2272§ (10)
2245 (168)	2252 (95)	2259 (96)	2266 (26)	2273§ (48)
2246 (98)	2253 (158)	2260 (97)	2267 (29)	

Several of these engines were sold out of service to the Manchester Collieries and are still at work at Walkden, Lancs. in 1966.

No. 2271 was repainted some years ago in full N.S.R. red livery as No. 2 for exhibition at Stoke-on-Trent, and still runs in this condition.

§ Built 1923.

0-10-0 Fowler Midland banking engine

Built 1919

Weight:
73 tons 13 cwt.

Boiler Pressure:
180 lbs.

Cylinders (4):
$16\frac{3}{4}'' \times 28''$

Driving Wheel Diameter:
$4' 7\frac{1}{2}''$

Tractive Effort:
43,4315 lbs.

Valve Gear:
Walschaerts

Number built : 1.

No. in service (1/1/23) 1; (1/1/48) 1. Withdrawn 1956.

2290

Renumbered 22290 in 1947 and became B.R. No. 58100 in 1949.

0-6-0 Beyer Peacock Stratford-on-Avon & Midland Junction

Built 1880-1908

Weight:
31 tons 3 cwt. (2300)
32 tons 1 cwt. (2301/2)
35 tons 0 cwt. (2304-6)
38 tons 6 cwt. (2307-9)
40 tons 5 cwt. (2310/1)

Boiler Pressure:
120 lbs. (2300-2)
140 lbs. (2304-6)
160 lbs. (2307-9)
165 lbs. (2310/1)

Cylinders:
$17'' \times 24''$ (to 2309)
$18'' \times 24''$ (2310/1)

Driving Wheel Diameter:
$4' 6\frac{1}{2}''$ (2300)
$5' 0\frac{1}{2}''$ (2301/2)
$5' 1\frac{1}{2}''$ (2304-6)
$4' 9''$ (2307-11)

Tractive Effort:
13,101 lbs. (2300)
11,791 lbs. (2301/2)
13,695 lbs. (2304-6)
16,549 lbs. (2307-9)
19,256 lbs. (2310/1)

Number built: 11.

These engines varied in detail. No. 2300-2/4-6 had curved frames over the coupling-rod cranks, and Nos. 2307-11 straight frames. (All were double framed engines.)

First loco withdrawn 1924; last loco withdrawn 1930.
No. in service (1/1/23) 11; (1/1/48) 0.

Former S.M.J. numbers in brackets:

2300 (2) 2301 (3)	2302 (4) 2304 (10)	2305 (11) 2306 (12)	2307 (14) 2308 (15)	2309 (16) 2310 (17)	2311 (18)

Nos. 2305/6 ran for a short time before withdrawal as No. 2398/9, owing to construction of new 2-6-4T's.

0-6-0 Stroudley Stratford-on-Avon & Midland Junction

Built Brighton 1884

(Purchased from L.B. & S.C.R. 1920)

Weight:
40 tons 7 cwt.

Driving Wheel Diameter:
5′ 0″

Boiler Pressure:
150 lbs.

Tractive Effort:
18,402 lbs.

Cylinders:
$18\frac{1}{2}'' \times 26''$

Valve Gear:
Stephenson

Number built (by L.B. & S.C.R.): 12.

No. in service (1/1/23) 1. Withdrawn 1924.

2303 late S.M.J.R. 7 (originally L.B. & S.C.R. 428)

0-6-0 Clare North Stafford IF

N.S.R. class E

Built 1871-1877

Weight:
33 tons 7 cwt.

Driving Wheel Diameter:
5′ 0″

Boiler Pressure:
150 lbs.

Tractive Effort:
13,056 lbs.

Cylinders:
$17'' \times 24''$

Valve Gear:
Stephenson

Number built: 30.

First loco withdrawn before 1923; last loco withdrawn 1934.
No. in service (1/1/23) 23; (1/1/48) 0.

Former N.S.R. numbers in brackets:

2320* (74A)	2325 (107)	2330* (112)	2335 (119A)	2340* (67)
2321 (75A)	2326* (108)	2331* (113)	2336* (120A)	2341* (68)
2322* (104)	2327* (109)	2332 (70A)	2337 (121A)	2342* (66)
2323 (105)	2328* (110)	2333 (116A)	2338* (122)	
2324* (106)	2329* (111)	2334 (118A)	2339* (123)	

In 1928 the surviving engines of the class, indicated *, were renumbered 8650-8664 to make way for new 2-6-4T's.

0-6-0 Longbottom North Stafford 2F
N.S.R. '100' class
Built 1896-1907

Weight:
37 tons 9 cwt.

Driving Wheel Diameter:
4′ 6″

Boiler Pressure:
150 lbs.

Tractive Effort:
14,739 lbs.

Cylinders:
17″×24″

Valve Gear:
Stephenson

Number built: 10.

First loco withdrawn 1928; last loco withdrawn 1931.
No. in service (1/1/23) 10; (1/1/48) 0.

Former N.S.R. numbers in brackets:

2343	(81)	2345	(80)	2347	(100)	2349	(102)	2357	(82)
2344	(79)	2346	(78)	2348	(101)	2350	(103)	2358	(83)

All renumbered 8665-8672 and 8679/80 in 1928 to make way for new 2-6-4T's.

0-6-0 Longbottom North Stafford 2F
N.S.R. '159' class
Built 1900

Weight:
40 tons 14 cwt.

Driving Wheel Diameter:
5′ 0″

Boiler Pressure:
150 lbs.

Tractive Effort:
17,901 lbs.

Cylinders:
18″×26″

Valve Gear:
Stephenson

Number built: 6.

First loco withdrawn 1929; last loco withdrawn 1936.
No. in service (1/1/23) 6; (1/1/48) 0.

Former N.S.R. numbers in brackets:

2351 (159)	2352 (160)	2353 (161)	2354 (162)	2355 (163)	2356 (164)

All renumbered 8673-8678 in 1928 to make way for new 2-6-4T's.

0-6-0 Adams North Stafford 3F
N.S.R. class H
Built 1909-1911

Weight:
42 tons 17 cwt. (2359-2362)
43 tons 12 cwt. (2363-2366)

Driving Wheel Diameter:
5′ 0″

Boiler Pressure:
175 lbs.

Tractive Effort:
22,227 lbs.

Cylinders:
$18\frac{1}{2}'' \times 26''$

Valve Gear:
Stephenson

Number built: 8.

First loco withdrawn 1928; last loco withdrawn 1930.
No. in service (1/1/23) 8; (1/1/48) 0.

Former N.S.R. numbers in brackets:

2359 (84) 2360 (85)	2361 (88) 2362 (169)	2363 (6)	2364 (90)	2365 (91)	2366 (92)

All renumbered 8681-8688 in 1928 to make way for new 2-6-4T's.

0-6-0 Hookham North Stafford 3F

This engine was a reconstruction of the 4-cylinder tank engine 1599 (page 33, which see for further details).

As a tender engine it ran from 1924 to 1928, when it was withdrawn from service.

2367 (N.S.R. 23). Renumbered 8689 shortly before withdrawal.

0-6-0 Kirtley Midland double framed 1F
(straight frames)
Built 1852-1862
Rebuilt Johnson

Weight:
36 tons

Driving Wheel Diameter:
5′ 2″

Boiler Pressure:
140 lbs.

Tractive Effort:
12,541 lbs.

Cylinders:
$16\frac{1}{2}'' \times 24''$

Number in existence 1907—98 (numbered 2300-2397).

First loco withdrawn before 1907; last loco withdrawn 1927.
No. in service (1/1/23) 22; (1/1/48) 0.

Some of the class were renumbered to make way for N.S.R. 0-6-0's (see page 46). Nos. 2314, 2335 and 2359 were not so dealt with as they were withdrawn in 1923 whilst the general L.M.S. renumbering scheme was being drawn up. Nos. 2311, allocated the number 2383 (the original engine of that number also being withdrawn in 1923), never actually carried it, and may for a short time have duplicated the S.M.J.R. 0-6-0 No. 18 (see page 44).

(Late M.R. numbers shown in brackets)

2311	2369	2385 (2320)	2389 (2337)	2393	2396 (2357)
2314	2382 (2303)	2386 (2328)	2390 (2347)	2394 (2356)	2397 (2360)
2335	2383	2387 (2333)	2391 (2349)	2395	2398 (2366)
2359	2384 (2315)	2388	2392 (2354)		

No. 2385 (late 2320) was repainted 1929 in old M.R. colours with its original number 421, for preservation, but it was subsequently broken up in 1932.

0-6-0 Kirtley Midland double framed 1F (curved frames over coupling-rod cranks)

Built 1863-1874

Rebuilt Johnson/Deeley

A number of engines latterly carried class 2F boilers in various guises, some of these being identical in appearance with the class 1F engines, others being altered by the provision of Deeley cabs, at first with higher pitched boilers and slightly extended smokeboxes, most of these eventually acquiring lower pitched Belpaire boilers with Ramsbottom safety valves in place of the Salter spring balance safety valves on the dome.

Weight:
37 tons 12 cwt.

Boiler Pressure:
140 lbs.
(class 2 engines, 160 lbs.)

Cylinders:
17″×24″
(class 2 engines, 18″×24″)

Driving Wheel Diameter:
5′ 3″

Tractive Effort:
13,101 lbs.
(class 2 engines, 16,786 lbs.)

Valve Gear:
Stephenson

Number in existance 1907: 470 (Numbered 2399-2867)

First loco withdrawn before 1907; last loco withdrawn 1951.
No. in service (1/1/23) 449; (1/1/48) 4.

2399	2408	2419	2431	2439	2447
2400	2410	2420	2432	2440	2448
2401	2411	2421	2433	2441	2449
2402	2413	2423	2434	2442	2451*
2403	2414	2424*	2435	2443	2452
2404	2415	2425	2436	2444	2453
2405	2416	2427	2437	2445	2454*
2407	2417	2430	2438	2446	2455

			2641		
2456	2522	2582	2642	2702	2762
2457	2523	2583	2643	2703	2763
2458	2524	2584	2644	2704	2764
2463	2525	2585	2645	2705	2766
2465	2526	2586	2646	2706	2767
2466	2527	2587	2647	2707	2768
2467	2528	2588	2648	2708	2769
2468	2530	2589*	2649	2709	2770
2469	2531	2590	2650	2710	2771
2470	2532	2591	2651*	2711	2772
2471	2533	2592	2652	2713	2773
2472*	2534	2593	2653	2714	2774
2473	2535	2594	2654	2715	2775
2474	2536	2595	2655	2716	2776
2475	2537	2596	2656	2717	2777
2476	2538	2597	2657	2718	2778
2477	2539	2598	2658	2719	2779
2478	2540	2599	2659	2720	2780
2479	2541	2600	2660	2721	2781
2480	2542	2601	2661	2722	2782
2481	2543	2602	2662	2723	2783
2483	2544	2603*	2663	2724	2784
2484	2545	2604	2664	2725	2785
2485	2546	2605	2665	2726	2786
2486	2547	2606	2666	2727	2787
2487	2548	2607	2667	2728	2788
2488	2549	2608	2668	2729	2789
2489	2550	2609	2669	2730	2790
2490	2551	2610	2670	2731	2791
2491	2552	2611	2671	2732	2792
2492	2553	2612	2672	2733	2793
2493	2554	2613	2673*	2734	2794
2494	2555	2614	2674	2735	2795
2495	2556	2615	2675	2736	2796
2496	2557	2616	2677*	2737	2797*
2497	2558	2617	2678*	2738	2798
2498	2559	2618	2679	2739	2799
2499	2560	2619	2680	2740	2800
2500	2561	2620	2681	2741	2801
2501	2562	2621	2682	2742	2802
2502	2563	2622	2683	2743	2803
2503	2564	2623	2684	2744	2804
2504	2565	2624	2685	2745	2805
2505	2566	2625	2686	2746	2806*
2506	2567*	2626	2687	2747	2807
2507	2568	2627	2688	2748	2808
2508	2569	2628	2689	2749	2809
2509	2570	2629	2690	2750	2810
2510	2571	2630*	2691	2751	2811
2511	2572	2631	2692	2752	2812
2512	2573	2632	2693	2753	2813*
2513	2574	2633	2694	2754	2814
2514	2575	2634	2695	2755	2815
2515	2576	2635	2696	2756	2816
2516	2577	2636	2697	2757	2817
2517	2578	2637	2698	2758	2818*
2518	2579*	2638	2699	2759	2819*
2519	2580	2639	2700	2760	2820
2520	2581	2640	2701	2761	2821*

2822*	2830	2838	2846*	2854	2862*
2823	2831	2839	2847*	2855	2863*
2824	2832	2840	2848	2856	2864
2825	2833	2841	2849*	2857	2865
2826	2834*	2842	2850	2858*	2866
2827	2835*	2843	2851	2859	2867
2828*	2836	2844	2852*	2860	
2829	2837	2845	2853*	2861*	

*Fitted with Class 2 boiler.

Nos. 2707-2788 (inclusive, but omitting 2712) were on loan during the first world war to the Railway Operating Division (W.D.) and most of them served in France. No. 2717 was captured by the Germans and used by them. All were returned to further service on the M.R.

In 1934-36 the surviving engines of the class had 20000 added to their numbers to make way for new engines. These became Nos. 22567, 22579, 22589, 22630, 22818, 22822/8, 22834, 22846/9, 22852/3, 22863.

The four surviving engines at Nationalisation, Nos. 22630, 22846, 22853, and 22863, were allocated B.R. Nos. 58110-58113, but only No. 58110 actually carried its new number. This engine was scrapped in 1951, then 81 years old.

0-6-0 Johnson S. & D.J.R. 2F

Built 1879-1890

(Taken into L.M.S. stock, 1930)

Weight:
34 tons 8 cwt.

Boiler Pressure:
140 lbs.†

Cylinders:
17″×24″

Driving Wheel Diameter:
4′ 6″

Tractive Effort:
12,844 lbs.†

†Some engines rebuilt with 160 lb. boilers with tractive effort 15,413 lbs.

Original number in class: 28.

First loco withdrawn before 1922; last loco withdrawn 1932.
No. in service (1930) 11; (1/1/48) nil.

2880 (34)	2882 (36)	2884 (38)	2886 (67)	2888 (69)	2890 (71)
2881 (35)	2883 (37)	2885 (51)	2887 (68)	2889 (70)	

0-6-0

L.T. & S.R. 2F

Built 1899

Weight:
38 tons 4 cwt.

Boiler Pressure:
150 lbs.

Cylinders:
18″ × 24″

Driving Wheel Diameter:
4′ 6½″

Tractive Effort:
18,026 lbs.

Valve Gear:
Stephenson

Number built: 2.

2898 withdrawn 1933; 22899 withdrawn 1936.
No. in service (1/1/23) 2; (1/1/48) 0.

2898 (late L.T. & S.R. 49)	2899 (late L.T. & S.R. 50)

No. 2899 became 22899 in 1935.

Notes on the M.R. Johnson 0-6-0's

When Mr. S. W. Johnson designed his first 0-6-0's soon after his appointment as C.M.E. to the Midland Railway in 1873 he inaugurated what was to be a long succession of a standard design which was gradually multiplied over a lengthy period by himself, and, with progressive enlargement, by his successors, culminating in the standard Class 4 goods introduced by Sir Henry Fowler in 1911. These were perpetuated right up to 1941, by which time a total of no less than 767* engines of this final version alone were in service, which in addition to the original Johnson/Deeley engines, totalling 935, resulted in the record number of 1702* locomotives all of which sprang from the original basic design of 1875. It is true that the class 4's were naturally of considerably larger dimensions and with such modern refinements as superheaters, etc., but nevertheless they can undoubtedly claim the ancestry of the original design.

Dealing with the Johnson engines in rather more detail, they may be divided broadly into two main classes. What became in later days known as Class 2 (the Midland system of power classification indicated by a small brass figure on the cabside, later adopted by the LMS with embellishments, such as "F", indicating the freight power load, and 2P corresponding passenger class) and Class 3, representing the first major enlargement of the design, and which first appeared in 1903, at the end of Mr. Johnson's term of office.

Deeley, who succeeded Johnson, continued the construction of this enlarged design until 1908, and at the same time turned his attention to rebuilding many of the Johnson engines with the larger boiler, thus converting them from Class 2 to Class 3.

As in the case of the 4-4-0's, however, it was mainly the later series which received attention, and again in the same way the earliest of them were never rebuilt to Class 3, although the majority did acquire new Class 2 Belpaire boilers, as will be mentioned shortly.

*These figures do not include 16 engines of the same design supplied to the Midland and Great Northern Joint Railway, and also another 43 to the Somerset and Dorset, most of which came eventually into LMS stock. The total of 1,761 easily constitutes a record for this country.

The initial order was for 120 engines, all built in 1875-6, the work being divided between four of the largest firms of the day, thirty engines coming each from Messrs. Kitson, Dubs, Beyer Peacock, and Neilson. These were what eventually became Nos. 2900-3019 under the 1907 renumbering scheme. They had 4′ 11″ driving wheels. They lasted until comparatively recent years, the Neilson batch in particular must have been very well constructed, as twenty out of the thirty were still at work in 1956. All have now of course gone.

Another 110 engines followed up to 1884, these were fitted with 5′ 3″ driving wheels. None of this early lot ever became Class 3.

Nos. 3130-3189 came next, in which a reversion to the 4′ 11″ diameter wheels was made, but thereafter 5′ 3″ became the standard for all subsequent construction, including the final Class 4 design.

The Class 2's eventually reached the number 3764, Nos. 3765 onwards being turned out new as Class 3.

No. 3136 was the earliest engine ever to receive a Class 3 boiler (although it later reverted to Class 2) and from thereon the number of rebuilds gradually increased until by the time the 3200's and 3300's are reached the proportion of unrebuilt to rebuilt engines is about 50/50, the 3's gradually increasing until most of the 3700's are in this category, although several with class 3 round top boilers were rebuilt with class 2 Belpaires during the period 1925-27. There were a good many changes of this sort, with the result that a complete detailed history of the class would be a complicated one.

Class 3, new engines, and rebuilds, at first still had round topped fireboxes and the small Johnson cab, but this later gave place to the larger Deeley type, and most of them eventually acquired Belpaire fireboxes, concurrently with which the large square panel over the rear driving wheels was replaced by a small sector of splasher running into the cabside, which was now vertical down to the running plate. The last twenty, Nos. 3815-3834, came out new with vertical cabfront combined with a sweeping splasher, but were later altered to conform with the rest of the class. In the case of the Class 2 conversions to Belpaire, the square panel was retained, even though Deeley cabs were fitted in most cases.

In 1917 No. 2933 was rebuilt with a small Class 2 boiler but with Belpaire firebox, and this became standard for future replacement on the Class 2 engines, most of them being eventually so treated, although some retained Johnson boilers with dome Salter safety valves to the end. The fitting of Deeley cabs to the Class 2 Belpaire rebuilds was by no means universal, however, and many retained the small Johnson type after conversion.

0-6-0 Johnson Midland 2F, 3F*

Built 1875-1908

Weight:
(2900-3019) 40 tons
(3020-3129) 40 tons
(3130-3189) 40 tons (class 2)
43 tons 17 cwt.* (class 3)
(3190-3774) 40 tons (class 2)
43 tons 17 cwt.* (class 3)
(3775-3834) 46 tons 3 cwt.* (class 3)

Boiler Pressure:
160 lbs.; 175 lbs.*

Cylinders:
(2900-3774) 18″ × 26″
(3775-3834) 18½″ × 26″

Number built for Midland: 935.

Driving Wheel Diameter:
(2900-3019) 4′ 11″
(3020-3129) 5′ 3″
(3130-3189) 4′ 11″
(3190-3834) 5′ 3″§

Tractive Effort:
(2900-3019) 19,420 lbs.
(3020-3129) 18,185 lbs.
(3130-3189) 19,420 lbs. (class 2)
21,240 lbs.* (class 3)
(3190-3774) 18,185 lbs. (class 2)
19,890 lbs.* (class 3)
(3775-3834) 21,010 lbs.* (class 3)

Valve Gear:
Stephenson

First loco withdrawn 1925; last loco withdrawn 1964.

No. in service (1/1/23) 935; (1/1/48) 603†.

†(Including ex-S. & D.J.R. locos.)

§ In 1923 No. 3333 was running with 6′ 0″ driving wheels being one of three (the others were 3326 and 3387) so converted in 1906. They reverted to standard in 1922, 1924 and 1918 respectively.

2900	2950	3000	3050	3100	3150
2901	2951	3001	3051	3101	3151
2902	2952	3002	3052	3102	3152
2903	2953	3003	3053	3103	3153
2904	2954	3004	3054	3104	3154
2905	2955	3005	3055	3105	3155*
2906	2956	3006	3056	3106	3156*
2907	2957	3007	3057	3107	3157
2908	2958	3008	3058	3108	3158
2909	2959	3009	3059	3109	3159*
2910	2960	3010	3060	3110	3160
2911	2961	3011	3061	3111	3161
2912	2962	3012	3062	3112	3162
2913	2963	3013	3063	3113	3163
2914	2964	3014	3064	3114	3164
2915	2965	3015	3065	3115	3165
2916	2966	3016	3066	3116	3166
2917	2967	3017	3067	3117	3167
2918	2968	3018	3068	3118	3168
2919	2969	3019	3069	3119	3169*
2920	2970	3020	3070	3120	3170
2921	2971	3021	3071	3121	3171
2922	2972	3022	3072	3122	3172
2923	2973	3023	3073	3123	3173*
2924	2974	3024	3074	3124	3174*
2925	2975	3025	3075	3125	3175
2926	2976	3026	3076	3126	3176
2927	2977	3027	3077	3127	3177
2928	2978	3028	3078	3128	3178*
2929	2979	3029	3079	3129	3179*
2930	2980	3030	3080	3130	3180*
2931	2981	3031	3081	3131	3181*
2932	2982	3032	3082	3132	3182
2933	2983	3033	3083	3133	3183*
2934	2984	3034	3084	3134	3184
2935	2985	3035	3085	3135	3185*
2936	2986	3036	3086	3136*	3186*
2937	2987	3037	3087	3137*	3187*
2938	2988	3038	3088	3138	3188*
2939	2989	3039	3089	3139	3189*
2940	2990	3040	3090	3140	3190
2941	2991	3041	3091	3141	3191*
2942	2992	3042	3092	3142	3192
2943	2993	3043	3093	3143	3193*
2944	2994	3044	3094	3144	3194
2945	2995	3045	3095	3145	3195
2946	2996	3046	3096	3146	3196
2947	2997	3047	3097	3147*	3197*
2948	2998	3048	3098	3148	3198*
2949	2999	3049	3099	3149	3199

3200*	3259*	3318*	3377	3436*	3495*
3201*	3260	3319*	3378*	3437	3496*
3202	3261*	3320*	3379*	3438	3497*
3203*	3262	3321*	3380	3439*	3498
3204*	3263*	3322	3381*	3440*	3499*
3205*	3264	3323*	3382	3441*	3500
3206	3265*	3324*	3383	3442	3501
3207*	3266*	3325*	3384	3443*	3502*
3208*	3267*	3326*	3385	3444*	3503
3209	3268*	3327*	3386*	3445	3504
3210*	3269*	3328*	3387*	3446*	3505
3211*	3270	3329*	3388*	3447*	3506*
3212*	3271*	3330*	3389*	3448*	3507*
3213*	3272	3331*	3390*	3449*	3508
3214*	3273*	3332*	3391	3450*	3509*
3215	3274*	3333*	3392*	3451	3510*
3216	3275*	3334*	3393	3452*	3511
3217	3276	3335*	3394*	3453*	3512
3218	3277*	3336*	3395*	3454*	3513
3219*	3278*	3337*	3396*	3455*	3514*
3220	3279	3338*	3397	3456*	3515*
3221	3280	3339*	3398*	3457*	3516*
3222*	3281*	3340*	3399*	3458*	3517
3223*	3282*	3341*	3400*	3459*	3518
3224*	3283*	3342*	3401*	3460	3519
3225*	3284*	3343	3402*	3461	3520*
3226*	3285*	3344*	3403*	3462*	3521*
3227	3286*	3345	3404*	3463*	3522*
3228*	3287*	3346	3405*	3464*	3523*
3229	3288*	3347	3406*	3465	3524*
3230	3289	3348	3407	3466	3525
3231*	3290*	3349	3408*	3467*	3526
3232*	3291	3350	3409*	3468*	3527
3233*	3292*	3351*	3410*	3469*	3528
3234*	3293*	3352	3411*	3470*	3529*
3235*	3294*	3353	3412	3471	3530
3236	3295*	3354	3413*	3472*	3531*
3237*	3296*	3355*	3414	3473	3532
3238*	3297*	3356*	3415*	3474*	3533
3239*	3298*	3357*	3416	3475	3534*
3240*	3299*	3358*	3417	3476*	3535
3241*	3300*	3359*	3418	3477	3536
3242*	3301*	3360	3419*	3478*	3537
3243*	3302	3361*	3420	3479	3538*
3244*	3303	3362	3421	3480	3539
3245*	3304	3363	3422	3481	3540*
3246*	3305*	3364*	3423	3482*	3541*
3247*	3306*	3365	3424	3483*	3542*
3248	3307*	3366	3425	3484*	3543
3249*	3308*	3367*	3426*	3485	3544*
3250*	3309*	3368*	3427	3486	3545
3251*	3310*	3369*	3428*	3487*	3546*
3252*	3311	3370*	3429*	3488*	3547
3253*	3312*	3371*	3430	3489*	3548*
3254*	3313*	3372	3431*	3490*	3549
3255	3314*	3373*	3432	3491*	3550*
3256*	3315*	3374*	3433*	3492*	3551
3257*	3316*	3375*	3434	3493	3552*
3258*	3317*	3376	3435*	3494*	3553*

3554	3601*	3648	3695	3742*	3789*
3555	3602	3649	3696	3743*	3790*
3556*	3603*	3650*	3697*	3744*	3791*
3557	3604*	3651*	3698*	3745*	3792*†
3558*	3605*	3652*	3699	3746*	3793*
3559	3606*	3653*	3700*	3747*	3794*
3560*	3607*	3654	3701*	3748*	3795*
3561	3608*	3655*	3702*	3749*	3796*
3562*	3609*	3656*	3703	3750*	3797*
3563*	3610	3657*	3704*	3751*	3798*
3564*	3611	3658*	3705*	3752*	3799*
3565*	3612*	3659	3706*	3753*	3800*
3566	3613*	3660*	3707	3754*	3801*
3567*	3614*	3661*	3708*	3755*	3802*
3568*	3615*	3662*	3709*	3756*	3803*
3569	3616*	3663*	3710*	3757*	3804*
3570*	3617	3664*	3711*	3758*	3805*
3571	3618*	3665*	3712*	3759*	3806*†
3572*	3619*	3666*	3713*	3760*	3807*
3573*	3620*	3667*	3714*	3761*	3808*
3574*	3621*	3668*	3715*	3762*	3809*
3575*	3622*	3669*	3716*	3763*	3810*
3576	3623*	3670*	3717*	3764*	3811*
3577	3624*	3671*	3718	3765*	3812*
3578*	3625*	3672*	3719*	3766*	3813*
3579*	3626	3673*	3720*	3767*	3814*
3580*	3627*	3674*	3721*	3768*	3815*
3581*	3628*	3675*	3722*	3769*	3816*
3582*	3629*	3676*	3723*	3770*	3817*
3583*	3630*	3677	3724*	3771*	3818*
3584*	3631*	3678*	3725*	3772*	3819*
3585*	3632	3679*	3726*	3773*	3820*
3586*	3633*	3680*	3727*	3774*	3821*
3587*	3634*	3681*	3728*	3775*	3822*
3588*	3635*	3682*	3729*	3776*	3823*
3589*	3636*	3683*	3730*	3777*	3824*
3590	3637*	3684*	3731*	3778*	3825*
3591*	3638*	3685*	3732*	3779*	3826*
3592	3639*	3686*	3733*	3780*	3827*
3593*	3640*	3687*	3734*	3781*	3828*
3594*	3641*	3688*	3735*	3782*	3829*
3595*	3642	3689*	3736*	3783*	3830*
3596*	3643	3690*	3737*	3784*	3831*
3597	3644*	3691	3738*	3785*	3832*
3598*	3645*	3692*	3739*	3786*	3833*
3599*	3646*	3693*	3740*	3787*	3834*
3600*	3647*	3694*	3741*	3788*	

Engines marked * are those which are known to have carried Class 3 boilers at some period, but as mentioned in the notes on this class, some of them eventually reverted to Class 2.

†Nos. 3792 and 3806 had received superheaters and extended smokeboxes, later removed.

It should be noted that engines latterly carrying the numbers 3194, 3198, 3201, 3204, 3211, 3216, 3218, 3228, 3248 and 3260 (all class 3 Belpaire) were not the original M.R. engines, but acquired from the S. & D.J.R. in 1930 (see page 56).

In 1934 a certain amount of renumbering of post-grouping standard designs was undertaken, under which scheme the Nos. 2900-2984 were required for standard 2-6-0's. The surviving Johnson 0-6-0's in this range were therefore renumbered correspondingly 22900-22984.

Again in 1947 when the Ivatt Class 4 2-6-0's were brought out as Nos. 3000-3019*, the old Midland engines, such as still remained, became 23000-23019.

The intervening numbers between these two series, 2985-2999, were not required under either of the above schemes, and these M.R. engines remained unaltered until the B.R. renumbering of 1948. Under this scheme, all of the Class 2 0-6-0's still surviving, 205 engines in all, were completely renumbered in a new series, 58114-58310, except for 23016, 3021, 3050, 3153, 3195, 3424, 3473 and 3602 withdrawn early in 1948 before the renumbering scheme was prepared. The Class 3 0-6-0's took their ordinary place in the more general scheme of adding 40000 to their numbers, and thus after an interval of some forty years the two classes were at last sorted out into separate series.

*Further construction of these engines in 1952 resulted in Class 3 0-6-0 No. 43137 becoming No. 43750.

0-6-0 Johnson S. & D.J.R. 3F

Built 1896-1902

(Taken into L.M.S. stock 1930)

Constructed as standard Johnson class 2, later rebuilt to class 3 Belpaire similar to M.R. locos (q.v.).

For dimensional details see M.R. 3190-3774 series (rebuilds).

Number built: 10.

First loco withdrawn 1947: last loco withdrawn 1962.
No. in service (1930) 10; (1/1/48) 9.

3194 (62)	3201 (64)	3211 (66)	3218 (73)	3248 (75)	3260 (76)
3198 (63)	3204 (65)	3216 (72)	3228 (74)		

All except 3198 and 3260 survived to have 40000 added to their numbers by B.R.

0-6-0 Fowler Midland 4F

Built 1911-1922

Weight:
48 tons 15 cwt.

Boiler Pressure:
175 lbs.

Cylinders:
20″×26″

Driving Wheel Diameter:
5′ 3″

Tractive Effort:
24,555 lbs.

Valve Gear:
Stephenson

Number built (M.R.): 192.
(575 engines later constructed by L.M.S. and 5 acquired from S. & D.J.R.)

First loco withdrawn 1954; last M.R. loco withdrawn 1965.
No. in service (1/1/23) 192; (1/1/48) 772.

3835	3867	3899	3931	3963	3995
3836	3868	3900	3932	3964	3996
3837	3869	3901	3933	3965	3997
3838	3870	3902	3934	3966	3998
3839	3871	3903	3935	3967	3999
3840	3872	3904	3936	3968	4000
3841	3873	3905	3937	3969	4001
3842	3874	3906	3938	3970	4002
3843	3875	3907	3939	3971	4003
3844	3876	3908	3940	3972	4004
3845	3877	3909	3941	3973	4005
3846	3878	3910	3942	3974	4006
3847	3879	3911	3943	3975	4007
3848	3880	3912	3944	3976	4008
3849	3881	3913	3945	3977	4009
3850	3882	3914	3946	3978	4010
3851	3883	3915	3947	3979	4011
3852	3884	3916	3948	3980	4012
3853	3885	3917	3949	3981	4013
3854	3886	3918	3950	3982	4014
3855	3887	3919	3951	3983	4015
3856	3888	3920	3952	3984	4016
3857	3889	3921	3953	3985	4017
3858	3890	3922	3954	3986	4018
3859	3891	3923	3955	3987	4019
3860	3892	3924	3956	3988	4020
3861	3893	3925	3957	3989	4021
3862	3894	3926	3958	3990	4022
3863	3895	3927	3959	3991	4023
3864	3896	3928	3960	3992	4024
3865	3897	3929	3961	3993	4025
3866	3898	3930	3962	3994	4026

Further locos of this class constructed or acquired subsequent to the grouping were as follows:—

4027-4036	Built 1924/5.	4382-4399	Built 1926.
4037-4216	Built 1924-6.	4400-4446	Built 1927.
4217-4286	Built 1926.	4447-4476	Built 1928.
4287-4301	Built 1927.	4477-4506	Built 1927.
4302-4311	Built 1926.	4507-4556	Built 1928.
4312-4322	Built 1927.	4557-4561	S. & D.J.R. engines—see below.
4323-4331	Built 1928.	4562-4576	Built 1937.
4332-4346	Built 1926.	4577-4596	Built 1939.
4347-4381	Built 1927.	4597-4606	Built 1940/1.

Twelve of the engines were still in service on 1/1/66.

0-6-0 Fowler S. & D.J.R. 4F

Built 1922

(Taken into L.M.S. stock, 1930)

For dimensional details see M.R. 3835-4026.

Number built: 5.

First loco withdrawn 1962; last loco withdrawn 1965.
No. in service (1930) 5; (1/1/48) 5.

4557 (57)	4558 (58)	4559 (59)	4560 (60)	4561 (61)

2-2-2 Trevithick L.N.W.R. (unclassified)
Built 1847

This famous engine is believed to have been originally built as a 2-2-2, but very soon afterwards altered to 4-2-2 type, and at first had the boiler *underneath* the driving axle to obtain a low centre of gravity. Only the very large 8′ 6″ diameter of the driving wheels (the largest wheels ever used in this country apart from the 9′ 0″ broad gauge engines of the Bristol and Exeter Railway) made this possible. However, it was completely reconstructed by John Ramsbottom in 1858 with the boiler in the orthodox position and remained practically unchanged thereafter. It ran in ordinary service until 1902, when it was laid aside until 1907, in which year it was put to work hauling an inspection saloon. As such it was transferred to the Departmental Stock and consequently was not included in the renumbering scheme at the grouping, otherwise it would have undoubtedly received the number 5000 in accordance with the general pattern, and the 2-4-0's would probably have started at 5010 or possibly 5100.

It was tried out for a short time about 1921 working a pull and push train, but perhaps not surprisingly was not very successful in this capacity. Apart from this it remained on its departmental duties until 1927, when it was finally retired and is now preserved.

Boiler pressure:
140 lbs.

Cylinders:
$17\frac{1}{2}'' \times 24''$

Driving Wheel Diameter:
8′ 6″

Tractive Effort:
8,575 lbs.

3020 ' CORNWALL ' (originally L.N.W.R. 173, placed on duplicate list in 1886)

2-4-0 Webb L.N.W.R. 'Precedent' class 1P
Built 1874-1901

Weight:
35 tons 12 cwt.

Boiler Pressure:
150 lbs.

Cylinders:
$17'' \times 24''$

Driving Wheel Diameter:
6′ 9″

Tractive Effort:
10,918 lbs.

Valve Gear:
Allan

Number built: 166.

First loco withdrawn 1908; last loco withdrawn 1934.
No. in service (1/1/23) 80; (1/1/48) 0.

L.N.W.R. pre-grouping numbers in brackets:

5000 (2190) Princess Beatrice
5001 (2191) Snowdon*
5002 (1170) General
5003 (512) Lazonby
5004 (271) Minotaur
5005 (1522) Pitt
5006 (1527) Raleigh
5007 (379) Sedgwick
5008 (941) Blenkinsop
5009 (1517) Princess Helena
5010 (1480) Newton
5011 (696) Director
5012 (1211) John Ramsbottom
5013 (1212) Pioneer

5014 (1488) Murdock	5047 (253) President Garfield
5015 (1685) Gladiator	5048 (364) Henry Pease
5016 (1748) Britannia	5049 (883) Phantom
5017 (1521) Gladstone	5050 (860) Merrie Carlisle
5018 (1672) Talavera	5051 (890) Sir Hardman Earle
5019 (1531) Cromwell	5052 (749) Mercury
5020 (1674) Delhi	5053 (945) Humphrey Davy
5021 (2006) Princess	5054 (2183) Antelope
5022 (1525) Abercrombie	5055 (514) Lawrence
5023 (1668) Dagmar	5056 (477) Caractacus
5024 (1675) Vimiera	5057 (866) Courier
5025 (1518) Countess	5058 (2185) Alma
5026 (1519) Duchess	5059 (2193) Salopian
5027 (1520) Franklin	5060 (619) Mabel
5028 (1666) Ariadne	5061 (2176) Robert Benson
5029 (1684) Speke	5062 (506) Sir Alexander Cockburn
5030 (2002) Madge	5063 (864) Pilot
5031 (790) Hardwicke	5064 (1187) Chandos
5032 (1213) The Queen	5065 (478) Commodore
5033 (1678) Airey	5066 (2194) Cambrian
5034 (1745) Glowworm	5067 (2186) Lowther
5035 (304) Hector	5068 (1194) Miranda
5036 (1682) Novelty	5069 (2187) Penrith Beacon
5037 (381) Patterdale	5070 (262) Wheatstone
5038 (787) Clarendon	5071 (480) Duchess of Lancaster
5039 (1667) Corunna	5072 (193) Rocket
5040 (919) Nasmyth	5073 (2180) Perseverance
5041 (2005) Lynx	5074 (857) Prince Leopold
5042 (1173) The Auditor	5075 (862) Balmoral
5043 (2192) Caradoc	5076 (2189) Avon
5044 (871) Prosperine	5077 (1105) Hercules
5045 (265) Thomas Carlyle	5078 (870) Fairbairn
5046 (865) Envoy	5079 (861) Amazon

*No. 5001 was renumbered 25001 for a few months before withdrawal in 1934 (the last of the class) owing to the construction of new Stanier class 5 4-6-0's.

No. 5031 is preserved in its original condition as 790 ' HARDWICKE '

Several of these engines never carried their new L.M.S. number.

2-4-0 Webb L.N.W.R. 'Waterloo' class 1P

Built 1889-1896

Weight:
36 tons 1 cwt.

Driving Wheel Diameter:
6′ 3″

Boiler Pressure:
150 lbs.

Tractive Effort:
12,283 lbs.

Cylinders:
17″×24″

Valve Gear:
Allan

Original number: 90.

First loco withdrawn 1907; last loco withdrawn 1936.
No. in service (1/1/23) 30; (1/1/48) 0.

L.N.W.R. numbers in brackets:

5080	(748)	Waterloo	5095	(628)	Tartarus
5081	(1045)	Whitworth	5096	(817)	Constance
5082	(733)	Chimera	5097	(824)	Adelaide
5083	(814)	Henrietta	5098	(486)	Skiddaw
5084	(642)	Bee	5099†	(792)	Theorem
5085	(901)	Hero	5100†	(737)	Roberts
5086†	(468)	Wildfire	5101†	(793)	Martin
5087	(604)	Narcissus	5102	(1168)	Cuckoo
5088	(735)	Charon	5103	(732)	Hecla
5089	(934)	North Star	5104	(794)	Woodlark
5090	(124)	Marquis Douro	5105	(2158)	Sister Dora
5091	(634)	Ellesmere	5106	(773)	Centaur
5092	(763)	Violet	5107	(424)	Sirius
5093	(764)	Shap	5108	(1166)	Wyre
5094†	(609)	The Earl of Chester	5109	(2157)	Unicorn

Several of these engines never carried their new L.M.S. numbers.

Engines 5086, 5094, 5099, 5100 and 5101 transferred to Engineer's Dept. in 1923/4, becoming respectively " Engineer Northampton ", " Engineer Walsall ", " Engineer " (spare engine), " Engineer Lancaster ", and " Engineer Watford ". The names were removed, and they never carried their L.M.S. numbers. They replaced other engines which were withdrawn in 1923†. There were also five others similarly attached to the service list, as follows:—

" Engineer " (spare engine)	formerly L.N.W.R. 885 Vampire†
" Engineer Crewe "*	formerly L.N.W.R. 209 Petrel
" Engineer Liverpool "	formerly L.N.W.R. 742 Spitfire
" Engineer Bangor "	formerly L.N.W.R. 1166 Wyre†
" Engineer Manchester "	formerly L.N.W.R. 2156 Sphinx.

* Later "Engineer South Wales".

† These engines were of an earlier but similar class known as the "Samsons", built in the 1870's. They had 6′ 0″ driving wheels and 16″×20″ cylinders. It will be noted that two different engines (see No. 5108 above) had carried the number and name 1166 Wyre.

4-4-0 Webb L.N.W.R. 4-cyl. Compound 'Jubilee' Class 2P

Built 1897-1900

Weight:
54 tons 10 cwt.

Driving Wheel Diameter:
7′ 1″

Boiler Pressure:
200 lbs.

Tractive Effort:
(at 80% B.P.) 29,152 lbs.

Cylinders:
2HP(O)—15″×24″; 2LP(I)—20½″×24″

Valve Gear:
Joy

Original number in class: 40.

First loco withdrawn 1923; last unrebuilt loco withdrawn 1925.
No. in service (1/1/23) 9; (1/1/48) 0.

L.N.W.R. numbers in brackets:

5110† (1903) Iron Duke	5114† (1915) Implacable
5111 (1904) Rob Roy	5115 (1923) Agamemnon
5112† (1911) Centurion	5116† (1927) Goliath
5113† (1912) Colossus	5117† (1929) Polyphemus

Also 1908 Royal George withdrawn 1923 without being allocated an L.M.S. number. Nos. 5111 and 5115 did not carry their alloted numbers.

†Subsequently rebuilt as 2-cylinder simple engines, 'Renown' class (q.v. for further particulars).

4-4-0 Webb L.N.W.R. 4-cyl. Compound 'Alfred the Great' class 2P

Built 1901-3

Weight:
57 tons 12 cwt.

Driving Wheel Diameter:
7′ 1″

Boiler Pressure:
200 lbs.

Tractive Effort:
(at 80% B.P.) 30,544 lbs.

Cylinders:
2HP(O) 16″×24″; 2LP(I) 20½″×24″

Valve Gear:
Joy

Original Number in class: 40.

First loco withdrawn 1923; last unrebuilt loco withdrawn 1928.
No. in service (1/1/23) 15; (1/1/48) 0.

5118 (1944) Victoria and Albert	5125† (1967) Cressy
5119† (1952) Benbow	5126† (1969) Dominion
5120† (1953) Formidable	5127† (1970) Good Hope
5121† (1954) Galatea	5128* (1974)Howe
5122 (1955) Hannibal	5129† (1977) Mars
5123† (1964) Caesar	5130 (1979) Nelson
5124 (1966) Commonwealth	

Also 1956 Illustrious and 1976 Lady Godiva, both withdrawn 1923 without being allocated L.M.S. numbers.

*No. 1974 Howe, which although allocated L.M.S. No. 5128 never carried it, was superheated in 1921, the only one of the class to be so treated. It ran as 1974 Howe until scrapped in 1928. Nos. 5118, 5122, 5124, 5125 and 5130 also did not carry their alloted numbers.

†Subsequently rebuilt as 2-cylinder simple engine 'Renown' class (q.v. for further particulars).

4-4-0 Webb L.N.W.R. Renown class 2P

Built 1897-1903 as 4-cylinder compound
Rebuilt 1908-24 as 2 cylinder simples

Weight:
56 tons

Boiler Pressure:
200 lbs.

Cylinders:
$18\frac{1}{2}'' \times 24''$

Driving Wheel Diameter:
7′ 1″

Tractive Effort:
16,428 lbs.

Valve Gear:
Joy

Eventual number of rebuilds: 70.

First loco withdrawn 1925; last loco withdrawn 1931.
No. in service (1/1/23) 56; (1/1/48) 0.

5131	(1918)	Renown
5132	(1913)	Canopus
5133	(1935)	Collingwood
5134	(1921)	John of Gaunt
5135	(1971)	Euryalus
5136	(1951)	Bacchante
5137	(1905)	Black Diamond
5138	(1946)	Diadem
5139	(1945)	Magnificent
5140	(1961)	Albemarle
5141	(1948)	Camperdown
5142	(1930)	Ramillies
5143	(1959)	Revenge
5144	(1257)	Invincible
5145	(1943)	Queen Alexandra
5146	(1922)	Intrepid
5147	(1925)	Warrior
5148	(1957)	Orion
5149	(1906)	Robin Hood
5150	(1936)	Royal Sovereign
5151	(1965)	Charles H. Mason
5152	(1949)	King Arthur
5153	(1960)	Francis Stevenson
5154	(1937)	Superb
5155	(1916)	Irresistible
5156	(1901)	Jubilee
5157	(1902)	Black Prince
5158	(1939)	Temeraire
5159	(1909)	Crusader
5160	(1919)	Resolution
5161	(1938)	Sultan
5162	(1932)	Anson
5163	(1963)	Boadicea
5164	(1968)	Cumberland
5165	(1934)	Blenheim
5166	(1920)	Flying Fox
5167	(1975)	Jupiter
5168	(1972)	Hindostan
5169	(1933)	Barfleur
5170	(1940)	Trafalgar
5171	(1962)	Aurora
5172	(1910)	Cavalier
5173	(1928)	Glatton
5174	(1947)	Zillah
5175	(1973)	Hood
5176	(1931)	Agincourt
5177	(1978)	Merlin
5178	(1907)	Black Watch
5179	(1941)	Alfred the Great
5180	(1926)	La France
5181	(1958)	Royal Oak
5182	(1980)	Neptune
5183	(1924)	Powerful
5184	(1917)	Inflexible
5185	(1942)	King Edward VII
5186	(1950)	Victorious

Several of these engines never carried their new L.M.S. numbers.

4-4-0 Whale L.N.W.R. Precursor 2P, 3P*

Built 1904-7

Weight:
59 tons 15 cwt.

Boiler Pressure:
175 lbs.

Cylinders:
$19'' \times 26''$; $20\frac{1}{2}'' \times 26''$*

Driving Wheel Diameter:
6′ 9″

Tractive Effort:
18,222 lbs.; 20,640 lbs.*

Valve Gear:
Joy

Number built: 130.

*No. 5270 onwards are the engines which had already been rebuilt with superheaters prior to the grouping. Some of the earlier ones were also so treated subsequently. Most of the class carried Belpaire fireboxes in later years.

First loco withdrawn 1927; last loco withdrawn 1949.
No. in service (1/1/23) 130; (1/1/48) 1.

5187†	(2023)	Helvellyn
5188†	(412)	Marquis
5189	(510)	Albatross
5190	(639)	Ajax
5191	(648)	Archimedes
5192	(685)	Cossack
5193	(1102)	Thunderbolt
5194	(1117)	Vandal
5195	(622)	Euphrates
5196	(638)	Huskisson
5197	(645)	Mammoth
5198	(40)	Niagara
5199	(1104)	Cedric
5200	(1111)	Cerberus
5201	(1431)	Egeria
5202	(520)	Panopea
5203	(2031)	Waverley
5204	(184)	Havelock
5205	(1115)	Apollo
5206	(1545)	Cyclops
5207†	(2061)	Eglinton
5208	(619)	Messenger
5209	(2120)	Trentham
5210	(1430)	Victor
5211†	(113)	Aurania
5212†	(315)	Harrowby
5213	(311)	Emperor
5214	(1509)	America
5215	(2257)	Vulture
5216†	(911)	Herald
5217	(1114)	Knowsley
5218†	(1116)	Pandora
5219	(1510)	Psyche
5220	(1784)	Python
5221	(2202)	Vizier
5222	(117)	Alaska
5223†	(127)	Snake
5224	(229)	Stork
5225†	(1301)	Candidate
5226	(1396)	Harpy
5227	(2007)	Oregon
5228	(2012)	Penguin
5229	(2115)	Servia
5230	(2576)	Arab
5231	(2579)	Ganymede
5232	(2580)	Problem
5233	(2581)	Peel
5234	(2582)	Rowland Hill
5235	(2583)	Moonstone
5236	(2585)	Watt
5237	(234)	Pearl
5238	(526)	Ilion
5239	(723)	Coptic
5240	(837)	Friar
5241	(1311)	Napoleon
5242	(1312)	Ionic
5243	(1642)	Lapwing
5244	(2017)	Tubal
5245†	(561)	Antaeus
5246	(675)	Adjutant
5247	(772)	Admiral
5248	(804)	Amphion
5249	(988)	Bellerophon
5250	(1433)	Faerie Queene
5251	(1650)	Richard Trevithick
5252	(1787)	Hyperion
5253	(1)	Clive
5254	(218)	Daphne
5255	(419)	Monarch
5256	(665)	Mersey
5257	(1011)	Locke
5258	(1364)	Clyde
5259	(2053)	Edith
5260	(2181)	Eleanor
5261	(276)	Doric
5262	(754)	Celtic
5263	(807)	Oceanic
5264	(976)	Pacific
5265	(1297)	Phalaris
5266	(1516)	Alecto
5270	(469)	Marmion
5271	(802)	Gaelic
5272†	(1363)	Brindley
5273	(2064)	Jason
5274	(688)	Hecate
5275	(1439)	Tiger
5276	(7)	Titan
5277†	(2164)	Oberon
5278	(513)	Precursor
5279†	(2062)	Sunbeam
5280	(2166)	Shooting Star
5281	(564)	Erebus
5282†	(515)	Champion
5283	(2011)	Brougham
5284	(333)	Ambassador
5285	(1419)	Tamerlane
5286†	(1573)	Dunrobin
5287†	(365)	Alchymist
5288†	(1469)	Tantalus
5289	(301)	Leviathan
5290	(310)	Achilles
5291†	(1395)	Harbinger
5292†	(366)	Medusa
5293†	(2513)	Levens

5294†	(106)	Druid	5307†	(305)	Senator
5295	(1723)	Scorpion	5308	(2)	Simoom
5296	(659)	Dreadnought	5309	(2578)	Fame
5297†	(643)	Sirocco	5310†	(1120)	Thunderer
5298†	(60)	Dragon	5311†	(811)	Express
5299†	(1137)	Vesuvius	5312	(2584)	Velocipede
5300†	(1617)	Hydra	5313	(2577)	Etna
5301	(300)	Emerald	5314	(282)	Alaric
5302†	(1309)	Shamrock	5315	(2051)	Delamere
5303	(323)	Argus	5316	(1737)	Viscount
5304†	(302)	Greyhound	5317	(374)	Empress
5305	(303)	Himalaya	5318	(806)	Swiftsure
5306	(1387)	Lang Meg	5319†	(990)	Bucephalus

†Surviving engines in 1934 had 20000 added to their numbers consequent on the construction of new class 5 4-6-0's.

No. 25297 'Sirocco' the only surviving engine in 1948, was allocated B.R. No. 58010 but never carried it.

4-4-0 Bowen-Cooke L.N.W.R. 'George the Fifth' Class 2P

Built 1910-1915

Weight:
59 tons 17 cwt.

Driving Wheel Diameter:
6′ 9″

Boiler Pressure:
180 lbs.

Tractive Effort:
20,640 lbs.

Cylinders:
$20\frac{1}{2}'' \times 26''$

Valve Gear:
Joy

Number built: 90.

First loco withdrawn 1935; last loco withdrawn 1948.
No. in service (1/1/23) 90; (1/1/48) 3.

5320	(2663)	George the Fifth	5338	(2512)	Thomas Houghton
5321†	(1059)	Lord Loch	5339†	(2168)	Henry Maudslay
5322†	(1294)	F. S. P. Wolferstan	5340	(956)	Bulldog
5323†	(1583)	Henry Ward	5341	(1489)	Wolfhound
5324†	(1725)	John Bateson	5342	(1504)	Boarhound
5325†	(2025)	Sir Thomas Brooke	5343	(1513)	Otterhound
5326†	(2155)	W. C. Brocklehurst	5344†	(1532)	Bloodhound
5327	(228)	E. Nettlefold	5345†	(1628)	Foxhound
5328	(445)	P. H. Chambres	5346	(1662)	Deerhound
5329	(2664)	Queen Mary	5347†	(1706)	Elkhound
5330	(1550)	Westminster	5348†	(5000)	Coronation
5331†	(2271)	J. P. Bickersteth	5349	(502)	British Empire
5332	(896)	George Whale	5350†	(868)	India
5333	(1559)	Drake	5351	(882)	Canada
5334†	(2151)	Newcomen	5352	(1218)	Australia
5335	(2507)	Miles MacInnes	5353	(1792)	Staghound
5336	(238)	F. W. Webb	5354	(2081)	New Zealand
5337	(1195)	T. J. Hare	5355	(2212)	South Africa

Stroudley 0-6-0T No. 57B 'Lochgorm', still running in H.R. colours as late as 1929, one of the last engines on the L.M.S. to retain pre-grouping livery. Although dating back to 1872 it survived a general overhaul, emerging as 16119 (without name)and was not scrapped until 1932.

0-6-0T No. 16380, one of three built by Drummond in 1904, utilising parts of withdrawn 2-4 0 tender engines.

'Barney' 0-6-0 No. 17702, retaining the typical Drummond 'pop' safety valves mounted on the dome, and in this case also the firebox cross water tubes. These features were eventually removed on the whole class and in most cases the engines received C.R. type boilers.

The original Jones 4-6-0, the first engine of its wheel arrangement in the British Isles, now restored as Highland Railway 103.

North Stafford rail motor No. 3 out of service at Stoke in 1923.
[W. H. Whitworth

Lancashire and Yorkshire rail motor at Edlington in 1933.

L.N.W.R. rail motor taking water at Moffat in 1931

Wolverton and Stony Stratford tram engine at Wolverton in 1925
[K. A. C. R. Nunn

G. & S.W.R. Stirling 0-4-2 No. 17029. [L. R. Tomsett

G. & S.W.R. Smellie 0-6-0 No. 17117, fitted with Stirling round topped cab [L. R. Tomsett

G. & S.W.R. Manson small 0-4-4T No. 16085. [L. R. Tomsett

G. & S.W.R. Drummond 2-6-0 No. 17830.

Highland Railway 'Strath' class 4-4-0 ,No. 14275 'Glentruim'.

Last survivor of the earlier 'Bruce' class 4-4-0's.

'Skye bogie' No. 14284, one of a class of nine engines specially built for the Kyle of Lochalsh line.

'Large Ben'. development of Mr. Drummonds' 'Small Ben' class (not illustrated) introduced in 1898. As later rebuilt with extended smokebox.

5356†	(2291)	Gibraltar	5383	(89)	John Mayall
5357†	(2495)	Bassethound	5384	(132)	S. R. Graves
5358	(2177)	Malta	5385	(1138)	William Froude
5359	(2498)	Cyprus	5386	(1193)	Edward Tootal
5360†	(361)	Beagle	5387†	(2154)	William Siemens
5361	(888)	Challenger	5388	(2282)	Richard Arkwright
5362†	(1360)	Fire Queen	5389†	(404)	Eclipse
5363	(1394)	Harrier	5390	(681)	St. George
5364	(1623)	Nubian	5391	(845)	Saddleback
5365†	(1631)	Racehorse	5392†	(1188)	Penmaenmawr
5366	(1644)	Roebuck	5393†	(1680)	Loyalty
5367	(2089)	Traveller	5394	(2086)	Phaeton
5368	(2494)	Perseus	5395†	(2279)	Henry Crosfield
5369†	(1371)	Quail	5396	(1481)	Typhon
5370	(1417)	Landrail	5397	(2197)	Planet
5371†	(1472)	Moorhen	5398	(2242)	Meteor
5372†	(1595)	Wild Duck	5399	(2428)	Lord Stalbridge
5373†	(1681)	Ptarmigan	5400	(363)	Llandudno
5374†	(2220)	Vanguard	5401	(789)	Windermere
5375	(1713)	Partridge	5402	(984)	Carnarvon
5376†	(1730)	Snipe	5403	(104)	Leamington Spa
5377†	(1733)	Grouse	5404	(226)	Colwyn Bay
5378†	(1777)	Widgeon	5405	(1086)	Conway
5379	(1799)	Woodcock	5406†	(2153)	Llandrindod
5380†	(82)	Charles Dickens	5407	(2233)	Blackpool
5381	(752)	John Hick	5408†	(2106)	Holyhead
5382†	(2124)	John Rennie	5409†	(2370)	Dovedale

†Surviving engines in 1934 had 20000 added to their numbers consequent on the anticipated construction of new class 5 4-6-0's.

Nos. 25350 (which had by then lost its name) and 25373 Ptarmigan the only surviving engines in 1948, were allocated B.R. Nos. 58011 and 58012 but neither lasted long enough to carry them.

4-6-0 Whale L.N.W.R. Experiment Class 3P

Built 1905-10

One engine Rebuilt 1915*

Weight:
65 tons 15 cwt.

Driving Wheel Diameter:
6′ 3″

Boiler Pressure:
175 lbs.

Tractive Effort:
18,616 lbs.; 20,232 lbs.*

Cylinders:
(2) 19″×26″
(4) 14″×26″*

Valve Gear:
Joy
Dendy-Marshall*

Original number in class: 105

Many of the later survivors were rebuilt with Belpaire fireboxes.

First loco withdrawn 1925; last loco withdrawn 1935.
No. in service (1/2/23) 105; (1/1/48) 0.

5450 (66) Experiment
5451 (306) Autocrat
5452 (353) Britannic
5453 (372) Belgic
5454 (507) Sarmatian
5455 (565) City of Carlisle
5456† (893) City of Chester
5457† (1074) City of Dublin
5458 (1357) City of Edinburgh
5459 (165) City of Lichfield
5460† (828) City of Liverpool
5461† (978) City of London
5462† (1405) City of Manchester
5463 (1575) City of Paris
5464 (1669) City of Glasgow
5465 (1986) Clanricarde
5466† (1987) Glendower
5467 (1988) Hurricane
5468 (1989) Lady of the Lake
5469 (1990) North Western
5470 (1991) Palmerston
5471 (1992) President
5472 (1993) Richard Moon
5473† (1994) Scottish Chief
5474 (61) Atalanta
5475 (222) Ivanhoe
5476 (291) Leander
5477 (667) Mazeppa
5478 (1304) Prometheus
5479† (1676) Shakespeare
5480 (1709) Princess May
5481 (1995) Tornado
5482 (2027) Queen Empress
5483 (2052) Stephenson
5484 (2269) William Cawkwell
5485 (496) Harlequin
5486 (830) Phosphorus
5487† (902) Combermere
5488† (937) Princess Alice
5489 (1014) Henry Bessemer
5490 (2112) Victoria
5491† (1135) Prince George
5492 (1526) Sanspareil
5493 (2161) Jeannie Deans
5494 (322) Adriatic
5495 (884) Greater Britain
5496 (887) Fortuna
5497† (1020) Majestic
5498 (1483) Redgauntlet
5499 (1490) Wellington
5500 (1553) Faraday
5501 (1571) Herschel
5502† (2076) Pheasant
5503 (2116) Greystoke
5504† (2621) Ethelred
5505 (2622) Eunomia
5506† (2623) Lord of the Isles
5507 (2624) Saracen
5508† (2625) Buckland
5509† (2626) Chillington
5510 (2627) President Lincoln
5511† (2628) Banshee
5512 (2629) Terrier
5513 (2630) Buffalo
5514† (1406) George Findlay
5515 (1413) Henry Cort
5516 (1477) Hugh Myddleton
5517 (1498) Thomas Savery
5518 (1566) John Penn
5519 (1603) Princess Alexandra
5520 (1649) Sisyphus
5521 (1661) Wordsworth
5522 (1781) Lightning
5523† (2022) Marlborough
5524 (2637) Babylon
5525† (2638) Byzantium
5526† (2639) Bactria
5527 (2640) Belisarius
5528† (2641) Bellona
5529 (2642) Berenice
5530 (2643) Bacchus
5531† (2644) Berengaria
5532† (2645) Britomart
5533 (2646) Boniface
5534 (1412) Bedfordshire
5535 (1418) Cheshire
5536 (1420) Derbyshire
5537 (1455) Herefordshire
5538 (1611) Hertfordshire
5539† (1616) Lancashire
5540 (71) Oxfordshire
5541 (275) Shropshire
5542 (677) Staffordshire
5543 (1002) Warwickshire
5544 (1534) Westmorland
5545 (1624) Leicestershire
5546 (1652) Middlesex
5547 (1689) Monmouthshire
5548† (1703) Northumberland
5549 (1471) Worcestershire
5550 (1561) Yorkshire
5551† (1618) Carnarvonshire
5552† (1621) Denbighshire
5553 (1658) Flintshire
5554* (1361) Prospero

†Surviving engines in 1934 had 20000 added to their numbers consequent on the renumbering and construction of ' Baby Scot ' and ' Jubilee ' class 4-6-0s' and anticipated building of further class 5 4-6-0's.

4-6-0 Bowen-Cooke 'Prince of Wales' Class 3P
Built 1911-1921

Weight:
66 tons 10 cwt.

Driving Wheel Diameter:
6′ 3″

Boiler Pressure:
175 lbs.

Tractive Effort:
21,760 lbs.

Cylinders:
$20\frac{1}{2}'' \times 26''$

Valve Gear:
Joy*

Number built: 246.

*Nos. 5632, 5672, 5688 and 5726 were rebuilt in 1923/4 with outside Walschaerts valve gear, and one additional engine, No. 5845, was constructed after the grouping, in 1924, to this design. Many of the later survivors were rebuilt with Belpaire fireboxes.

First loco withdrawn 1933; last loco withdrawn 1949.
No. in service (1/1/23) 245; (1/1/48) 4.

5600	(819)	Prince of Wales
5601	(1388)	Andromeda
5602	(1452)	Bonaventure
5603	(1454)	Coquette
5604	(1537)	Enchantress
5605	(1691)	Pathfinder
5606	(1704)	Conqueror
5607	(1721)	Defiance
5608	(2021)	Wolverine
5609	(2359)	Hermione
5610	(362)	Robert Southey
5611	(892)	Charles Wolfe
5612	(1081)	John Keats
5613	(1089)	Sydney Smith
5614	(1134)	Victor Hugo
5615	(2040)	Oliver Goldsmith
5616	(2075)	Robert Burns
5617	(321)	Henry W. Longfellow
5618	(479)	Thomas B. Macaulay
5619	(951)	Bulwer Lytton
5620	(2198)	John Ruskin
5621	(2205)	Thomas Moore
5622	(2213)	Charles Kingsley
5623	(1679)	Lord Byron
5624	(2249)	Thomas Campbell
5625	(2283)	Robert L. Stevenson
5626	(86)	Mark Twain
5627	(146)	Lewis Carroll
5628	(307)	R. B. Sheridan
5629	(637)	Thomas Gray
5630	(979)	W. M. Thackeray
5631	(1400)	Felicia Hermans
5632*	(964)	Bret Harte
5633	(985)	Sir W. S. Gilbert
5634	(1321)	William Cowper
5635	(2152)	Charles Lamb
5636	(2293)	Percy Bysshe Shelley
5637	(2377)	Edward Gibbon
5638	(2443)	Charles James Lever
5639	(2520)	G. P. Neele
5640	(27)	General Joffre
5641	(88)	Czar of Russia
5642	(122)	King of the Belgians
5643	(160)	King of Serbia
5644	(185)	King of Italy
5645	(877)	Raymond Poincare
5646	(1333)	Sir John French
5647	(2275)	Edith Cavell
5648	(2396)	Queen of the Belgians
5649	(2408)	Admiral Jellicoe
5650	(606)	Castor
5651	(745)	Pluto
5652	(810)	Onyx
5653	(1352)	The Nile
5654	(1379)	Witch
5655	(1484)	Smeaton
5656	(1084)	Shark
5657	(1346)	Trent
5658	(2417)	Atlas
5659	(2442)	Odin
5660	(90)	Kestrel
5661	(95)	Gallipoli
5662	(126)	Anzac
5663	(136)	Minerva
5664	(173)	Livingstone
5665	(233)	Suvla Bay
5666	(257)	Plynlimmon
5667	(401)	Zamiel
5668	(446)	Pegasus
5669	(525)	Vulcan
5670	(610)	Albion
5671	(849)	Arethusa
5672*	(867)	Condor
5673	(1100)	Lusitania

5674	(1132)	Scott
5675	(1466)	Sphinx
5676	(1744)	Petrel
5677	(1749)	Precedent
5678	(2055)	Milton
5679	(2063)	Hibernia
5680	(2175)	Loadstone
5681	(2203)	Falstaff
5682	(2339)	Samson
5683	(1324)	Falaba
5684	(2092)	Arabic
5685	(2276)	Persia
5686	(2295)	Anglia
5687	(2300)	Hotspur
5688*	(2340)	Tara
5689	(2392)	Caliban
5690	(28)	
5691	(263)	
5692	(295)	
5693	(391)	
5694	(740)	
5695	(805)	
5696	(863)	
5697	(940)	Richard Cobden
5698	(1196)	
5699	(1546)	
5700	(621)	Telford
5701	(707)	
5702	(1373)	
5703	(1453)	
5704	(1584)	Scotia
5705	(57)	
5706	(504)	Canning
5707	(974)	Hampden
5708	(1673)	
5709	(2184)	
5710	(33)	
5711	(388)	
5712	(1123)	
5713	(1215)	
5714	(1351)	
5715	(1437)	
5716	(1670)	
5717	(1732)	
5718	(2073)	
5719	(2285)	
5720	(444)	
5721	(497)	
5722	(501)	
5723	(522)	Stentor
5724	(601)	
5725	(783)	
5726*	(56)	
5727	(924)	
5728	(1125)	
5729	(1290)	Lucknow
5730	(1307)	
5731	(67)	
5732	(435)	
5733	(686)	
5734	(812)	
5735	(969)	
5736	(1325)	Disraeli
5737	(1341)	
5738	(1355)	
5739	(1620)	
5740	(35)	
5741	(395)	
5742	(487)	
5743	(1178)	Prince Albert
5744	(889)	
5745	(1113)	
5746	(1408)	
5747	(1422)	
5748	(1478)	
5749	(1535)	
5750	(1542)	Marathon
5751	(1549)	
5752	(1557)	
5753	(1694)	Premier
5754	(2516)	Dalton
5755	(120)	
5756	(123)	
5757	(125)	
5758	(129)	
5759	(135)	
5760	(140)	
5761	(141)	
5762	(142)	
5763	(145)	
5764	(148)	
5765	(224)	
5766	(227)	
5767	(232)	
5768	(237)	
5769	(239)	
5770	(240)	
5771	(241)	
5772	(242)	
5773	(243)	
5774	(244)	
5775	(246)	
5776	(247)	
5777	(248)	
5778	(249)	
5779	(251)	
5780	(252)	
5781	(258)	
5782	(259)	
5783	(261)	
5784	(266)	
5785	(267)	
5786	(268)	
5787	(269)	
5788	(270)	
5789	(272)	
5790	(273)	
5791	(274)	

5792	(394)	5820	(354)
5793	(277)	5821	(491)
5794	(281)	5822	(493)
5795	(284)	5823	(518)
5796	(292)	5824	(551)
5797	(293)	5825	(554)
5798	(296)	5826	(549)
5799	(313)	5827	(557)
5800	(324)	5828	(558)
5801	(325)	5829	(778)
5802	(331)	5830	(1099)
5803	(355)	5831	(1179)
5804	(357)	5832	(1316)
5805	(359)	5833	(1339)
5806	(435)	5834	(53)
5807	(436)	5835	(197)
5808	(438)	5836	(433)
5809	(440)	5837	(614)
5810	(442)	5838	(1083)
5811	(443)	5839	(1320)
5812	(452)	5840	(1349)
5813	(483)	5841	(1323)
5814	(489)	5842	(1344)
5815	(490)	5843	(1742)
5816	(492)	5844	(2043)
5817	(17)	5845*	(built 1924, never had a L.N.W.R. number.
5818	(153)		
5819	(198)		

*No. 5845 was exhibited at Wembley Exhibition before being put into traffic, during which time it was temporarily named " Prince of Wales ".

Nearly all of this class were renumbered in 1934 but the addition of 20000, owing to the projected construction of " Jubilee " class 4-6-0's, although in fact these engines never reached beyond 5742.

Exceptions which were never renumbered owing to the engines already having been withdrawn were as follows: 5600, 5606, 5609, 5610, 5622, 5632, 5639, 5649, 5652 and 5688.

Four engines which survived into Nationalisation days, Nos. 25648, 25673, 25752 and 25787, were allocated B.R. Nos. 58000-3, but none lasted long enough to carry them.

4-6-0 Bowen-Cooke L.N.W.R. ' Claughton ' Class 5P, 5XP

Built 1913-1921

*Some rebuilt with large boilers, 1928

Weight:
77 tons 15 cwt.
89 tons*

Boiler Pressure:
175 lbs.
200 lbs.*

Cylinders:
(4) $15\frac{3}{4}'' \times 26''$ (some engines had $15\frac{1}{2}''$ diameter and others 16″ diameter)

Driving Wheel Diameter:
6′ 9″

Tractive Effort:
27,072 lbs.
29,570 lbs.*

Valve Gear:
Walschaerts*
10 engines were later fitted with Caprotti valve gear.

Number built: 130.

First loco withdrawn 1929 (accident); last loco withdrawn 1949.
No. in service (1/1/23) 130; (1/1/48) 1.

5900	(2222)	Sir Gilbert Claughton
5901	(1161)	Sir Robert Turnbull
5902	(1191)	Sir Frank Ree
5903	(21)	Duke of Sutherland
5904	(163)	Holland Hibbert
5905	(650)	Lord Rathmore
5906†	(1159)	Ralph Brocklebank
5907	(1319)	Sir Frederick Harrison
5908*†	(1327)	Alfred Fletcher
5909	(2046)	Charles N. Lawrence
5910†	(250)	J. A. Bright
5911	(260)	W. E. Dorrington
5912	(1131)	Lord Faber
5913	(1429)	Colonel Lockwood
5914	(209)	J. Bruce Ismay
5915	(668)	Rupert Guinness
5916	(856)	E. Tootal Broadhurst
5917	(1567)	Charles J. Cropper
5918	(2239)	Frederick Baynes
5919	(2401)	Lord Kitchener
5920	(511)	George Macpherson
5921	(695)	Sir Arthur Lawley
5922*	(968)	Lord Kenyon
5923	(1093)	Sir Guy Calthrop
5924	(1345)	James Bishop
5925	(2174)	E. C. Trench
5926	(2204)	Sir Herbert Walker K.C.B.
5927*†	(2221)	Sir Francis Dent
5928	(2338)	Charles H. Dent
5929	(2395)	J. A. F. Aspinall
5930	(37)	G. R. Jebb
5931	(154)	Captain Fryatt
5932	(155)	Sir Thomas Williams
5933	(162)	
5934	(186)	
5935	(713)	
5936	(1334)	
5937	(2042)	
5938	(2097)	
5939	(2230)	Clio
5940	(1019)	Columbus
5941	(1335)	
5942	(2366)	
5943	(2373)	Tennyson
5944	(2411)	
5945	(2420)	Ingestre
5946*†	(2427)	Duke of Connaught
5947	(2431)	
5948*†	(2445)	Baltic
5949	(2450)	
5950	(116)	
5951	(159)	
5952	(171)	
5953†	(986)	Buckingham
5954	(1085)	
5955	(1103)	
5956	(2122)	
5957*†	(2368)	
5958	(2416)	
5959	(2426)	
5960	(69)	
5961	(178)	
5962*†	(194)	
5963	(972)	
5964	(1914)	Patriot
5965	(484)	
5966	(1177)	Bunsen
5967	(1407)	L./Cpl. J. A. Christie, V.C.
5968	(1599)	John o' Groat
5969	(2179)	
5970†	(2499)	Patience
5971	(2511)	Croxteth
5972†	(1726)	
5973	(1741)	
5974	(1747)	
5975*†	(12)	Talisman
5976	(2035)	Private E. Sykes, V.C.
5977	(2083)	
5978	(2231)	
5979	(2268)	Frobisher
5980	(85)	
5981	(98)	
5982	(103)	
5983	(201)	
5984	(499)	
5985	(808)	
5986†	(1092)	
5987	(1096)	
5988	(1097)	Private W. Wood, V.C.
5989	(1133)	
5990	(1326)	
5991	(2059)	C. J. Bowen-Cooke
5992	(2090)	
5993†	(2095)	
5994	(6)	
5995	(8)	
5996	(10)	
5997	(11)	
5998	(2101)	
5999†	(2430)	Vindictive
6000	(15)	
6001	(23)	
6002	(30)	Thalaba
6003	(32)	
6004†	(42)	Princess Louise
6005	(63)	
6006	(68)	
6007	(102)	
6008	(110)	Lady Godiva
6009	(119)	
6010	(149)	

6011 (150) Illustrious	6021 (192) Bevere
6012 (152)	6022 (205)
6013*†(156)	6023*†(207) Sir Charles Cust
6014 (157)	6024 (208)
6015 (158) Private E. Sykes, V.C.§	6025 (210)
6016 (161)	6026 (211)
6017† (169) Breadalbane	6027 (517)
6018 (179) Private W. Wood, V.C.§	6028 (1216)
6019 (180) Llewellyn	6029† (1220)
6020 (183)	

†Rebuilt large boiler. *Rebuilt Caprotti valve gear.

No. 6004 was the only engine to survive Nationalisation, and although allotted the No. 46004 did not carry it. It outlasted its sisters by several years, the last previous withdrawal having been in 1941. Its name had been removed in 1936.

§Names added 1926.

0-4-2PT Webb L.N.W.R. 1P

Built 1896-1901

Weight:
35 tons

Boiler Pressure:
150 lbs.

Cylinders:
17″×24″

Driving Wheel Diameter:
4′ 3″

Tractive Effort:
16,530 lbs.

Valve Gear:
Stevenson

Number built: 20.

First loco withdrawn 1929; last loco withdrawn 1956.
No. in service (1/1/23) 20; (1/1/48) 2.

6400 (3464)	6404 (3468)	6408 (3472)	6411 (3525)	6414 (3528)	6417 (3531)
6401 (3465)	6405 (3469)	6409 (3473)	6412 (3526)	6415 (3529)	6418 (3532)
6402 (3466)	6406 (3470)	6410 (3524)	6413 (3527)	6416 (3530)	6419 (3533)
6403 (3467)	6407 (3471)				

It appears that these engines were erroneously classified as passenger engines, which was odd as they were not even fitted with vacuum brakes.

Only Nos. 6402, 6403, 6407, 6414 and 6418 actually carried these first allotted L.M.S. numbers, and in 1927 the whole class was more correctly renumbered 7850-7869 in the freight group. The two engines which survived Nationalisation duly became B.R. Nos. 47862 and 47865.

2-4-0T Webb L.N.W.R. 1P

Built 1876-1885

Weight:
38 tons 4 cwt.

Boiler Pressure:
150 lbs.

Cylinders:
17″×20″

Driving Wheel Diameter:
4′ 6″

Tractive Effort:
13,045 lbs.

Valve Gear:
Stephenson

Number built: 15.

First loco withdrawn 1924; last loco withdrawn 1952.
No. in service (1/1/23) 15; (1/1/48) 1.

6420 (2234)	6423 (2243)	6426 (2248)	6429 (2280)	6431 (1000)	6433 (1443)
6421 (2238)	6424 (2244)	6427 (2252)	6430 (999)	6432 (1001)	6434 (386)
6422 (2240)	6425 (2247)	6428 (2278)			

No. 6428, the last survivor by many years (the last previous withdrawal having been in 1936) became 26428 in 1948 and B.R. 58092 in 1949.

Several were scrapped without carrying their L.M.S. numbers.

4-4-0T Adams North London inside-cylinder 1P

Built 1865-1869

Weight:
51 tons

Boiler Pressure:
160 lbs.

Cylinders:
$17\frac{1}{2}'' \times 24''$

Driving Wheel Diameter:
5′ 11″

Tractive Effort:
13,964 lbs.

Valve Gear:
Stephenson

Number built: 11.

First loco withdrawn before 1909; last loco withdrawn 1925.
No. in service (1/1/23) 4; (1/1/48) 0.

First No. in brackets is original N.L.R. number, Second No., L.N.W.R. number.

6435 (109, 2874)	6436 (114, 2648)	6437 (117, 2649)	6438 (103, 2647)

Nos. 2647-2649 were taken over by the L.N.W.R. in 1909, and 2874 in 1923. None of them actually carried their L.M.S. numbers.

4-4-0T Park North London outside-cylinder 1P

Built 1886-1907 (most were nominal rebuilds of older engines constructed from 1871 onwards)

Weight:
49 tons 13 cwt.

Boiler Pressure:
160 lbs.

Cylinders:
$17'' \times 24''$

Driving Wheel Diameter:
5′ 5″

Tractive Effort:
14,511 lbs.

Valve Gear:
Stephenson

Number built: 74.

First loco withdrawn 1914; last loco withdrawn 1929.
No. in service (1/1/23) 74; (1/1/48) 0.

First No. in brackets is former N.L.R. number. Second No. L.N.W.R. number. The engines were absorbed into L.N.W.R. stock early in 1923 and temporarily renumbered into the L.N.W.R. list pending the L.M.S. scheme, but some of them went straight from N.L.R. to L.M.S. numbers; although many others never actually carried their allotted numbers in the new L.M.S. list.

6439 (8, 2807)	6458 (35, 2828)	6477 (49, 2842)	6496 (38, 2831)
6440 (9, 2808)	6459 (30, 2824)	6478 (50, 2843)	6497 (33, 2826)
6441 (22, 2816)	6460 (31, 2825)	6479 (51, 2844)	6498 (39, 2832)
6442 (25, 2819)	6461 (67, 2853)	6480 (53, 2845)	6499 (81, 2861)
6443 (125, 2872)	6462 (68, 2854)	6481 (54, 2846)	6500 (82, 2862)
6444 (5, 2804)	6463 (69, 2855)	6482 (55, 2847)	6501 (83, 2863)
6445 (6, 2805)	6464 (70, 2856)	6483 (56, 2848)	6502 (84, 2864)
6446 (10, 2809)	6465 (36 ,2829)	6484 (11, 2810)	6503 (85, 2865)
6447 (20, 2814)	6466 (37, 2830)	6485 (12, 2811)	6504 (86, 2866)
6448 (127, 2873)	6467 (43, 2836)	6486 (13, 2812)	6505 (87, 2867)
6449 (7. 2806)	6468 (44, 2837)	6487 (14, 2813)	6506 (88, 2868)
6450 (124, 2871)	6469 (71, 2857)	6488 (57, 2849)	6507 (89, 2869)
6451 (21, 2815)	6470 (72, 2858)	6489 (58, 2850)	6508 (90, 2870)
6452 (28, 2822)	6471 (73, 2859)	6490 (59, 2851)	6509 (1, 2800)
6453 (29, 2823)	6472 (74, 2860)	6491 (60, 2852)	6510 (2, 2801)
6454 (41, 2834)	6473 (45, 2838)	6492 (23, 2817)	6511 (3, 2802)
6455 (40, 2833)	6474 (46, 2839)	6493 (24, 2818)	6512 (4, 2803)
6456 (42, 2835)	6475 (47, 2840)	6494 (26, 2820)	
6457 (34, 2827)	6476 (48, 2841)	6495 (27, 2821)	

The last engine to remain, in 1929, No. 6445, was retained at Derby with a view to preservation, but unfortunately was broken up in 1932.

2-4-2T Webb L.N.W.R. 1P

Built 1882-1890

Weight:
Not available

Boiler Pressure:
150 lbs.

Cylinders:
17″×20″

Driving Wheel Diameter:
4′ 6″

Tractive Effort:
12,577 lbs.

Valve Gear:
Joy

Number built: 88.

First loco withdrawn 1913 (sold to Wirral Railway); last loco withdrawn 1932.
No. in service (1/1/23) 86; (1/1/48) 0.

6515 (798)	6523 (298)	6531 (2504)	6539 (5)	6547 (977)	6555 (1365)
6516 (691)	6524 (299)	6532 (2505)	6540 (708)	6548 (980)	6556 (1438)
6517 (891)	6525 (521)	6533 (2509)	6541 (763)	6549 (998)	6557 (1440)
6518 (286)	6526 (523)	6534 (2510)	6542 (1056)	6550 (1003)	6558 (1441)
6519 (287)	6527 (529)	6535 (2514)	6543 (1073)	6551 (1008)	6559 (1442)
6520 (288)	6528 (769)	6536 (2515)	6544 (2523)	6552 (1072)	6560 (1444)
6521 (294)	6529 (2493)	6537 (2519)	6545 (603)	6553 (1358)	6561 (1445)
6522 (297)	6530 (2500)	6538 (2521)	6546 (765)	6554 (1362)	6562 (1446)

6563	(383)	6570	(839)	6577	(721)	6583	(786)	6589	(816)	6595	(975)
6564	(384)	6571	(844)	6578	(756)	6584	(788)	6590	(820)	6596	(2501)
6565	(385)	6572	(846)	6579	(760)	6585	(791)	6591	(430)	6597	(2506)
6566	(387)	6573	(2065)	6580	(761)	6586	(663)	6592	(825)	6598	(946)
6567	(389)	6574	(2067)	6581	(781)	6587	(729)	6593	(907)	6599	(2069)
6568	(390)	6575	(2068)	6582	(785)	6588	(730)	6594	(908)	6600	(1176)
6569	(835)	6576	(712)								

Several scrapped without carrying their L.M.S. number.

2-4-2T Webb L.N.W.R. 1P

Built 1890-1897

Weight:
50 tons 10 cwt.

Boiler Pressure:
150 lbs.

Cylinders:
17″×24″

Driving Wheel Diameter:
5′ 6″

Tractive Effort:
12,910 lbs.

Valve Gear:
Joy

Number built: 160.

First loco withdrawn 1921; last loco withdrawn 1955.
No. in service (1/1/23) 157; (1/1/48) 43.

6601*	(910)	6633	(1761)	6665	(1174)	6697	(2145)	6729	(2262)
6602	(214)	6634	(1762)	6666*	(2146)	6698	(31)	6730	(2263)
6603*	(459)	6635*	(1763)	6667	(2148)	6699	(50)	6731	(2264)
6604*	(465)	6636	(1765)	6668	(2149)	6700	(290)	6732	(2265)
6605	(466)	6637*	(1766)	6669	(202)	6701*	(342)	6733	(2266)
6606	(655)	6638	(1767)	6670	(204)	6702	(620)	6734	(2267)
6607	(133)	6639	(1768)	6671	(886)	6703	(649)	6735	(1153)
6608	(199)	6640	(338)	6672	(1157)	6704	(923)	6736	(838)
6609	(546)	6641	(408)	6673	(1197)	6705	(960)	6737	(2147)
6610	(608)	6642	(409)	6674	(2135)	6706	(1018)	6738	(1367)
6611	(613)	6643*	(431)	6675	(2136)	6707	(2232)	6739	(1374)
6612	(657)	6644	(481)	6676	(2137)	6708	(255)	6740	(1383)
6613	(658)	6645	(1144)	6677	(2138)	6709	(426)	6741	(1386)
6614	(660)	6646	(1152)	6678	(2139)	6710	(626)	6742	(1398)
6615	(661)	6647	(1165)	6679	(2140)	6711	(680)	6743	(1402)
6616*	(662)	6648	(1169)	6680*	(2141)	6712*	(847)	6744	(1409)
6617	(897)	6649	(2125)	6681	(2142)	6713	(1180)	6745	(1410)
6618	(900)	6650	(2126)	6682	(2143)	6714	(70)	6746	(1423)
6619	(921)	6651	(2127)	6683*	(2144)	6715	(144)	6747	(1425)
6620*	(922)	6652	(2128)	6684	(2215)	6716	(151)	6748	(1378)
6621	(1769)	6653	(2129)	6685	(2216)	6717	(187)	6749	(1381)
6622	(1750)	6654*	(2130)	6686	(2217)	6718	(340)	6750	(1389)
6623	(1751)	6655	(2131)	6687*	(2218)	6719	(341)	6751	(1391)
6624	(1752)	6656*	(2132)	6688	(2219)	6720	(371)	6752	(1392)
6625	(1753)	6657	(2133)	6689	(427)	6721	(402)	6753	(1393)
6626	(1754)	6658*	(2134)	6690	(697)	6722	(853)	6754	(1451)
6627	(1755)	6659	(406)	6691	(1143)	6723	(1156)	6755	(1458)
6628	(1756)	6660	(413)	6692	(1145)	6724	(516)	6756	(1463)
6629	(1757)	6661	(425)	6693	(1147)	6725	(1151)	6757*	(1468)
6630	(1758)	6662	(718)	6694	(1148)	6726	(2259)		
6631	(1759)	6663	(779)	6695	(1149)	6727*	(2260)		
6632	(1760)	6664	(1150)	6696	(1155)	6728	(2261)		

No. 6616 was renumbered 26616 in 1945, apparently in error as no more of the class received the 20000 addition. It retained this number however until it became B.R. 46616 in 1948. Others which survived to have 40000 added to their numbers are indicated *.

2-4-2T Webb Wirral Railway 1P

Built 1877-1884

(Purchased from L.N.W.R., 1913-1921)

Boiler Pressure:
150 lbs.

Cylinders:
17″×20″

Valve Gear:
Joy

Driving Wheel Diameter:
4′ 6″

Tractive Effort:
12,577 lbs.

No. purchased by Wirral Railway:
4

First loco withdrawn 1924; last loco withdrawn 1928.
No. in service (1/1/23) 4; (1/1/48) 0.

First No. in brackets, original L.N.W.R. number. Second No., late W.R. number.

6758 (2282, 4)	6759 (969, 11)	6760 (889, 16)	6761 (284, 17)

Only No. 6761 actually carried its L.M.S. number.

2-4-2T Aspinall Wirral Railway 2P

Built 1889

(Purchased from L. & Y.R. 1921)

Weight:
56 tons

Boiler Pressure:
180 lbs.

Cylinders:
18″×26″

Driving Wheel Diameter:
5′ 8″

Tractive Effort:
19,416 lbs.

Valve Gear:
Joy

Number purchased by Wirral Railway: 1.

No. in service (1/1/23) 1; (1/1/48) 1. Withdrawn 1952.

6762 (W.R. 6). It was originally L. & Y.R. 1041, and was actually allocated the number 10638 in the L.M.S. list, taking its natural place amongst the L. & Y.R. engines, but for some reason it became L.M.S. 6762 instead. It survived to carry B.R. No. 46762, the only Wirral engine to last into Nationalisation days.

0-4-4T Wirral Railway 1P

Built 1887-8

Weight:
40 tons 16 cwt.

Boiler Pressure:
140 lbs.

Cylinders:
16″×24″

Driving Wheel Diameter:
5′ 2″

Tractive Effort:
11,696 lbs.

Valve Gear:
Stephenson

Number built: 5.

First loco withdrawn 1923; last loco withdrawn 1924.
No. in service (1/1/23) 4; (1/1/48) 0.

6770 (2)	6771 (5)	6772 (8)	6773 (9)

None of these engines actually carried its allotted L.M.S. number.

0-4-4T Wirral Railway 1P
Built 1894

Weight:
47 tons 18 cwt.

Boiler Pressure:
160 lbs.

Cylinders:
17″×24″

Driving Wheel Diameter:
5′ 2″

Tractive Effort:
15,211 lbs.

Valve Gear:
Stephenson

Number built: 2.

First loco withdrawn 1923; last loco withdrawn 1924.
No. in service (1/1/23) 2; (1/1/48) 0.

6774 (7)	6775 (10)

Neither engine actually carried its allotted L.M.S. number.

0-4-4T Wirral Railway 2P
Built 1914

Weight:
54 tons 10 cwt.

Boiler Pressure:
160 lbs.

Cylinders:
18″×26″

Driving Wheel Diameter:
5′ 2″

Tractive Effort:
18,479 lbs.

Valve Gear:
Stephenson

Number built: 1.

Withdrawn 1928.

6776 (3)

This is believed to be the only one of the pure Wirral built engines actually to have carried its L.M.S. number, although two of the 2-4-2T's, purchased from the L.N.W.R. and L. & Y.R., Nos. 6761 and 6762, also did so.

4-4-2T Whale L.N.W.R. 2P

Built 1906-1909

Weight:
74 tons 15 cwt.

Driving Wheel Diameter:
6′ 3″

Boiler Pressure:
175 lbs.

Tractive Effort:
15,216 lbs.

Cylinders:
19″×26″

Valve Gear:
Joy

Number built: 50.

First loco withdrawn 1927; last loco withdrawn 1940.
No. in service (1/1/23) 50; (1/1/48) 0.

6780 (528)	6789 (1985)	6798 (1508)	6806 (1589)	6814 (827)	6822 (1164)
6781 (531)	6790 (97)	6799 (2210)	6807 (1671)	6815 (875)	6823 (1219)
6782 (784)	6791 (111)	6800 (139)	6808 (1714)	6816 (1427)	6824 (1523)
6783 (1295)	6792 (181)	6801 (653)	6809 (2165)	6817 (1764)	6825 (1536)
6784 (1305)	6793 (196)	6802 (834)	6810 (44)	6818 (2196)	6826 (1551)
6785 (1981)	6794 (562)	6803 (874)	6811 (527)	6819 (2446)	6827 (2077)
6786 (1982)	6795 (616)	6804 (1506)	6812 (612)	6820 (920)	6828 (2223)
6787 (1983)	6796 (803)	6805 (1572)	6813 (762)	6821 (935)	6829 (2228)
6788 (1984)	6797 (1356)				

4-4-2T Wirral Railway 1P

Built 1892

Weight:
48 tons

Driving Wheel Diameter:
5′ 2″

Boiler Pressure:
140 lbs.

Tractive Effort:
11,790 lbs.

Cylinders:
16″×24″

Valve Gear:
Stephenson

Number built: 1.

Withdrawn 1924.
No. in service (1/1/23) 1; (1/1/48) 0.

6830 (1). It never actually carried its allotted L.M.S. number.

4-4-4T Barker Wirral Railway IP

Built 1903

Weight:
60 tons 5 cwt.

Boiler Pressure:
170 lbs.

Cylinders:
17″×24″

Driving Wheel Diameter:
5′ 3″

Tractive Effort:
15,910 lbs.

Valve Gear:
Stephenson

Number built: 3.

First loco withdrawn 1919; last loco withdrawn 1924.
No. in service (1/1/23) 2; (1/1/48) 0.

6850 (14)	6851 (15)

Neither engine actually carried its allotted L.M.S. number.

0-6-2T Webb L.N.W.R. IP

Built 1898-1902

Weight:
52 tons 6 cwt.

Boiler Pressure:
150 lbs.

Cylinders:
18″×24″

Driving Wheel Diameter:
5′ 0″

Tractive Effort:
15,865 lbs.

Valve Gear:
Joy

Number built: 80.

First loco withdrawn 1920; last loco withdrawn 1953.
No. in service (1/1/23) 77; (1/1/48) 15.

6860	(1560)	6876	(1626)	6892	(2016)	6908	(583)	6924	(741)
6861	(1562)	6877	(1627)	6893	(2019)	6909	(586)	6925	(1095)
6862	(1563)	6878	(1635)	6894	(2020)	6910	(587)	6926	(2113)
6863	(1564)	6879	(29)	6895	(2026)	6911	(593)	6927	(2211)
6864	(1574)	6880	(76)	6896	(2028)	6912*	(599)	6928	(775)
6865	(1587)	6881	(80)	6897	(2037)	6913	(624)	6929	(938)
6866	(1588)	6882	(115)	6898	(280)	6914	(646)	6930	(973)
6867	(1590)	6883	(118)	6899	(283)	6915	(654)	6931	(983)
6868	(1593)	6884	(167)	6900*	(309)	6916	(656)	6932	(1023)
6869	(1596)	6885	(182)	6901	(312)	6917	(664)	6933*	(1024)
6870	(1597)	6886	(189)	6902	(345)	6918	(46)	6934	(1032)
6871	(1598)	6887	(235)	6903	(356)	6919	(55)	6935	(1140)
6872	(1601)	6888	(4)	6904	(358)	6920	(78)	6936	(2382)
6873	(1608)	6889	(14)	6905	(368)	6921	(105)		
6874	(1615)	6890	(16)	6906	(377)	6922	(188)		
6875	(1622)	6891	(317)	6907	(398)	6923	(495)		

*Nos. 6900 and 6912 survived to become B.R. 46900 and 46912. No. 6933 temporarily renumbered 26933 in error for a short time in 1934.

0-6-4T Wirral Railway 2P

Built 1900

Weight:
62 tons

Driving Wheel Diameter:
5′ 2″

Boiler Pressure:
170 lbs.

Tractive Effort:
19,320 lbs.

Cylinders:
18″×26″

Valve Gear:
Stephenson

Number built: 2.

First loco withdrawn 1923; last loco withdrawn 1924.
No. in service (1/1/23) 2; (1/1/48) 0.

6948 (12)	6949 (13)

Neither engine actually carried its allotted L.M.S. number.

4-6-2T Bowen-Cooke L.N.W.R. 3P

Built 1910-1916

Weight:
77 tons

Driving Wheel Diameter:
5′ $8\frac{1}{2}$″

Boiler Pressure:
175 lbs.

Tractive Effort:
22,584 lbs.

Cylinders:
20″×26″

Valve Gear:
Joy

Number built: 47.

First loco withdrawn 1936; last loco withdrawn 1941.
No. in service (1/1/23) 47; (1/1/48) 0.

6950 (2665)	6958 (1366)	6966 (944)	6974 (1006)	6982 (1186)	6990 (878)
6951 (2666)	6959 (1797)	6967 (327)	6975 (1021)	6983 (1710)	6991 (2096)
6952 (2667)	6960 (91)	6968 (704)	6976 (1184)	6984 (1692)	6992 (2273)
6953 (2668)	6961 (375)	6969 (858)	6977 (632)	6985 (1638)	6993 (2292)
6954 (2669)	6962 (376)	6970 (962)	6978 (1533)	6986 (1416)	6994 (2298)
6955 (2670)	6963 (716)	6971 (2004)	6979 (1688)	6987 (96)	6995 (2384)
6956 (217)	6964 (915)	6972 (841)	6980 (1728)	6988 (316)	6996 (2418)
6957 (1183)	6965 (932)	6973 (963)	6981 (1734)	6989 (809)	

0-4-0WT Webb L.N.W.R. unclassified

Built 1880-1882

Weight:
15 tons 3 cwt.

Boiler Pressure:
140 lbs.

Cylinders:
9″ × 12″

Driving Wheel Diameter:
2′ 6″

Tractive Effort:
3,792 lbs.

Number built:
10.

First loco withdrawn 1926; last loco withdrawn 1942.
No. in service (1/1/23) 10; (1/1/48) 0.

7200 (3010)	7202 (3012)	7204 (3017)	3013*	3015*
7201 (3011)	7203 (3016)	7205 (3018)	3014*	3019*

*These were departmental engines, and were not included in the L.M.S. renumbering scheme.

None of the others actually carried their allotted L.M.S. numbers.

0-4-0ST Ramsbottom L.N.W.R. unclassified

Built 1864-1892

Weight
24 tons 14 cwt.

Boiler Pressure:
120 lbs.

Cylinders:
14″ × 20″

Driving Wheel Diameter:
4′ 3″

Tractive Effort:
8,075 lbs.

Number built:
17

First loco withdrawn 1919; last loco withdrawn 1947.
No. in service (1/1/23) 16; (1/1/48) 0.

7206 (3031)	7210 (3103)	7213 (3240)	7216 (3245)	3009*
7207 (3033)	7211 (3039)	7214 (3241)	3001*	3087*
7208 (3003)	7212 (3070)	7215 (3243)	3004*	3101*
7209 (3060)				

*These were departmental engines, and were not included in the L.M.S. renumbering scheme.

One engine of this class which was sold out of service prior to the grouping has been re-acquired by B.R. and preserved in its original colours under its former L.N.W.R. number 1439.

0-4-2ST Webb L.N.W.R. Crane engines Unclassified

Built 1892-1895

Weight:
31 tons 6 cwt.

Boiler Pressure:
120 lbs.

Cylinders:
14″ × 20″

Driving Wheel Diameter:
4′ 3″

Tractive Effort:
7,840 lbs.

Number built:
8

Jones Loch'' class in original condition. One of three engines, built in 1917, to the same design as the first fifteen, turned out in 1896.

'Loch' class as rebuilt with Caledonian boiler.

The last Highland express type, Cummings 'Clan' class of 1919.

One of the well known 'Castles', mainstay of H.R. main line working for a period of many years.

Jones 4-4-0T No. 15010, one of three engines originally constructed in 1878 as 2-4-0T's. All at one time had names appropriate to the branch on which they worked, this one being 'Aberfeldy'.

Jones 0-4-4T, built as a saddle tank in 1890, and named 'Strathpeffer' for working that branch. Later reconstructed and transferred to the Lybster branch, being renamed accordingly.

4-4-0T No. 15014, one of five built by Dubs & Co. 1891-3 for the Uruguay Eastern Railway, but never delivered, and taken over by the H.R. in 1892-3. This particular engine worked the Fortrose branch for a time, being named 'Munlochy' accordingly.

Drummond 0-6-4T No. 15307, one of a series of eight built mainly for banking duties from Blair Athol to Druimuachdar summit, 1488 feet above sea level, highest standard gauge altitude in the British Isles.

Leek and Manifold Valley Light Railway train with No. 2 'J. B. Earle' in pre-grouping days. [*L.P.C.*

N.S.R. Caldon Low quarry engines 'Frog' and 'Toad' [*L.P.C.*

L. & Y.R. narrow gauge engines 'Robin', 'Wasp' and 'Mouse'. [*W. Leslie Good*

N.S.R. Caldon Low quarry engine 'Bobs'. [*L.P.C.*

L.N.W.R. Pe
nent Way D
'Jim Crow'
ted with hi
chimney).
[W. A. Ca

L.N.W.R. Permanent Way Dept. 'Platelayer'
[L. W. Perkins

L.N.W.R. Per
nent Way D
'Kitchener'
[W. A. Ca

First loco withdrawn 1929; last loco withdrawn 1947.
No. in service (1/1/23) 8; (1/1/48) 0.

L.N.W.R. numbers:

3246	3251
3247	3252
3248	Carriage Dept. No. 2 Wolverton
3249	Carriage Dept. No. 5 Wolverton

These were all departmental engines, and were not included in the L.M.S. renumbering scheme. They consequently duplicated M.R. Johnson 0-6-0's which bore the same numbers.

They are tabulated at this point as had they been allocated L.M.S. numbers they would no doubt have followed the 7200 and 7206 classes just described.

0-4-2ST Sharp Stewart North London crane engine Unclassified

Built 1858 as 0-4-0ST for North & South Western Junction Railway, later taken over by N.L.R.
Rebuilt as 0-4-2ST 1872 and crane fitted

Weight:
32 tons 6 cwt.

Driving Wheel Diameter:
3′ 10″

Boiler Pressure:
120 lbs.

Tractive Effort:
6,370 lbs.

Cylinders:
13″ × 17″

Number built:
1

No. in service (1/1/23) 1; (1/1/48) 1. Withdrawn 1951.

7217 (N.L.R. 29A; L.N.W.R. 2896). Renumbered 27217 in 1935, and B.R. 58865 in 1949.

0-6-0ST Ramsbottom/Webb L.N.W.R. 1F (' Special tank ')

Built 1870-1880

Weight:
34 tons 10 cwt.

Driving Wheel Diameter:
4′ 6″

Boiler Pressure:
150 lbs.

Tractive Effort:
16,530 lbs.

Cylinders:
17″ × 24″

Valve Gear:
Stephenson

Number built: 258.

First loco withdrawn 1920; last loco withdrawn 1959.
No. in service (1/1/23) 243; (1/1/48) 6.

7220	(3581)	7268	(3175)	7316	(3417)	7364	(3587)	7411	(3373)
7221	(3035)	7269	(3221)	7317	(3586)	7365	(3256)	7412	(3374)
7222	(3047)	7270	(3308)	7318*	(3617)	7366	(3257)	7413	(3538)
7223	(3064)	7271	(3312)	7319	(3651)	7367	(3290)	7414	(3543)
7224	(3116)	7272	(3412)	7320	(3083)	7368	(3298)	7415	(3544)
7225	(3118)	7273	(3424)	7321	(3368)	7369*	(3300)	7416	(3567)
7226	(3123)	7274	(3426)	7322	(3027)	7370*	(3315)	7417	(3590)
7227	(3125)	7275	(3569)	7323	(3093)	7371	(3340)	7418	(3655)
7228*	(3244)	7276	(3579)	7324	(3158)	7372	(3411)	7419	(3603)
7229	(3347)	7277*	(3584)	7325	(3161)	7373	(3570)	7420	(3092)
7230	(3403)	7278	(3588)	7326	(3162)	7374	(3618)	7421	(3304)
7231	(3409)	7279	(3589)	7327	(3620)	7375	(3619)	7422	(3307)
7232	(3577)	7280	(3591)	7328	(3152)	7376	(3277)	7423*	(3595)
7233	(3609)	7281	(3600)	7329	(3160)	7377	(3296)	7424	(3313)
7234	(3611)	7282	(3615)	7330	(3178)	7378	(3349)	7425	(3324)
7235	(3612)	7283	(3661)	7331	(3185)	7379*	(3364)	7426	(3279)
7236*	(3613)	7284	(3104)	7332	(3401)	7380	(3404)	7427	(3327)
7237	(3616)	7285	(3211)	7333*	(3663)	7381	(3405)	7428	(3335)
7238	(3662)	7286	(3212)	7334*†	(3021)	7382	(3664)	7429	(3344)
7239	(3126)	7287	(3215)	7335†	(3186)	7383	(3032)	7430	(3351)
7240	(3133)	7288	(3216)	7336	(3190)	7384*	(3049)	7431	(3352)
7241	(3140)	7289	(3217)	7337*	(3191)	7385	(3051)	7432	(3361)
7242	(3156)	7290	(3218)	7338	(3192)	7386*	(3061)	7433	(3363)
7243	(3181)	7291	(3219)	7339	(3193)	7387	(3073)	7434	(3408)
7244	(3182)	7292	(3220)	7340	(3341)	7388	(3113)	7435	(3534)
7245	(3407)	7293	(3222)	7341	(3597)	7389	(3540)	7436	(3536)
7246	(3416)	7294	(3226)	7342	(3653)	7390*	(3542)	7437	(3596)
7247	(3513)	7295	(3227)	7343	(3659)	7391	(3207)	7438	(3110)
7248	(3598)	7296	(3346)	7344	(3440)	7392	(3281)	7439	(3111)
7249	(3601)	7297	(3578)	7345	(3599)	7393	(3283)	7440	(3260)
7250	(3602)	7298	(3580)	7346	(3196)	7394	(3299)	7441	(3539)
7251	(3607)	7299	(3583)	7347	(3201)	7395	(3311)	7442	(3545)
7252	(3608)	7300	(3592)	7348	(3202)	7396	(3316)	7443	(3665)
7253	(3610)	7301	(3656)	7349	(3203)	7397	(3406)	7444	(3369)
7254	(3652)	7302	(3657)	7350	(3204)	7398	(3582)	7445	(3371)
7255	(3658)	7303	(3028)	7351*	(3205)	7399	(3585)	7446	(3375)
7256	(3142)	7304	(3030)	7352	(3614)	7400	(3606)	7447	(3376)
7257	(3143)	7305	(3043)	7353*	(3208)	7401	(3321)	7448	(3377)
7258	(3144)	7306	(3048)	7354	(3253)	7402	(3326)	7449	(3378)
7259	(3146)	7307	(3050)	7355	(3254)	7403	(3334)	7450	(3379)
7260	(3148)	7308	(3052)	7356*	(3255)	7404	(3337)	7451	(3380)
7261	(3153)	7309*	(3059)	7357	(3258)	7405	(3537)	7452	(3568)
7262	(3164)	7310	(3065)	7358*	(3259)	7406	(3593)	7453	(3594)
7263	(3165)	7311	(3232)	7359	(3261)	7407	(3654)	7454	(3381)
7264	(3167)	7312	(3234)	7360	(3263)	7408	(3660)	7455	(3382)
7265	(3169)	7313	(3237)	7361	(3265)	7409	(3199)	7456	(3605)
7266	(3172)	7314	(3238)	7362	(3266)	7410	(3355)	7457	(3604)
7267	(3174)	7315	(3291)	7363	(3267)				

3323§
Carriage Dept. 1 Wolverton§
Carriage Dept. 3 Wolverton§
Carriage Dept. 4 Crewe§
Carriage Dept. 6 Wolverton§
Carriage Dept. 7 Wolverton§
Carriage Dept. 8 Earlestown§

Not all these engines actually carried their allocated L.M.S. numbers.

The last mentioned engine carried the name "Earlestown". It latterly worked at Wolverton.

†7334 Liverpool (3021); 7335 Euston (3186). These two engines had square pannier tanks and were fitted with condensing apparatus.

§These were departmental engines, and were not included in the L.M.S. renumbering scheme. No. 3323 carried B.R. No. 43323 for a short time in 1949, duplicating the M.R. Johnson 0-6-0 of that number, but later reverted to its L.N.W.R. No. 3323.

*Nos. 7228, etc., as indicated were renumbered 27228 and so on in 1934.

0-6-0PT Webb L.N.W.R. 1F

Built 1873-1892 as 0-6-0 tender engines
Rebuilt to pannier tanks, 1905-1907

Weight:
34 tons 10 cwt.

Driving Wheel Diameter:
4′ 6″

Boiler Pressure:
150 lbs.

Tractive Effort:
16,530 lbs.

Cylinders:
17″ × 24″

Number rebuilt:
45

First loco withdrawn 1924; last loco withdrawn 1948.
No. in service (1/1/23) 47; (1/1/48) 1.

7458	(3413)	7467*	(3694)	7476	(3179)	7485	(3677)	7494	(3328)
7459	(3680)	7468	(3695)	7477*	(3187)	7486	(3678)	7495	(3682)
7460	(3681)	7469*	(3696)	7478	(3671)	7487*	(3679)	7496*	(3683)
7461	(3189)	7470*	(3697)	7479	(3672)	7488	(3042)	7497	(3684)
7462*	(3345)	7471*	(3698)	7480*	(3197)	7489	(3666)	7498	(3685)
7463*	(3690)	7472	(3699)	7481	(3673)	7490	(3667)	7499	(3686)
7464	(3691)	7473*	(3700)	7482	(3674)	7491	(3668)	7500	(3687)
7465	(3692)	7474	(3177)	7483	(3675)	7492*	(3275)	7501	(3688)
7466	(3693)	7475*	(3088)	7484*	(3676)	7493	(3314)	7502	(3689)

*Renumbered 27462, etc., in 1934.

No. 27480 was allocated B.R. No. 58870 under the Nationalisation renumbering scheme, but never actually carried it.

0-6-0T Park North London Railway 1F

Built 1887-1905

Weight:
45 tons 10 cwt.

Driving Wheel Diameter:
4′ 4″

Boiler Pressure:
160 lbs.

Tractive Effort:
18,140 lbs.

Cylinders:
17″ × 24″

Valve Gear:
Stephenson

Number built: 30.

First loco withdrawn 1930; last loco withdrawn 1960.
No. in service (1/1/23) 30; (1/1/48) 14.

First No. in brackets is the original N.L.R. number. Second No. is L.N.W.R. number. Nine engines (Nos. 7503-7510 and 7531) were taken over by the L.N.W.R. in 1909, the remainder in 1923. These mostly carried their new L.N.W.R. numbers for a year or two until again renumbered under the general L.M.S. scheme.

7503	(115, 2634)	7511*	(63, 2881)	7519	(76, 2886)	7526	(91, 2891)
7504	(119, 2635)	7512*	(64, 2882)	7520*	(77, 2887)	7527*	(92, 2892)
7505*	(116, 2650)	7513*	(65, 2883)	7521*	78, 2888)(	7528*	(93, 2893)
7506*	(121, 2651)	7514*	(15, 2875)	7522	(79, 2889)	7529*	(94, 2894)
7507	(104, 2631)	7515*	(16, 2876)	7523*	(80, 2890)	7530*	(95, 2895)
7508*	(111, 2633)	7516	(17, 2877)	7524*	(61, 2879)	7531	(107, 2632)
7509*	(122, 2652)	7517*	(18, 2878)	7525*	(62, 2880)	7532*	(66, 2884)
7510*	(123, 2636)	7518	(75, 2885)				

*Surviving engines in 1934 had 20000 added to their numbers. Of these, Nos. 27505, 27509, 27510, 27512, 27513, 27514, 27515, 27517, 25720, 27522, 27527, 27528, 27530 and 27532 again became B.R. Nos. 58850-58863 on Nationalisation.

The last survivor, No. 58850, now runs on the Bluebell Railway under its 1909-1926 guise as L.N.W.R. 2650.

0-6-2T Webb L.N.W.R. 1F

Built 1881-1896

Weight:
43 tons 15 cwt.

Boiler Pressure:
150 lbs.

Cylinders:
17″×24″

Driving Wheel Diameter:
4′ 3″

Tractive Effort:
16,530 lbs.

Valve Gear:
Stephenson

Number built: 300.

First loco withdrawn 1921; last loco withdrawn 1958.
No. in service (1/1/23) 291; (1/1/48) 64.

7550	(3287)	7571*	(703)	7592	(3747)	7613	(3756)	7634	(2479)
7551*	(3737)	7572*	(766)	7593*	(3748)	7614	(693)	7635*	(2480)
7552*	(611)	7573	(957)	7594*	(3749)	7615	(3757)	7636*	(2481)
7553*	(770)	7574	(971)	7595	(3750)	7616*	(3758)	7637	(2482)
7554	(991)	7575*	(1060)	7596*	(3751)	7617	(3759)	7638	(2483)
7555*	(2490)	7576	(3708)	7597*	(2458)	7618*	(3760)	7639	(2484)
7556	(1015)	7577*	(3710)	7598	(2459)	7619*	(3761)	7640*	(2485)
7557	(3055)	7578	(3717)	7599	(2460)	7620	(3762)	7641	(2486)
7558*	(958)	7579	(3119)	7600*	(2461)	7621*	(3763)	7642	(2487)
7559	(3415)	7580*	(3154)	7601	(2462)	7622	(3764)	7643	(2488)
7560	(3420)	7581	(3206)	7602*	(2463)	7623*	(629)	7644	(2489)
7561*	(3776)	7582	(3292)	7603*	(679)	7624*	(673)	7645*	(2491)
7562*	(3155)	7583*	(850)	7604*	(682)	7625*	(747)	7646	(2492)
7563	(597)	7584	(3707)	7605*	(701)	7626*	(797)	7647	(607)
7564	(1199)	7585*	(3738)	7606*	(717)	7627*	(1009)	7648*	(615)
7565	(2356)	7586*	(3740)	7607	(996)	7628	(2473)	7649	(671)
7566	(3285)	7587	(3742)	7608	(997)	7629	(2474)	7650	(690)
7567	(3005)	7588	(3743)	7609*	(3053)	7630	(2475)	7651	(952)
7568	(602)	7589	(3744)	7610	(3716)	7631*	(2476)	7652	(617)
7569	(605)	7590*	(3745)	7611	(3725)	7632	(2477)	7653	(678)
7570	(627)	7591*	(3746)	7612	(3726)	7633	(2478)	7654*	(692)

7655*	(694)	7693	(3475)	7731	(2455)	7768	(3765)	7805	(1076)
7656	(698)	7694	(3702)	7732	(2456)	7769	(3766)	7806	(1031)
7657	(953)	7695	(3703)	7733	(2457)	7770	(3767)	7807	(1046)
7658	(780)	7696	(3704)	7734	(3058)	7771	(3768)	7808	(1048)
7659	(959)	7697	(3706)	7735	(3271)	7772	(3769)	7809	(1049)
7660*	(1004)	7698	(3719)	7736	(3320)	7773*	(3770)	7810	(1050)
7661	(1053)	7699	(3724)	7737	(3325)	7774	(3771)	7811	(1052)
7662*	(3705)	7700	(3727)	7738	(3418)	7775	(3772)	7812	(1077)
7663*	(3709)	7701	(3752)	7739	(3422)	7776	(3773)	7813	(1078)
7664*	(3720)	7702	(947)	7740	(3453)	7777	(3774)	7814	(1079)
7665	(3722)	7703	(949)	7741	(3741)	7778	(3775)	7815	(1080)
7666*	(3728)	7704	(950)	7742	(3044)	7779	(580)	7816	(1250)
7667	(3729)	7705	(1005)	7743	(3068)	7780	(582)	7817	(1251)
7668	(3735)	7706	(3423)	7744	(3105)	7781	(584)	7818	(1252)
7669*	(3753)	7707	(652)	7745	(3109)	7782	(585)	7819	(1253)
7670	(848)	7708	(699)	7746	(3353)	7783	(588)	7820	(1254)
7671	(1101)	7709*	(771)	7747	(3419)	7784	(589)	7821	(1255)
7672*	(1106)	7710	(796)	7748	(3509)	7785	(3421)	7822	(1256)
7673	(1109)	7711	(966)	7749	(3711)	7786	(3713)	7823	(1258)
7674*	(1112)	7712	(970)	7750	(3712)	7787	(3714)	7824	(1259)
7675	(3151)	7713	(1016)	7751	(3731)	7788	(3715)	7825	(709)
7676	(925)	7714	(1075)	7752	(3732)	7789	(590)	7826	(1198)
7677	(926)	7715	(1201)	7753	(3733)	7790	(591)	7827	(1200)
7678*	(927)	7716	(1202)	7754	(3734)	7791	(592)	7828	(3231)
7679	(928)	7717	(1203)	7755	(3739)	7792	(594)	7829	(3498)
7680*	(981)	7718	(1204)	7756	(3754)	7793	(595)	7830	(3669)
7681*	(1013)	7719	(1206)	7757	(3755)	7794	(596)	7831	(3670)
7682	(1118)	7720	(1207)	7758	(3356)	7795	(3062)	7832	(3701)
7683	(3029)	7721	(1208)	7759	(3387)	7796*	(3209)	7833	(2350)
7684	(3339)	7722	(1209)	7760	(3428)	7797	(706)	7834	(2351)
7685	(3448)	7723	(1210)	7761	(3736)	7798	(753)	7835	(2352)
7686	(3457)	7724	(2360)	7762	(1338)	7799	(1054)	7836	(2353)
7687	(3721)	7725	(2361)	7763	(2010)	7800	(1062)	7837	(2354)
7688	(751)	7726	(2362)	7764	(3414)	7801	(1063)	7838*	(2355)
7689	(948)	7727	(2363)	7765	(578)	7802	(1067)	7839	(2357)
7690	(1057)	7728	(2364)	7766	(579)	7803	(1068)	7840	(2358)
7691	(3723)	7729	(2453)	7767	(3447)	7804	(1069)	7841	(3730)
7692	(3336)	7730	(2454)						

*Engines indicated had 20000 added to their numbers in 1934, although 27709, 27773, 27796 and 27838 later reverted to their former Nos. At a later date, in 1945, No. 7830 became 27830. Sixty-four of the class survived Nationalisation, and of these, fifty-eight, Nos. 27553, 27561/2, 37580/5/6, 27951/6, 27602/3, 27619, 27621/5/7, 27635, 27645, 27669, 27674, 27681, 7692/9, 7703, 7710/1, 7720/1, 7730/3/7, 7740/1/6, 7751/2/6/7/9, 7765/9, 7773, 7780/2/7/9, 7791/4/9, 7802/3/8, 7816, 7821/2/9, 27830, 7833/6 and 7840, were allocated B.R. Nos. 58880-58937, although not all lasted long enough to carry them. The last survivor of all, No. 58926, has been preserved in its old L.N.W.R. colours as No. 1054.

0-8-2T Bowen-Cooke L.N.W.R. 4F

Built 1911-1917

Weight:
72 tons 10 cwt.
Boiler Pressure:
170 lbs.
Cylinders:
$20\frac{1}{2}'' \times 24''$

Driving Wheel Diameter:
$4' 5\frac{1}{2}''$
Tractive Effort:
27,240 lbs.
Valve Gear:
Joy

Number built: 30.

First loco withdrawn 1934; last loco withdrawn 1953.
No. in service (1/1/23) 30; (1/1/48) 9.

7870 (1185)	7875 (1494)	7880 (482)	7885 (1124)	7890 (24)	7895 (2105)
7871 (1548)	7876 (1592)	7881 (563)	7886 (1414)	7891 (92)	7896 (2294)
7872 (1665)	7877 (1659)	7882 (58)	7887 (1514)	7892 (714)	7897 (2341)
7873 (289)	7878 (1663)	7883 (736)	7888 (1515)	7893 (1291)	7898 (2348)
7874 (1163)	7879 (2013)	7884 (1090)	7889 (2277)	7894 (1331)	7899 (2391)

Of the nine survivors at Nationalisation, four lasted long enough to carry their new number, No. 47877, 47881, 47884 and 47896.

0-8-4T Beames L.N.W.R. 5F

Built 1923-4

(*Note:* These locomotives were not delivered till after Grouping.)

Weight:
88 tons

Driving Wheel Diameter:
4′ 5½″

Boiler Pressure:
185 lbs.

Tractive Effort:
29,815 lbs.

Cylinders:
20½″ × 24″

Valve Gear:
Joy

Number built: 30.

First loco withdrawn 1944; last loco withdrawn 1951.
No. in service (1/1/23) Nil; (1/1/48) 14.

7930 (380)	7935 (256)	7940 (468)	7945	7950	7955
7931 (782)	7936 (731)	7941 (792)	7946	7951	7956
7932 (1189)	7947 (739)	7942 (793)	7947	7952	7957
7933 (1677)	7938 (1908)	7943 (1904)	7948	7953	7958
7934 (1976)	7939 (1956)	7944 (609)	7949	7954	7959

The first fifteen of these engines, which did not appear until 1923, came out with L.N.W.R. numbers but the initials L.M.S. on the tank sides. It is thought that the last two of these, Nos. 7943 and 7944, came out with L.M.S. Nos. when new.

No. 7957 was temporarily renumbered 27957 for a short time in 1934, and No. 7943 became 27943 in 1945.

Two of the 1948 survivors, Nos. 7931 and 7937, became 47931 and 47937 under the B.R. renumbering scheme.

0-6-0 Ramsbottom Reb. Webb L.N.W.R. Special DX Class

Built 1858-1872

Weight:
Loco.: 27 tons

Boiler Pressure:
120 lbs.

Cylinders:
17″×24″

Driving Wheel Diameter:
5′ 2″

Tractive Effort:
11,410 lbs.

Valve Gear:
Stephenson

Number built for L.N.W.R.: 857.

First loco withdrawn 1902; last loco withdrawn 1930.
No. in service (1/1/23) 88; (1/1/48) 0.

8000 (3331)	8015 (3008)	8030 (3091)	8045 (3280)	8060 (3069)	8075 (3242)
8001 (3410)	8016 (3022)	8031 (3096)	8046 (3293)	8061 (3145)	8076 (3480)
8002 (3441)	8017 (3223)	8032 (3097)	8047 (3306)	8062 (3131)	8077 (3482)
8003 (3402)	8018 (3224)	8033 (3098)	8048 (3309)	8063 (3358)	8078 (3484)
8004 (3393)	8019 (3273)	8034 (3127)	8049 (3400)	8064 (3436)	8079 (3445)
8005 (3036)	8020 (3338)	8035 (3132)	8050 (3056)	8065 (3072)	8080 (3461)
8006 (3262)	8021 (3514)	8036 (3134)	8051 (3074)	8066 (3117)	8081 (3474)
8007 (3025)	8022 (3006)	8037 (3135)	8052 (3106)	8067 (3188)	8082 (3499)
8008 (3041)	8023 (3026)	8038 (3139)	8053 (3108)	8068 (3239)	8083 (3501)
8009 (3136)	8024 (3040)	8039 (3157)	8054 (3128)	8069 (3288)	8084 (3517)
8010 (3137)	8025 (3054)	8040 (3166)	8055 (3130)	8070 (3295)	8085 (3551)
8011 (3270)	8026 (3057)	8041 (3184)	8056 (3168)	8071 (3082)	8086 (3552)
8012 (3278)	8027 (3066)	8042 (3225)	8057 (3310)	8072 (3085)	8087 (3565)
8013 (3302)	8028 (3086)	8043 (3250)	8058 (3359)	8073 (3122)	
8014 (3002)	8029 (3090)	8044 (3274)	8059 (3430)	8074 (3173)	

The pioneer engine of the class, No. 8000, original built in 1858 as No. 355 Hardman, lasted until 1928.

0-6-0 Webb L.N.W.R. 17″ Coal Engines

Built 1873-1892

Weight:
Loco.: 32 tons

Boiler Pressure:
150 lbs.

Cylinders:
17″×24″

Driving Wheel Diameter:
4′ 5½″

Tractive Effort:
16,530 lbs.

Valve Gear:
Stephenson

Number built: 500.

First loco withdrawn about 1903; last loco withdrawn 1953.
No in service (1/1/23) 227; (1/1/48) 46.

8088*	(2085)	8134	(993)	8179	(936)	8224	(2409)	8269	(3038)
8089	(3176)	8135	(137)	8180	(3023)	8225	(3080)	8270	(3170)
8090	(3286)	8136	(3319)	8181	(3024)	8226*	(3129)	8271*	(2398)
8091*	(3289)	8137	(3392)	8182	(3045)	8227*	(3332)	8272	(3081)
8092	(3394)	8138*	(3479)	8183	(3078)	8228	(3399)	8273	(3171)
8093*	(3458)	8139*	(3114)	8184	(3138)	8229	(3425)	8274	(3365)
8094	(3489)	8140	(2207)	8185	(3150)	8230*	(3450)	8275	(3508)
8095*	(3502)	8141*	(2346)	8186*	(3439)	8231	(3483)	8276	(3548)
8096	(3519)	8142	(3200)	8187*	(3269)	8232	(3504)	8277	(3560)
8097*	(3561)	8143	(3297)	8188	(3435)	8233*	(3550)	8278*	(101)
8098	(2437)	8144	(3370)	8189	(3449)	8234*	(3566)	8279	(3095)
8099*	(3063)	8145*	(3459)	8190	(3486)	8235	(3574)	8280	(3342)
8100*	(3198)	8146	(873)	8191*	(3329)	8236	(3575)	8281	(3385)
8101	(3317)	8147	(1172)	8192	(3395)	8237	(2425)	8282	(3434)
8102	(3318)	8148	(3518)	8193	(3511)	8238	(2432)	8283	(3500)
8103	(3354)	8149	(45)	8194	(3573)	8239*	(3427)	8284	(3520)
8104*	(3367)	8150	(881)	8195	(3236)	8240*	(3451)	8285	(1340)
8105*	(3433)	8151	(3100)	8196	(3384)	8241	(3476)	8286	(3076)
8106*	(3443)	8152*	(3463)	8197	(3455)	8242	(3553)	8287	(3366)
8107*	(3490)	8153*	(2072)	8198	(961)	8243	(3554)	8288*	(3549)
8108	(3563)	8154	(2107)	8199*	(1330)	8244	(1082)	8289*	(2045)
8109	(2163)	8155	(2299)	8200	(1332)	8245*	(3386)	8290	(2049)
8110	(2214)	8156	(2302)	8201	(2170)	8246*	(2434)	8291	(3348)
8111	(3004)	8157	(3213)	8202*	(2397)	8247*	(3099)	8292	(3388)
8112	(3037)	8158*	(3322)	8203	(3107)	8248	(3102)	8293	(3391)
8113	(3075)	8159	(3462)	8204*	(3228)	8249	(3383)	8294	(3510)
8114	(3094)	8160	(3571)	8205*	(3372)	8250	(3431)	8295*	(1205)
8115*	(3159)	8161	(3276)	8206	(3512)	8251*	(3432)	8296*	(2415)
8116*	(3194)	8162	(3506)	8207	(3546)	8252	(3477)	8297	(3089)
8117*	(3282)	8163	(3229)	8208	(700)	8253*	(3495)	8298	(3115)
8118	(3284)	8164	(3305)	8209*	(3124)	8254	(3496)	8299	(3147)
8119	(3357)	8165	(3460)	8210	(3233)	8255	(3497)	8300	(3230)
8120	(3360)	8166*	(3521)	8211	(3456)	8256*	(3505)	8301	(3235)
8121	(3390)	8167	(3572)	8212	(3507)	8257	(3515)	8302	(3350)
8122	(3396)	8168	(3210)	8213	(3547)	8258	(3576)	8303*	(3454)
8123	(3397)	8169	(3330)	8214	(3556)	8259	(1087)	8304	(3558)
8124	(3398)	8170	(2347)	8215	(3557)	8260	(3071)	8305	(3516)
8125	(3442)	8171	(3214)	8216*	(2375)	8261*	(3264)	8306	(2098)
8126	(3452)	8172*	(3535)	8217	(3312)	8262*	(3444)	8307	(3180)
8127	(3481)	8173	(3046)	8218	(3294)	8263*	(3446)	8308*	(3183)
8128*	(3491)	8174	(3120)	8219	(3362)	8264	(3488)	8309*	(3195)
8129*	(3503)	8175	(3141)	8220	(3487)	8265	(3493)	8310	(3268)
8130	(3523)	8176	(3343)	8221*	(3522)	8266	(3272)	8311	(3333)
8131	(3555)	8177	(3438)	8222	(876)	8267	(1098)	8312*	(3389)
8132	(3559)	8178	(3492)	8223	(2403)	8268	(2419)	8313*	(3478)
8133*	(3564)							8314	(3485)

*Surviving engines in 1940 had 20000 added to their numbers to make way for the construction of new class 8 2-8-0's.

Of the forty six engines still in service at Nationalisation, forty-two were allocated B.R. Nos. 58320-58361, but not all survived long enough to carry them.

0-6-0 Webb L.N.W.R. 'Cauliflower' 2F

Built 1880-1902

Weight:
Loco. 36 tons 10 cwt.

Driving Wheel Diameter:
5′ 2½″

Boiler Pressure:
150 lbs.

Tractive Effort:
15,865 lbs. (except Nos. 8315-8327 and 8330-2 which were 14,145 lbs.)

Cylinders:
18″×24″ (except Nos. 8315-8327 and 8330-2 which had 17″×24″ cylinders)

Valve Gear:
Joy

Number built: 310.

Many of the later survivors were rebuilt with Belpaire fireboxes.
First loco withdrawn 1922; last loco withdrawn 1955.
No. in service (1/1/23) 308; (1/1/48) 69.

8315*	(726)	8355	(1029)	8393	(2305)	8431	(330)	8469	(1717)
8316	(930)	8356	(1030)	8394	(2306)	8432	(332)	8470	(1718)
8317	(1263)	8357	(722)	8395	(2307)	8433	(334)	8471	(1719)
8318*	(1268)	8358	(822)	8396	(2308)	8434	(335)	8472	(1720)
8319	(1269)	8359	(831)	8397	(2309)	8435	(336)	8473	(1722)
8320	(1146)	8360	(836)	8398	(2310)	8436	(1139)	8474	(74)
8321	(2319)	8361	(100)	8399	(2311)	8437	(337)	8475	(397)
8322	(1175)	8362	(1260)	8400	(2312)	8438	(339)	8476	(534)
8323	(1235)	8363	(1262)	8401*	(2313)	8439	(346)	8477	(543)
8324	(39)	8364	(1264)	8402	(2314)	8440	(347)	8478	(1033)
8325	(168)	8365	(1265)	8403*	(2315)	8441*	(348)	8479	(1034)
8326	(454)	8366	(1266)	8404*	(2316)	8442*	(349)	8480	(1501)
8327	(548)	8367*	(1267)	8405	(2317)	8443*	(350)	8481	(1502)
8330	(715)	8368	(625)	8406	(2318)	8444	(683)	8482*	(1724)
8331	(1641)	8369*	(195)	8407	(2320)	8445	(462)	8483	(1736)
8332	(879)	8370*	(623)	8408*	(2321)	8446	(909)	8484*	(9)
8333*	(2365)	8371	(666)	8409	(2322)	8447	(1470)	8485 *	(378)
8334	(2464)	8372*	(672)	8410*	(2323)	8448	(1473)	8486	(473)
8335*	(2465)	8373	(676)	8411	(2324)	8449	(1474)	8487*	(544)
8336	(2466)	8374	(689)	8412	(2325)	8450*	(1476)	8488	(1743)
8337*	(2467)	8375	(840)	8413	(2326)	8451*	(1491)	8489	(1771)
8338*	(2468)	8376	(854)	8414	(2327)	8452	(1493)	8490	(1773)
8339*	(2469)	8377	(855)	8415*	(2328)	8453	(1496)	8491	(1779)
8340	(2470)	8378	(912)	8416	(2329)	8454	(1499)	8492*	(1780)
8341	(2471)	8379	(967)	8417*	(2330)	8455	(415)	8493	(1232)
8342	(2472)	8380	(1007)	8418	(2331)	8456	(903)	8494*	(1234)
8343*	(147)	8381	(1160)	8419	(2332)	8457*	(954)	8495	(1238)
8344	(343)	8382	(1171)	8420*	(2333)	8458*	(1037)	8496	(1239)
8345*	(1382)	8383	(1182)	8421	(456)	8459	(1636)	8497	(1244)
8346	(1475)	8384	(1580)	8422*	(651)	8460*	(1646)	8498	(1246)
8347*	(34)	8385*	(505)	8423*	(799)	8461	(1651)	8499*	(1270)
8348	(532)	8386	(913)	8424	(2334)	8462	(1695)	8500	(1275)
8349	(598)	8387	(914)	8425	(2335)	8463	(1701)	8501	(2008)
8350*	(1022)	8388	(600)	8426	(200)	8464*	(1702)	8502	(52)
8351	(1025)	8389	(687)	8427	(314)	8465	(1705)	8503*	(54)
8352	(1026)	8390	(777)	8428*	(318)	8466	(1712)	8504	(59)
8353	(1027)	8391	(2303)	8429 *	(319)	8467	(1715)	8505*	(64)
8354	(1028)	8392*	(2304)	8430*	(320)	8468	(1716)	8506	(65)

8507*	(73)	8531*	(190)	8555*	(451)	8579	(536)	8602	(725)
8508*	(19)	8532*	(191)	8556*	(453)	8580*	(537)	8603*	(727)
8509*	(22)	8533*	(206)	8557	(455)	8581	(538)	8604	(728)
8510	(25)	8534	(212)	8558	(457)	8582	(539)	8605	(743)
8511*	(26)	8535*	(213)	8559*	(458)	8583 *	(541)	8606	(987)
8512*	(38)	8536	(219)	8560	(460)	8584	(542)	8607	(2388)
8513*	(47)	8537	(236)	8561*	(461)	8585*	(547)	8608*	(755)
8514	(49)	8538*	(245)	8562	(463)	8586*	(550)	8609	(759)
8515*	(51)	8539	(278)	8563	(1459)	8587*	(1221)	8610*	(774)
8516	(75)	8540	(399)	8564	(1798)	8588*	(552)	8611*	(776)
8517	(79)	8541	(400)	8565	(464)	8589*	(553)	8612	(800)
8518*	(423)	8542*	(416)	8566	(467)	8590	(555)	8613	(801)
8519	(744)	8543*	(420)	8567	(470)	8591	(556)	8614*	(1298)
8520	(1740)	8544*	(421)	8568	(471)	8592*	(559)	8615	(2121)
8521*	(84)	8545	(422)	8569	(472)	8593	(560)	8616*	(2227)
8522	(87)	8546*	(428)	8570	(474)	8594*	(566)	8617	(143)
8523	(109)	8547*	(432)	8571	(475)	8595	(577)	8618*	(174)
8524*	(114)	8548*	(439)	8572	(476)	8596	(581)	8619*	(684)
8525*	(121)	8549*	(540)	8573	(488)	8597*	(2206)	8620	(1010)
8526 *	(128)	8550*	(441)	8574	(494)	8598*	(225)	8621	(1130)
8527	(130)	8551*	(447)	8575*	(498)	8599	(702)	8622*	(2070)
8528	(164)	8552*	(448)	8576	(530)	8600	(710)	8623	(2344)
8529*	(166)	8553*	(449)	8577	(533)	8601*	(711)	8624	(2502)
8530	(177)	8554	(450)	8578	(535)				

*Surviving engines had 20000 added to their numbers between 1940 and 1944 to make way for the construction of new class 8 2-8-0's. Nos. 28315, 28367, 28369, 28487 (and also 28577, which did not survive to this later period) had already temporarily borne these numbers for a short period during 1934.

The sixty nine engines which were still in service at Nationalisation were allocated B.R. Nos. 58362-58430, and most of them lasted long enough to carry these numbers.

4-6-0 Whale L.N.W.R. 4F

Built 1906-9

Weight:
63 tons

Driving Wheel Diameter:
5′ 2½″

Boiler Pressure:
175 lbs.

Tractive Effort:
22,340 lbs.

Cylinders:
19″×26″

Valve Gear:
Joy

Number built: 170.

Most of the class received Belpaire fireboxes in later years.

First loco withdrawn 1931; last loco withdrawn 1950.
No. in service (1/1/23) 170; (1/1/48) 3.

8700	(285)	8734	(2522)	8768	(2111)	8802	(705)	8836	(1457)
8701	(414)	8735	(2586)	8769	(2159)	8803	(738)	8837	(1686)
8702	(833)	8736	(2587)	8770	(2601)	8804	(821)	8838	(1739)
8703	(1350)	8737	(2588)	8771	(2602)	8805	(933)	8839	(1782)
8704	(2229)	8738	(2589)	8772	(2603)	8806	(1058)	8840	(2009)
8705	(3)	8739	(2590)	8773	(2604)	8807	(1292)	8841	(2241)
8706	(77)	8740	(2591)	8774	(2605)	8808	(1293)	8842	(370)
8707	(392)	8741	(2592)	8775	(2606)	8809	(1479)	8843	(1579)
8708	(1302)	8742	(2593)	8776	(2607)	8810	(1482)	8844	(1786)
8709	(2003)	8743	(2594)	8777	(2608)	8811	(1524)	8845	(939)
8710	(2087)	8744	(2595)	8778	(2609)	8812	(1552)	8846	(1399)
8711	(2209)	8745	(2596)	8779	(2610)	8813	(1565)	8847	(1447)
8712	(832)	8746	(618)	8780	(524)	8814	(1602)	8848	(2084)
8713	(1136)	8747	(719)	8781	(630)	8815	(1605)	8849	(2518)
8714	(1303)	8748	(1434)	8782	(917)	8816	(2188)	8850	(1342)
8715	(1428)	8749	(1512)	8783	(1296)	8817	(1544)	8851	(1376)
8716	(1460)	8750	(2270)	8784	(1610)	8818	(1708)	8852	(1397)
8717	(1653)	8751	(2597)	8785	(1640)	8819	(1731)	8853	(1450)
8718	(1772)	8752	(2598)	8786*	(1654)	8820	(2611)	8854	(1461)
8719	(2078)	8753	(2599)	8787*	(1683)	8821	(2612)	8855	(1465)
8720	(393)	8754	(2600)	8788	(1738)	8822	(2613)	8856	(1467)
8721	(989)	8755	(992)	8789	(2123)	8823	(2614)	8857	(1538)
8722	(1141)	8756	(1372)	8790	(636)	8824	(2615)	8858	(1554)
8723	(1656)	8757	(1390)	8791	(929)	8825	(724)	8859	(1558)
8724	(2029)	8758	(1415)	8792	(995)	8826	(852)	8860	(1421)
8725	(2044)	8759	(1569)	8793	(1328)	8827	(1126)	8861	(1541)
8726	(2173)	8760	(1594)	8794	(81)	8828	(1368)	8862	(1576)
8727	(1996)	8761	(1604)	8795	(746)	8829	(2616)	8863	(1581)
8728	(1997)	8762	(1607)	8796	(1119)	8830	(2617)	8864	(1612)
8729	(1998)	8763	(1632)	8797	(1707)	8831	(2618)	8865	(1613)
8730	(1999)	8764	(1643)	8798	(2110)	8832	(2619)	8866	(1625)
8731	(2000)	8765	(1645)	8799	(2508)	8833	(2620)	8867	(1630)
8732	(2424)	8766	(1795)	8800	(254)	8834	(1375)	8868	(1711)
8733	(2503)	8767	(1796)	8801	(418)	8835	(1377)	8869	(1770)

No. 8786 became 28786 in 1943, and No. 8787 had been temporarily renumbered 28787 for a short time during 1934.

General Notes on the L.N.W.R. 0-8-0's and 2-8-0's whose numbers during the period of the L.M.S. ranged between 8892 and 9615

The history of this class is a complicated one, owing to extensive rebuilding, but is summarised in the following pages in as concise a manner as possible to give general particulars without the necessity of an abundance of detail such as is outside the scope of this overall treatise.

The first L.N.W.R. 8-coupled freight engine was built by F. W. Webb in 1892, and was the first of a long line of locomotives of the 0-8-0 wheel arrangement which in many various forms eventually totalled 572 engines, all but one of which lasted into L.M.S. days.

Although Mr. Webb was at this time much taken up with compound propulsion, nevertheless this first 0-8-0 of his, No. 2524, was a 2-cylinder simple. However, a 3-cylinder compound version followed shortly afterwards in the shape of No. 50, and 110 more similar engines had been built by the time of the turn of the century. They seem to have been as successful as any of the Webb compounds, but notwithstanding Mr. Whale converted them all to 2-cylinder simples between 1904 and 1912, some with their original small boilers and others with the larger G type which eventually became standard for the class until the superheated G1 boiler was introduced in 1912, culminating in the final G2 version of 1921.

Meanwhile, however, before he retired, Mr. Webb had introduced a 4-cylinder compound design in 1901, and 170 of this new type were built, although most of them were subsequently converted to 2-cylinder simples, a number of them still remained in compound form at the grouping, fifty seven in their original condition as 0-8-0's, and a further sixteen which had been converted to the 2-8-0 wheel arrangement, again divided into two varieties, with small and large boilers. Most of all these remaining compounds were converted to standard 2-cylinder simples during the first few years of the grouping, but a few were scrapped without ever being rebuilt.

In the meantime construction continued of 2-cylinder simple 0-8-0's under the superintendency of Whale and Bowen-Cooke, the later ones from 1912 onwards being superheated, culminating in the final design known as G2A which appeared in 1922, and to which many of the earlier series were eventually converted. In more recent years a further modification has been the provision of Belpaire fireboxes. The last engines to remain in active service were withdrawn in 1964, but one of them is being retained for preservation.

0-8-0 8892-8899—see 9600-9615.

0-8-0 Webb L.N.W.R. Class B 4-cylinder compound 3F

Built 1901-1904

Weight:
53 tons 10 cwt.

Boiler Pressure:
200 lbs.

Cylinders:
H.P. (2) 15″ ×24″
L.P. (2) 20½″×24″

Driving Wheel Diameter:
4′ 5½″

Tractive Effort at 80% B.P.:
17,406 lbs.

Valve Gear:
Joy

Original number in class: 170.

First loco withdrawn 1921†; last unrebuilt loco withdrawn 1928. (Remainder converted to 2-cylinder simples, class G1. Last rebuild withdrawn 1962)

No. in service (1/1/23) 53; (1/1/48) 43.

†Boiler explosion at Buxton, engine No. 134.

8900*	(1881)	8911	(2496)	8922	(1051)	8933	(1404)	8944	(1308)
8901	(1890)	8912	(2556)	8923*	(1061)	8934	(2024)	8945	(1310)
8902	(1892)	8913	(2557)	8924	(1088)	8935	(2571)	8946*	(1547)
8903	(813)	8914	(2559)	8925	(1091)	8936	(2572)	8947*	(1370)
8904	(823)	8915	(2560)	8926	(1225)	8937*	(1281)	8948	(918)
8905	(826)	8916*	(2561)	8927	(1226)	8938*	(1282)	8949*	(1555)
8906	(843)	8917	(2564)	8928*	(1233)	8939	(1283)	8950	(644)
8907	(405)	8918	(1039)	8929	(1237)	8940	(2080)	8951	(1436)
8908	(2074)	8919*	(2565)	8930	(1248)	8941	(1284)	8952	(1543)
8909	(2342)	8920	(1040)	8931	(1249)	8942	(1287)		
8910	(2369)	8921	(2567)	8932	(1272)	8943	(1288)		

*These engines were withdrawn as compounds in 1927 and 1928. Remainder all converted to 2-cylinder simples.

0-8-0 Webb L.N.W.R. 4F
Class C (formerly Class A)

Built 1894-1899 as 3-cylinder compound
Rebuilt Whale 1904-6 as 2-cylinder simple

Weight:
49 tons 5 cwt.

Driving Wheel Diameter:
4′ 5½″

Boiler Pressure:
175 lbs.

Tractive Effort:
25,440 lbs.

Cylinders:
19½″×24″

Valve Gear:
Joy

Number built: 15.

First loco withdrawn 1927; last loco withdrawn 1961.
No. in service (1/1/23) 15; (1/1/48) 5.

8953 (2541)	8956 (1860)	8959 (1805)	8962 (2538)	8964 (1855)	8966 (1842)
8954 (2529)	8957 (1828)	8960 (1814)	8963 (2549)	8965 (1823)	8967 (1803)
8955 (1810)	8958 (2553)	8961 (1807)			

0-8-0 Webb L.N.W.R. 3F
Class C1

Built 1896-1899 as 3-cylinder compound
Rebuilt Whale 1909 as 2-cylinder simple with small boiler

Weight:
47 tons

Driving Wheel Diameter:
4′ 5½″

Boiler Pressure:
175 lbs.

Tractive Effort:
25,440 lbs.

Cylinders:
19½″×24″

Valve Gear:
Joy

Number built: 34

First loco withdrawn 1927; last loco withdrawn 1933.
No. in service (1/1/23) 34; (1/1/48) 0.

8968 (1862)	8974 (1875)	8980 (2545)	8986 (2535)	8992 (1851)	8997 (2554)
8969 (2546)	8975 (1840)	8981 (2543)	8987 (1849)	8993 (1852)	8998 (2555)
8970 (1850)	8976 (2550)	8982 (1847)	8988 (1829)	8994 (1859)	8999 (1817)
8971 (1809)	8977 (1801)	8983 (1841)	8989 (1869)	8995 (1826)	9000 (2534)
8972 (1861)	8978 (2531)	8984 (1806)	8990 (2542)	8996 (1858)	9001 (1835)
8973 (1867)	8979 (2533)	8985 (1844)	8991 (1811)		

0-8-0 Webb L.N.W.R. 4F Class D

Built 1893-1900 as 3-cylinder compound
Rebuilt Whale 1906-9 as 2-cylinder simple

Weight:
49 tons 5 cwt.

Driving Wheel Diameter:
4′ 5½″

Boiler Pressure:
175 lbs.

Tractive Effort
25,440 lbs.

Cylinders:
19½″ × 24″

Valve Gear:
Joy

Number built: 63.
Number rebuilt: 63.

First loco withdrawn 1948; last loco withdrawn 1962.
No. in service (1/1/23) 63; (1/1/48) 63.

9002	(1866)	9015	(1872)	9028	(1834)	9041	(1830)	9054	(1874)
9003	(1845)	9016	(1802)	9029	(2532)	9042	(1857)	9055	(1837)
9004	(2548)	9017	(1804)	9030	(1871)	9043	(2526)	9056	(1868)
9005	(1822)	9018	(1827)	9031	(2539)	9044	(1815)	9057	(1870)
9006	(1863)	9019*	(2537)	9032	(1838)	9045	(1816)	9058	(1819)
9007	(1873)	9020	(2540)	9033	(2536)	9046	(1877)	9059	(1846)
9008†	(2525)	9021	(1876)	9034	(2551)	9047	(1808)	9060	(1813)
9009	(1833)	9022	(1848)	9035	(1824)	9048	(1843)	9061	(1836)
9010	(1839)	9023	(1854)	9036	(1853)	9049	(2530)	9062	(1865)
9011	(2524)	9024	(1878)	9037	(1880)	9050	(1820)	9063	(1864)
9012	(2547)	9025	(1879)	9038	(1832)	9051	(2527)	9064	(1821)
9013	(1818)	9026	(1856)	9039	(1831)	9052	(2552)		
9014*	(1812)	9027	(2528)	9040	(2544)	9053	(1825)		

*Temporarily renumbered 29014 and 29019 for a short time during 1934.
†Originally No. 50, the first 0-8-0 compound, built in 1893.

0-8-0 Whale L.N.W.R. 4F Class G

Built 1910

(Some engines were rebuilds of 0-8-0 Compounds class B)

Weight:
53 tons 10 cwt.

Boiler Pressure:
175 lbs.

Cylinders:
$20\frac{1}{2}'' \times 24''$

Driving Wheel Diameter:
$4'\ 5\frac{1}{2}''$

Tractive Effort:
29,015 lbs.

Valve Gear:
Joy

Number built new: 60 (plus 32 rebuilds from class B)

First loco withdrawn 1948; last loco withdrawn 1962.
No. in service (1/1/23) 89; (1/1/48) 0.

9065	(1900)	9083	(1380)	9101	(1464)	9119	(2032)	9137	(1700)
9066	(1895)	9084	(1411)	9102	(1511)	9120	(1070)	9138	(1727)
9067	(2251)	9085	(1893)	9103	(1570)	9121	(1385)	9139	(1735)
9068	(503)	9086	(2659)	9104	(1578)	9122	(1449)	9140	(1775)
9069	(509)	9087	(2660)	9105	(1600)	9123	(1492)	9141	(1794)
9070	(1229)	9088	(2661)	9106	(1647)	9124	(1507)	9142	(1228)
9071	(1274)	9089	(2662)	9107	(1664)	9125	(1539)	9143	(1788)
9072	(2569)	9090	(508)	9108	(1687)	9126	(1577)	9144	(2014)
9073	(1245)	9091	(1322)	9109	(1699)	9127	(1606)	9145	(1271)
9074	(1299)	9092	(1456)	9110	(1503)	9128	(1648)	9146	(898)
9075	(1401)	9093	(1497)	9111	(1540)	9129	(1690)	9147	(1231)
9076	(1190)	9094	(1556)	9112	(1609)	9130	(1774)	9148	(1887)
9077	(2654)	9095	(1582)	9113	(1634)	9131	(1776)	9149	(1277)
9078	(2655)	9096	(1591)	9114	(1637)	9132	(818)	9150	(1243)
9079	(2656)	9097*	(1619)	9115	(1639)	9133	(1035)	9151	(641)
9080*	(2657)	9098	(1629)	9116	(1660)	9134	(1403)	9152	(2562)
9081	(2658)	9099	(1122)	9117	(1789)	9135	(1424)	9153	(2566)
9082	(1354)	9100	(1280)	9118*	(2030)	9136	(1462)		

*Temporarily renumbered 29080, 29097 and 29118 for a short time during 1934.

0-8-0 Bowen-Cooke L.N.W.R. 6F Class G1

Built 1912-1918

(Some engines were rebuilds of 0-8-0 Compounds class B including Nos. 9335-9394)

Weight:
60 tons 5 cwt.

Boiler Pressure:
160 lbs.

Cylinders:
$20\frac{1}{2}'' \times 24''$

Driving Wheel Diameter:
$4'\ 5\frac{1}{2}''$

Tractive Effort:
24,705 lbs.

Valve Gear:
Joy

Number built (inc. rebuilds): 241.

First loco withdrawn 1947; last loco withdrawn 1964.

No. in service (1/1/23) 236; (1/1/48) 235.

9154	(2653)	9203	(1192)	9251	(203)	9299	(2376)	9347	(1286)
9155	(1329)	9204	(2245)	9252	(931)	9300	(2410)	9348	(1891)
9156	(1384)	9205	(107)	9253	(2094)	9301	(2422)	9349	(1038)
9157	(1426)	9206	(93)	9254	(2224)	9302	(2441)	9350	(1224)
9158	(1633)	9207	(138)	9255	(170)	9303	(880)	9351	(1236)
9159	(1697)	9208	(670)	9256	(545)	9304	(1043)	9352	(1279)
9160	(1778)	9209	(734)	9257	(885)	9305	(1071)	9353	(1586)
9161	(1791)	9210	(767)	9258	(942)	9306	(1657)	9354	(916)
9162	(2001)	9211	(1127)	9259*	(982)	9307*	(1693)	9355	(1041)
9163	(2015)	9212	(1128)	9260	(1167)	9308	(2066)	9356	(2038)
9164	(2034)	9213	(2201)	9261	(1217)	9309	(2199)	9357	(2387)
9165	(1568)	9214	(2378)	9262	(1528)	9310	(2235)	9358	(1240)
9166	(1655)	9215	(43)	9263	(1729)	9311	(2253)	9359	(2056)
9167	(1696)	9216	(669)	9264	(2288)	9312	(757)	9360	(2272)
9168	(1698)	9217	(1314)	9265	(500)	9313	(829)	9361	(1289)
9169	(1783)	9218	(1343)	9266	(1884)	9314	(894)	9362	(41)
9170	(1162)	9219	(2117)	9267	(1885)	9315	(1107)	9363	(1227)
9171	(1505)	9220	(2195)	9268	(94)	9316	(1435)	9364	(2208)
9172	(1790)	9221	(2246)	9269	(112)	9317	(1495)	9365	(1036)
9173	(2018)	9222	(2258)	9270	(360)	9318	(1785)	9366	(1318)
9174	(2104)	9223	(2390)	9271	(851)	9319	(1883)	9367	(2570)
9175	(2119)	9224	(2452)	9272	(1066)	9320	(2054)	9368	(1223)
9176	(2284)	9225	(20)	9273	(1448)	9321	(2160)	9369*	(1110)
9177	(2254)	9226	(131)	9274	(2088)	9322	(2236)	9370	(1897)
9178	(2337)	9227*	(795)	9275	(2256)	9323	(172)	9371	(2057)
9179	(2345)	9228	(329)	9276	(2290)	9324	(1094)	9372	(1369)
9180	(2349)	9229*	(1181)	9277	(2296)	9325	(1261)	9373	(2573)
9181	(2385)	9230	(1214)	9278	(2274)	9326	(1306)	9374	(437)
9182	(2393)	9231	(1486)	9279	(2423)	9327	(1487)	9375	(815)
9183	(674)	9232	(1500)	9280	(83)	9328	(1793)	9376	(1044)
9184	(1746)	9233	(2033)	9281*	(720)	9329	(2287)	9377	(1055)
9185	(955)	9234	(2200)	9282	(750)	9330	(279)	9378	(1230)
9186	(1108)	9235	(108)	9283	(943)	9331	(410)	9379	(1300)
9187	(2162)	9236	(175)	9284	(1121)	9332	(1158)	9380	(1896)
9188	(2225)	9237	(351)	9285	(1313)	9333	(1359)	9381	(1278)
9189	(2281)	9238	(965)	9286	(2082)	9334	(2497)	9382	(1899)
9190	(2289)	9239	(1142)	9287	(2167)	9335	(1353)	9383	(640)
9191	(2301)	9240	(1485)	9288	(2172)	9336	(859)	9384	(1432)
9192	(2374)	9241	(2336)	9289	(2412)	9337	(904)	9385	(1898)
9193	(328)	9242	(2379)	9290	(1129)	9338	(842)	9386	(2114)
9194	(631)	9243	(2058)	9291*	(1614)	9339	(1285)	9387	(1047)
9195	(1529)	9244	(2156)	9292	(2118)	9340	(1065)	9388	(1242)
9196	(2091)	9245*	(2237)	9293	(2150)	9341	(2036)	9389	(1276)
9197	(2286)	9246	(48)	9294	(2250)	9342	(2568)	9390	(1886)
9198	(2380)	9247	(62)	9295	(2297)	9343	(2574)	9391	(1894)
9199	(2405)	9248	(72)	9296	(2343)	9344	(1882)	9392	(2060)
9200	(2421)	9249	(99)	9297	(230)	9345	(1889)	9393	(2169)
9201	(326)	9250	(176)	9298	(264)	9346	(1241)	9394	(2575)
9202	(633)								

Locomotives 9389-9394 rebuilt to this class during 1923. They were actually still running as compounds on 1st January, 1923, but as conversion took place before the renumbering scheme was devised they are included here for the sake of simplification.

*Temporarily renumbered 29227, 29229, 29245, 29259, 29281 29291, 29307 and 29369 for a short time during 1934.

0-8-0 Beames L.N.W.R. 7F Class G2

Built 1921-2

Weight:
60 tons 5 cwt.

Driving Wheel Diameter:
4′ 5½″

Boiler Pressure:
175 lbs.

Tractive Effort:
29,015 lbs.

Cylinders:
20½″ × 24″

Valve Gear:
Joy

Number built: 60.

First loco withdrawn 1959; last loco withdrawn 1964.

No. in service (1/1/23) 60; (1/1/48) 60.

9395† (485)	9405 (367)	9415 (567)	9425 (134)	9435 (872)	9445 (2399)
9396 (742)	9406 (369)	9416 (568)	9426 (869)	9436 (895)	9446 (1012)
9397 (215)	9407 (373)	9417 (569)	9427 (2047)	9437 (2182)	9447 (2414)
9398 (216)	9408 (382)	9418 (570)	9428 (2050)	9438 (2372)	9448 (2429)
9399 (220)	9409 (396)	9419 (571)	9429 (2171)	9439 (36)	9449 (2517)
9400 (221)	9410 (407)	9420 (572)	9430 (2226)	9440 (994)	9450 (13)
9401 (253)	9411 (411)	9421 (573)	9431 (2255)	9441 (2381)	9451 (231)
9402 (434)	9412 (417)	9422 (574)	9432 (2367)	9442* (758)	9452 (308)
9403 (1154)	9413 (429)	9423 (575)	9433 (2371)	9443 (2383)	9453 (403)
9404 (223)	9414 (1530)	9424 (576)	9434 (344)	9444 (2386)	9454 (2178)

*Temporarily renumbered 29442 for a short time during 1934.

†Retained for preservation.

A large number of the various L.N.W.R. 0-8-0 classes just described survived to carry B.R. numbers formed by the addition of 40000, including several of the conversions from the original compounds, such as 48893, 48895, 48898, 48899, 48901, etc., and the whole of the final G2 class, Nos. 49395 to 49454.

2-8-0 Webb L.N.W.R. 4-cylinder compound, small boiler 3F
Class E

Built 1901-4
Rebuilt to 2-8-0 1904-7

Weight:
56 tons 10 cwt.

Boiler Pressure:
200 lbs.

Cylinders:
H.P. (2) 15″ ×24″
L.P. (2) 20½″×24″

Driving Wheel Diameter:
4′ 5½″

Tractive Effort at 80% boiler pressure:
17,406 lbs.

Valve Gear:
Joy

Number rebuilt: 26.

First loco withdrawn 1927; last unrebuilt loco withdrawn 1928 (remainder converted to class G1). Last rebuilt engine withdrawn 1964.
No. in service (1/1/23) 10; (1/1/48) 0.

9600*	(1888)	9602	(18)	9604*	(2563)	9606	(1042)	9608	(1222)
9601	(905)	9603	(2558)	9605	(1017)	9607*	(1064)	9609*	(1585)

*Nos. 9600/4/7/9 were renumbered 8892-8895 on conversion to 0-8-0 simples. The remainder were scrapped as compounds.

2-8-0 Whale L.N.W.R. 4-cylinder compound, large boiler 3F
Class F

Built 1901-4 as 0-8-0
Rebuilt to 2-8-0 1904-7

Weight:

Boiler Pressure:
175 lbs.

Cylinders:
H.P. (2) 15″ ×24″
L.P. (2) 20½″×24″

Driving Wheel Diameter:
4′ 5½″

Tractive Effort at 80% boiler pressure:
15,221 lbs.

Valve Gear:
Joy

Number built: 12.

First loco withdrawn 1927; last unrebuilt loco withdrawn 1928. (Remainder converted to G1.) Last rebuilt engine withdrawn 1962.
No. in service (1/1/23) 6; (1/1/48) 0.

9610*	(899)	9612*	(906)	9613*	(1247)	9614	(1273)	9615*	(647)
9611	(352)								

*Nos. 9610/2/3/5 were renumbered 8896-8899 on conversion to 0-8-0 simples. The remainder were scrapped as compounds.

2-8-0 Robinson G.C.R. design

Built 1917-1919

Sold by War Dept. to L.N.W.R.

Weight:
73 tons 4 cwt.

Boiler Pressure:
180 lbs.

Cylinders:
21″ × 28″

Driving Wheel Diameter:
4′ 8″

Tractive Effort:
31,325 lbs.

Valve Gear:
Stephenson

Number purchased by L.N.W.R.: 50.

First loco withdrawn 1928; last loco withdrawn 1932.
No. in service (1/1/23) 50; (1/1/48) 0.

9616 (2400)	9625 (2041)	9634 (2413)	9643 (2444)	9652 (2886)	9661 (*)
9617 (2407)	9626 (2048)	9635 (1348)	9644 (2447)	9653 (2866)	9662 (2918)
9618 (2406)	9627 (2071)	9636 (2103)	9645 (2451)	9654 (2929)	9663 (2938)
9619 (1315)	9628 (2079)	9637 (2108)	9646 (2940)	9655 (2862)	9664 (2873)
9620 (1317)	9629 (2093)	9638 (2109)	9647 (2930)	9656 (2969)	9665 (2890)
9621 (1336)	9630 (2099)	9639 (2389)	9648 (2932)	9657 (2860)	
9622 (1337)	9631 (2100)	9640 (2394)	9649 (2934)	9658 (2895)	
9623 (1347)	9632 (2102)	9641 (2404)	9650 (2936)	9659 (2950)	
9624 (2039)	9633 (2402)	9642 (2439)	9651 (*)	9660 (2937)	

*Nos. 9651 and 9661 were never allocated L.N.W.R. numbers, and were renumbered into the L.M.S. stock straight from their W.D. Nos. 1924 and 1602. They came from the Great Eastern Railway to which line they had been on loan. It is doubtful whether any of the rest of the last twenty, Nos. 9646-9665 ever carried their allotted L.N.W.R. Nos.

In 1931 the survivors of this class, Nos. 9616-9, 9621, 9627-9633, 9635-8, 9640-5/7-9, 9652/4/5 became 9455-9482 in consequence of the construction of new Fowler 0-8-0's.

2-8-0 Fowler S. & D.J.R. 7F

Built 1914-1925

(Taken into L.M.S. stock, 1930)

Weight:
64 tons 15 cwt.

Boiler Pressure:
190 lbs.

Cylinders:
21″ × 28″

Driving Wheel Diameter:
4′ 8½″

Tractive Effort:
35,295 lbs.

Valve Gear:
Walschaerts

Number built: 11.

The five later engines, Nos. 86-90, built in 1925 had larger boilers than the original six, but all were latterly fitted with the smaller boilers as on Nos. 80-85.

First loco withdrawn 1959; last loco withdrawn 1964.

9670 (80) 9671 (81)	9672 (82) 9673 (83)	9674 (84) 9675 (85)	9676 (86) 9677 (87)	9678 (88) 9679 (89)	9680 (90)

In 1932 they were renumbered 13800-13810 in consequence of the construction of new Fowler 0-8-0's, and all in due course became B.R. Nos. 53800-53810.

2-4-0 Ramsbottom L. & Y.R. 1P Reb. Aspinall

Built 1873

(Built for L.N.W.R.—Sold to L. & Y.R. 1873)

Weight:
32 tons

Driving Wheel Diameter:
6′ 7½″

Boiler Pressure:
160 lbs.

Tractive Effort:
11,791 lbs.

Cylinders:
17″×24″

Valve Gear:
Stephenson

Original number in class: 10.

First loco withdrawn 1897; last loco withdrawn 1926.
No. in service (1/1/23) 1; (1/1/48) 0.

(L. & Y.R. No. in Brackets.)

10000 (731)

2-4-0 Furness Railway Unclassified

Built 1872-1882

Weight:
Not available

Driving Wheel Diameter:
5′ 6″

Boiler Pressure:
120 lb.

Tractive Effort:
7,915 lbs.

Cylinders:
16″×20″

Valve Gear:
Stephenson

Original number in class: 18.

First loco withdrawn before 1923; last loco withdrawn 1925.
No. in service (1/1/23) 2; (1/1/48) 0.

(F.R. No. in brackets.)

10002 (44A) (The L.M.S. number was never actually carried.)	45A (Not allocated L.M.S. number.)

2-4-0 Smellie Maryport & Carlisle Unclassified

Built 1874-1878

Weight:
33 tons 2 cwt.

Driving Wheel Diameter:
6′ 1½″

Boiler Pressure:
135 lbs.

Tractive Effort:
10,828 lbs.

Cylinders:
17″ × 24″

Valve Gear:
Stephenson

Number built: 3.

First loco withdrawn 1924; last loco withdrawn 1925.
No. in service (1/1/23) 3; (1/1/48) 0.

(M. & C.R. No. in brackets.)

10005 (13)	10006 (8)	10007 (10)

It is doubtful whether any actually carried their L.M.S. numbers.

0-4-2 Smellie Maryport & Carlisle 1P

Built 1879-1895

Weight:
33 tons 10 cwt.*

Driving Wheel Diameter:
5′ 7½″

Boiler Pressure:
150 lbs.*

Tractive Effort:
13,100 lbs.*

Cylinders:
17″ × 24″

Valve Gear:
Stephenson

Number built: 4.

*Engine No. 10011 had 140 lbs. boiler pressure, tractive effort of 11,800 lbs. and weighed 32 tons.

First loco withdrawn 1928; last loco withdrawn 1928.
No. in service (1/1/23) 4; (1/1/48) 0.

(M. & C.R. No. in brackets.)

10010 (4)	10011 (2)	10012 (15)	10013 (16)

4-4-0 Barton Wright L. & Y.R. 1P (L. & Y.R. Class J2)

Built 1885-7

Weight:
43 tons 5 cwt.

Boiler Pressure:
160 lbs.

Cylinders:
17½″×26″

Driving Wheel Diameter:
6′ 0″

Tractive Effort:
15,040 lbs.

Valve Gear:
Stephenson

Number built: 36.

First loco withdrawn 1906; last loco withdrawn 1930.
No. in service (1/1/23) 2; (1/1/48) 0.

(L. & Y.R. No. in brackets.)

10100 (922)	10101 (924)

4-4-0 Barton Wright L. & Y.R. 1P (L. & Y.R. Class J3)

Built 1888-9

*Three locos rebuilt Hughes 1910-1915 with Belpaire firebox and extended smokebox.

Weight:
43 tons 5 cwt.
44 tons 12 cwt.*

Boiler Pressure:
160 lbs.; 180 lbs.*

Cylinders:
18″×26″

Driving Wheel Diameter:
6′ 0″

Tractive Effort:
15,910 lbs.; 17,900 lbs.*

Valve Gear:
Joy

Number built: 30.

First loco withdrawn 1930†; last loco withdrawn 1935.
No. in service (1/1/23) 29; (1/1/48) 0.

†One engine scrapped 1901 after a collision.

10102	(978)	10108	(984)	10114	(991)	10120	(997)	10126*	(1003)
10103	(979)	10109	(985)	10115	(992)	10121	(998)	10127	(1004)
10104	(980)	10110	(986)	10116	(993)	10122*	(999)	10128	(1005)
10105	(981)	10111	(988)	10117	(994)	10123	(1000)	10129	(1006)
10106*	(982)	10112	(989)	10118	(995)	10124	(1001)	10130	(1007)
10107	(983)	10113	(990)	10119	(996)	10125	(1002)		

4-4-0 Furness 1P

Built 1890

Weight:
36 tons 2 cwt.

Driving Wheel Diameter:
5′ 7½″

Boiler Pressure:
140 lbs.

Tractive Effort:
12,228 lbs.

Cylinders:
17″×24″

Valve Gear:
Stephenson

Number built: 4.

First loco withdrawn 1924; last loco withdrawn 1927.
No. in service (1/1/23) 4; (1/1/48) 0.

10131 (120)	10132 (121)	10133 (122)	10134 (123)

4-4-0 Pettigrew Furness 1P

Built 1896-1900

Weight:
41 tons 6 cwt.

Driving Wheel Diameter:
6′ 0″

Boiler Pressure:
150 lbs.

Tractive Effort:
13,770 lbs.

Cylinders:
18″×24″

Valve Gear:
Stephenson

Number built: 8.

First loco withdrawn 1929; last loco withdrawn 1931.
No. in service (1/1/23) 8; (1/1/48) 0.

10135 (36) 10136 (37)	10137 (44) 10138 (45)	10139 (46) 10140 (47)	10141 (124) 10142 (125)

4-4-0 Pettigrew Furness 1P

Built 1900-1

Weight:
43 tons

Driving Wheel Diameter:
6′ 6″

Boiler Pressure:
160 lbs.

Tractive Effort:
14,688 lbs.

Cylinders:
18″×26″

Valve Gear:
Stephenson

Number built: 4.

First loco withdrawn 1930; last loco withdrawn 1931.
No. in service (1/1/23) 4; (1/1/48) 0.

10143 (126)	10144 (127)	10145 (128)	10146 (129)

4-4-0 Aspinall L. & Y.R. 2P
L. & Y.R. Class J4

Built 1891-4
(Six engines rebuilt Hughes 1908-9)

Weight:
44 tons 16 cwt.

Driving Wheel Diameter:
7′ 3″

Boiler Pressure:
180 lbs.

Tractive Effort:
14,814 lbs.

Cylinders:
18″×26″

Valve Gear:
Joy

Original number in class: 40.

First loco withdrawn 1925; last loco withdrawn 1930.
No. in service (1/1/23) 34; (1/1/48) 0.
6 rebuilt; See 10190-5

10150	(1093)	10157	(1101)	10164	(1111)	10171	(1226)	10178	(344)
10151	(1094)	10158	(1102)	10165	(1220)	10172	(1227)	10179	(368)
10152	(1095)	10159	(1103)	10166	(1221)	10173	(1228)	10180	(429)
10153	(1096)	10160	(1106)	10167	(1222)	10174	(1229)	10181	(430)
10154	(1097)	10161	(1107)	10168	(1223)	19175	(318)	10182	(488)
10155	(1099)	10162	(1108)	10169	(1224)	10176	(338)	10183	(498)
10156	(1100)	10163	(1109)	10170	(1225)	10177	(339)		

4-4-0 Pettigrew Furness 2P

Built 1913-4

Weight:
47 tons 12 cwt.

Driving Wheel Diameter:
6′ 0″

Boiler Pressure:
170 lbs.

Tractive Effort:
16,907 lbs.

Cylinders:
18″×26″

Valve Gear:
Stephenson

Number built: 4.

First loco withdrawn 1932; last loco withdrawn 1933.
No. in service (1/1/23) 4; (1/1/48) 0.

10185 (130)	10186 (131)	10187 (132)	10188 (133)

4-4-0 Aspinall Rebuilt Hughes L. & Y.R. 3P
L. & Y.R. Class J5

Built 1891-4
Rebuilt with superheater 1908-9

Weight:
48 tons 15 cwt.

Boiler Pressure:
180 lbs.

Cylinders:
19″×26″; 20″×26″*

Driving Wheel Diameter:
7′ 3″

Tractive Effort:
17,576 lbs.: 18,290 lbs.*

Valve Gear:
Joy; Walschaerts*

Number of rebuilds: 2,; 4*.

First loco withdrawn 1926, 1925*; last loco withdrawn 1926, 1926*.
No. in service (1/1/23) 6; (1/1/48) 0.

10190 (1112)	10192* (1104)	10193* (1098)	10194* (1105)	10195 (455)
10191* (1110)				

4-4-2 Aspinall L. & Y.R. 2P
L. & Y.R. Class L1

Built 1899-1902

Weight:
58 tons 15 cwt.

Boiler Pressure:
180 lbs.

Cylinders:
19″×26″

Driving Wheel Diameter:
7′ 3″

Tractive Effort:
16,506 lbs.

Valve Gear:
Joy

Number built: 40.

First loco withdrawn 1926; last loco withdrawn 1934.
No. in service (1/1/23) 40; (1/1/48) 0.

10300 (1400)	10308 (1399)	10316 (711)	10324 (1409)	10332 (1417)
10301 (1392)	10309 (1401)	10317 (718)	10325 (1410)	10333 (1418)
10302 (1393)	10310 (1402)	10318 (735)	10326 (1411)	10334 (1419)
10303 (1394)	10311 (1403)	10319 (737)	10327 (1412)	10335 (1420)
10304 (1395)	10312 (1404)	10320 (1405)	10328 (1413)	10336 (1421)
10305 (1396)	10313 (700)	10321 (1406)	10329 (1414)	10337 (1422)
10306 (1397)	10314 (702)	10322 (1407)	10330 (1415)	10338 (1423)
10307 (1398)	10315 (708)	10323 (1408)	10331 (1416)	10339 (1424)

4-6-0

Hughes L. & Y.R. 3P
L. & Y.R. Class N1

Built 1908-9

Weight:
77 tons 1 cwt.

Boiler Pressure:
180 lbs.

Cylinders (4):
16″×26″

Driving Wheel Diameter:
6′ 9″

Tractive Effort:
23,156 lbs.

Valve Gear:
Joy

Original number in class: 20.

First loco withdrawn 1925; last loco withdrawn 1926.
No. in service (1/1/23) 5; (1/1/48) 0.

10400 (1507)	10401 (1508)	10402 (1512)	10403 (1513)	10404 (1515)

4-6-0

Hughes L. & Y.R. 5P
L. & Y.R. Class N1

Built 1921-1925

Weight:
79 tons 1 cwt.

Boiler Pressure:
180 lbs.

Cylinders (4):
$16\frac{1}{2}$″×26″*†

Driving Wheel Diameter:
6′ 3″

Tractive Effort:
28,880 lbs.*

Valve Gear:
Walschaerts

*Some engines had $15\frac{3}{4}$″×26″ cylinders with 26,315 lbs. tractive effort. Nos. 10405-10419 were rebuilt from the original 1908 class with Joy's valve gear.

†In 1926 No. 10456 was rebuilt as compound with two inside cylinders 22″×26″ and two outside cylinders $15\frac{1}{2}$″×26″.

Original Number in class: 14. Plus 15 rebuilds and 41 further locos constructed 1923-1925.

First loco withdrawn 1934; last loco withdrawn 1951.
No. in service (1/1/23) 29; (1/1/48) 7.

See Nos. 11110-11119 for Tank version of this class.

10405 (1522)	10413 (1525)	10421 (1650)	10429 (1658)	10437 (1666)
10406 (1514)	10414 (1509)	10422 (1651)	10430 (1659)	10438 (1667)
10407 (1523)	10415 (1520)	10423 (1652)	10431 (1660)	10439 (1668)
10408 (1510)	10416 (1517)	10424 (1653)	10432 (1661)	10440 (1669)
10409 (1511)	10417 (1524)	10425 (1654)	10433 (1662)	10441 (1670)
10410 (1506)	10418 (1519)	10426 (1655)	10434 (1663)	10442 (1671)
10411 (1521)	10419 (1518)	10427 (1656)	10435 (1664)	10443 (1672)
10412 (1516)	10420 (1649)	10428 (1657)	10436 (1665)	10444 (1673)

10445 (1674)	10451* (1680)	10457* (1696)	10463* (1702)	10469* (1708)
10446* (1675)	10452* (1681)	10458* (1697)	10464* (1703)	10470* (1709)
10447* (1676)	10453* (1682)	10459* (1698)	10465* (1704)	10471* (1710)
10448* (1677)	10454* (1683)	10460* (1699)	10466* (1705)	10472* (1711)
10449* (1678)	10455* (1694)	10461* (1700)	10467* (1706)	10473* (1712)
10450* (1679)	†10456* (1695)	10462* (1701)	14068* (1707)	10474* (1713)

Nos. 1663-1674 although turned out early in 1923 with L. & Y.R. numbers, carried the initials L.M.S.R. on the tenders, whilst Nos. 10446* onwards carried L.M.S. numbers from the start and never bore their allotted L. & Y.R. numbers.

One engine, No. 10455, survived long enough to carry its B.R. No. 50455.

For 10600-10617, see page 186.

0-4-4T Maryport & Carlisle Unclassified

Built 1897

Cylinders:
16″×22″

Driving Wheel Diameter:
5′ 1½″

(Other particulars unavailable)

Number built: 1.

Loco withdrawn 1924.
No. in service (1/1/23) 1; (1/1/48) 0.

10618 (26) L.M.S. number never actually carried

2-4-2T Furness Unclassified

Built as 2-4-0 1875
Rebuilt 1891

Weight:
unavailable.

Driving Wheel Diameter:
5′ 6″

Boiler Pressure:
120 lbs.

Tractive Effort:
7,915 lbs.

Cylinders:
16″×20″

Valve Gear:
Stephenson

Number rebuilt: 7.

First loco withdrawn before 1923; last loco withdrawn 1924.
No. in service (1/1/23) 2; (1/1/48) 0.

10619 (71A)	10620 (72A)

Neither carried its L.M.S. number.

2-4-2T

Aspinall L. & Y.R. 2P
L. & Y.R. Class K2
Built 1889-1910

Many later rebuilt with lengthened bunkers and others with superheaters and Belpaire firebox. Some built new in these forms.

Weight:
55 tons 19 cwt. (to 10836)
59 tons 3 cwt. (10837 onwards)

Driving Wheel Diameter:
5′ 8″

Boiler Pressure:
160 lbs.
180 lbs. (Belpaire)*

Tractive Effort:
16,848 lbs. (17½″ cyls.)
17,330 lbs. (18″ cyls.)
19,496 lbs. (Belpaire)*

Cylinders:
17½″×26″
18″ ×26″

Valve Gear:
Joy

Number built: 309.

First loco withdrawn 1927; last loco withdrawn 1961.
No. in service (1/1/23) 278; (1/1/48) 110.

10621*	(1008)	10656	(1165)	10690	(147)	10724*	(1275)	10758	(1325)
10622	(1009)	10657	(1166)	10691*	(189)	10725	(24)	10759	(1326)
10623	(1010)	10658	(10)	10692*	(206)	10726	(31)	10760	(1327)
10624	(1011)	10659	(1167)	10693*	(208)	10727	(63)	10761	(1328)
10625	(1012)	10660	(1168)	10694	(299)	10728	(76)	10762	(1329)
10626	(1013)	10661	(1169)	10695	(1210)	10729	(84)	10763	(1330)
10627	(1014)	10662	(287)	10696	(1211)	10730	(88)	10764	(1331)
10628	(1015)	10663	(289)	10697	(1212)	19731	(97)	10765	(1332)
10629	(1016)	10664	(321)	10698	(1213)	10732	(104)	10766	(1333)
10630	(1017)	10665	(323)	10699	(1214)	10733	(107)	10767	(1334)
10631	(1033)	10666*	(334)	10700	(1215)	10734	(110)	10768	(1335)
10632*	(1034)	10667*	(337)	10701	(1216)	10735	(129)	10769	(1336)
10633	(1036)	10668	(1170)	10702	(1217)	10736*	(156)	10770	(1337)
10634	(1037)	10669	(1171)	10703	(1218)	10737	(185)	10771	(1338)
10635	(1038)	10670	(1172)	10704	(1219)	10738	(296)	10772	(1339)
10636	(1039)	10671	(1173)	10705	(36)	10739	(319)	10773	(1340)
10637	(1040)	10672	(1174)	10706	(39)	10740	(329)	10774	(1341)
10639	(1042)	10673	(1175)	10707	(1258)	10741	(362)	10775	(1342)
10640	(1043)	10674	(1176)	10708	(1259)	10742	(369)	10776	(1343)
10641	(1044)	10675	(1177)	10709	(1260)	10743	(415)	10777	(1344)
10642	(1045)	10676*	(1178)	10710	(1261)	10744	(1311)	10778	(1345)
10643	(1046)	10677	(1179)	10711	(1262)	10745	(1312)	10779	(1346)
10644	(1047)	10678	(16)	10712	(1263)	10746	(1313)	10780	(1347)
10645	(1048)	10679	(37)	10713	(1264)	10747	(1314)	10781	(1348)
10646	(1049)	10680	(301)	10714	(1265)	10748	(1315)	10782	(1349)
10647	(1052)	10681	(340)	10715	(1266)	10749	(1316)	10783	(1350)
10648	(1157)	10682	(345)	10716	(1267)	10750	(1317)	10784	(1361)
10649	(1158)	10683	(349)	10717	(1268)	10751	(1318)	10785	(1362)
10650*	(1159)	10684	(638)	10718	(1269)	10752	(1319)	10786	(1367)
10651*	(1160)	10685	(651)	10719	(1270)	10753	(1320)	10787	(1370)
10652*	(1161)	10686	(680)	10720	(1271)	10754	(1321)	10788	(1371)
10653	(1162)	10687	(46)	10721	(1272)	10755	(1322)	10789	(1372)
10654	(1163)	10688	(54)	10722*	(1273)	10756	(1323)	10790	(1373)
10655	(1164)	10689	(119)	10723	(1274)	10757	(1324)	10791	(1374)

10792	(1375)	10814	(723)	10839	(645)	10862	(716)	10883	(1465)
10793	(1376)	10815*	(724)	10840	(646)	10863	(722)	10884	(1466)
10794	(1377)	10816	(725)	10841	(653)	10864	(740)	10885	(1467)
10795	(1378)	10817	(728)	10842	(658)	10865	(741)	10886*	(1468)
10796	(1379)	10818	(730)	10843	(664)	10866	(742)	10887*	(1470)
10797	(1381)	10819	(732)	10844	(667)	10867	(743)	10888	(1526)
10798	(1382)	10820	(733)	10845	(668)	10868	(746)	10889	(1527)
10799	(1383)	10821	(734)	10847	(671)	10869	(790)	10890	(1530)
10800	(1384)	10822	(5)	10848	(672)	10870	(816)	10891	(1531)
10801	(1385)	10823	(34)	10849*	(674)	10871	(817)	10892	(1535)
10802	(1386)	10824	(90)	10850	(675)	10872	(819)	10893	(1537)
10803	(1387)	10825	(98)	10851	(678)	10873	(833)	10894	(1538)
10804	(1388)	10827	(183)	10852	(514)	10874	(839)	10895	(1540)
10805	(1389)	10828	(191)	10853	(515)	10875	(842)	10896	(1541)
10806	(1390)	10829*	(192)	10854	(516)	10876	(867)	10897	(1542)
10807	(1391)	10830	(297)	10855	(525)	10877	(868)	10898	(1544)
10808	(686)	10831	(316)	10856	(641)	10878	(878)	10899	(1545)
10809	(696)	10833	(346)	10857*	(669)	10879	(1461)	10951	(670)
10810	(699)	10834	(353)	10858	(689)	10880	(1462)	10952	(332)
10811	(701)	10835	(371)	10859	(705)	10881	(1463)	10953	(120)
10812	(703)	10837	(629)	10860	(707)	10882	(1464)	10954	(379)
10813	(721)	10838	(643)	10861	(714)				

All but the last twenty to be built were constructed with $17\frac{1}{2}''$ cylinders, but in most cases all were subsequently enlarged to 18″.

10826/32/6/46 were rebuilt 1923/4 to next class and numbered 10953/2/4/1. The other missing number, 10638, was allocated to but not carried by the engine sold to the Wirral Railway which became 6762 (q.v.).

†The original engine has been preserved as L. & Y.R. 1008.

*Rebuilt with Belpaire firebox and extended smokebox.

Many of this class survived to have 40000 added to their numbers by B.R., becoming 50621, etc.

2-4-2T Hughes L. & Y.R. Superheater 3P
L. & Y.R. Class K3

Built new 1911
Others rebuilt 1914-1925 from class K2

Weight:
63 tons

Boiler Pressure:
180 lbs.

Cylinders:
$20\frac{1}{2}'' \times 26''$

Driving Wheel Diameter:
5′ 8″

Tractive Effort:
24,584 lbs.

Valve Gear:
Joy

Number built: New: 20. Rebuilds: 44.

First loco withdrawn 1929; last loco withdrawn 1952.
No. in service (1/1/23) 51; (1/1/48) 14.

Rebuilding to this class from K2 continued after the grouping, and the first four engines thus dealt with, Nos. 10846, 10832, 10826, and 10836, were renumbered 10951-10954 following the engines already converted, but this practice was then discontinued and subsequent rebuilds retained their numbers in the 10621-10899 series. All of this class had Belpaire fireboxes and extended smokeboxes, in addition to being superheated.

10900	(18)	10911	(230)	10922	(38)	10933	(58)	10944	(632)
10901	(70)	10912	(253)	10923	(267)	10934	(1533)	10945	(1543)
10902	(111)	10913	(275)	10924	(1539)	10935	(48)	10946	(661)
10903	(112)	10914	(276)	10925	(1536)	10936	(1051)	10947	(644)
10904	(151)	10915	(285)	10926	(627)	10937	(630)	10948	(351)
10905	(162)	10916	(480)	10927	(693)	10938	(1469)	10949	(649)
10906	(188)	10917	(519)	10928	(26)	10939	(869)	10950	(356)
10907	(221)	10918	(618)	10929	(45)	10940	(1532)	10951	(670)
10908	(223)	10919	(637)	10930	(1050)	10941	(1534)	10952	(332)
10909	(224)	10920	(1529)	10931	(1380)	10942	(380)	10953	(120)
10910	(227)	10921	(1528)	10932	(1035)	10943	(719)	10954	(379)

Nos. 10909 and 10925 survived long enough to carry B.R. Nos. 50909 and 50925.

4-4-2T Pettigrew Furness 1P

Built 1915-6

Weight:
59 tons 10 cwt.

Boiler Pressure:
160 lbs.

Cylinders:
$17\frac{1}{2}'' \times 24''$

Driving Wheel Diameter:
5′ 8″

Tractive Effort:
14,700 lbs.

Valve Gear:
Stephenson

Number built: 6.

First loco withdrawn 1930; last loco withdrawn 1933.
No. in service (1/1/23) 6; (1/1/48) 0.

11080	(38)	11081	(39)	11082	(40)	11083	(41)	11084	(42)	11085	(43)

4-6-4T Rutherford Furness 3P

Built 1921

Weight:
92 tons 15 cwt.

Boiler Pressure:
170 lbs.

Cylinders:
$19\frac{1}{2}'' \times 26''$

Driving Wheel Diameter:
5′ 8″

Tractive Effort:
21,006 lbs.

Valve Gear:
Stephenson

Number built: 5.

First loco withdrawn 1934; last loco withdrawn 1940.
No. in service (1/1/23) 5; (1/1/48) 0.

11100	(115)	11101	(116)	11102	(117)	11103	(118)	11104	(119)

4-6-4T Hughes L. & Y.R. 5P
L. & Y.R. Class P1

Built 1924

Although these engines did not appear until after the grouping, they were essentially a Lancashire & Yorkshire design, and are included on that account. They were in all respects a tank version of the 4-6-0's being constructed at the same time (Nos. 10455-10474), in fact the latter were intended to be 4-6-4T's, but in the event the frames were cut down and they became 4-6-0 tender engines instead.

Weight:
99 tons 19 cwt.

Boiler Pressure:
180 lbs.

Cylinders (4):
$16\frac{1}{2}'' \times 26''$

Driving Wheel Diameter:
6′ 3″

Tractive Effort:
28,880 lbs.

Valve Gear:
Walschaerts

Number built: 10.

First loco withdrawn 1938; last loco withdrawn 1942.
No. in service (1/1/23) 0.; (1/1/48) 0.

11110	(1684)	11112	(1686)	11114	(1688)	11116	(1690)	11118	(1692)
11111	(1685)	11113	(1687)	11115	(1689)	11117	(1691)	11119	(1693)

No. 11114 was exhibited at Wembley Exhibition in 1925.

*The L. & Y.R. numbers quoted, although allocated, were never actually carried.

0-4-0ST Aspinall L. & Y.R. Unclassified
(L. & Y.R. Class B7)

Built 1886*, 1891-1910

Weight:
21 tons 5 cwt.

Boiler Pressure:
140 lbs.*
160 lbs.

Cylinders:
$13'' \times 18''$

Driving Wheel Diameter:
3′ 0″

Tractive Effort:
10,060 lbs.*
11,492 lbs.

Valve Gear:
Stephenson

Number built: 3*; 57.

First loco withdrawn 1912; last loco withdrawn 1963.
No. in service (1/1/23) 1*, 57; (1/1/48) 0*, 23.

11200*	(916)	11212	(1232)	11224	(399)	11236	(865)	11248	(71)
11201	(1153)	11213	(1286)	11225	(402)	11237	(879)	11249	(75)
11202	(1154)	11214	(1287)	11226	(403)	11238	(2)	11250	(118)
11203	(1155)	11215	(1288)	11227	(476)	11239	(3)	11251	(226)
11204	(1156)	11216	(1289)	11228	(260)	11240	(8)	11252	(271)
11205	(32)	11217	(1290)	11229	(813)	11241	(12)	11253	(298)
11206	(310)	11218	(68)	11230	(814)	11242	(17)	11254	(481)
11207	(504)	11219	(113)	11231	(821)	11243	(19)	11255	(517)
11208	(654)	11220	(139)	11232	(823)	11244	(28)	11256	(613)
11209	(729)	11221	(155)	11233	(825)	11245	(43)	11257	(614)
11210	(1230)	11222	(377)	11234	(832)	11246	(56)		
11211	(1231)	11223	(389)	11235	(840)	11247	(64)		

A considerable number of these engines survived to become B.R. Nos. 51202, etc. No. 51218 has been acquired by the Keighley & Worth Valley Preservation Society.

0-4-0ST Furness Unclassified

Built 1874

Weight:
24 tons 10 cwt.

Driving Wheel Diameter:
4′ 8″

Boiler Pressure:
120 lbs.

Tractive Effort:
11,191 lbs.

Cylinders:
16″×24″

Number built:
2

First loco withdrawn before 1923; last loco withdrawn 1924.
No. in service (1/1/23) 1; (1/1/48) 0.

11258 (97A) It never carried its allocated L.M.S. Number

0-4-0T Maryport & Carlisle Unclassified

Built 1880-1

Cylinders:
14″×20″

Driving Wheel Diameter:
3′ 8″

(Other dimensional details unavailable) **Number built:** 2

First loco withdrawn 1924; last loco withdrawn 1924.
No. in service (1/1/23) 2; (1/1/48) 0.

11259 (R3)	11260 (R2)

L.M.S. numbers never actually carried.

C.R. Lambie 4-4-0T No. 15026

C.R. Brittain 0-4-2 No. 17018.

C.R. An old 0-6-0 built for the Solway Junction Railway in 1868.
[W. H. Whitworth

C.R. McIntosh 0-8-0 No. 17997. This was the highest number in the L.M.S. list as at first drawn up at the grouping.
[W. H. Whitworth

G. & S.W.R. Smellie 4-4-0 No. 14116. A familiar sight at St. Enoch in the late 1920's and early 1930's, where it was normally engaged on station pilot duty.

G. & S.W.R. Manson 4-4-0's Nos. 14247 and 14248, the latter running with an unusual type of 8-wheeled tender.

G. & S.W.R. 4-6-0 No. 511, later L.M.S. No. 14672. [L.P.C.

G. & S.W.R. Large Whitelegg 4-6-4T No. 15405.

One of the well known L. & Y.R. 2-4-2T's which did such yeoman service on that line for many years. [L. R. Tomsett

Aspinall L. & Y.R. Atlantic No. 10327 [L.P.C.

L. & Y.R. Barton Wright 4-4-0 No. 997 (later L.M.S. 10120) at Manchester Victoria in 1926.

Hughes 4-6-0 No. 10474 temporarily fitted for oil burning during 1926. [W. H. Whitworth

Hoy L. & Y.R. 2-6-2T No. 11711, designed as an enlargement of the popular 2-4-2T's, but in the event a most unsuccessful class. [W. H. Whitworth

L. & Y.R. 4-cylinder compound 0-8-0 No. 12767. [W. H. Whitworth

Barton Wright 0-6-0ST converted from 0-6-0 tender engine. Dating back to 1891, a numerous and most useful class, the last of which was not withdrawn until 1964.

Two of Aspinall's L. & Y.R. 0-4-0ST's. The somewhat primitive spark arresters were fitted to those engines used for shunting in the Liverpool dock area.

0-6-0ST Garstang & Knott End Railway Unclassified

Built 1897-1900

Weight:
30 tons

Driving Wheel Diameter:
3′ 6″

Boiler Pressure:
140 lbs.

Tractive Effort:
12,950 lbs.

Cylinders:
15″ × 20″

Valve Gear:
Stephenson

Number built: 2.

First loco withdrawn 1925; last loco withdrawn 1926.

No. in service (1/1/23) 2; (1/1/48) 0.

11300	Jubilee Queen	11301	New Century

No. 11301 never carried its L.M.S. number.

Locos unnumbered on G. & K.E.R., known by name only.

0-6-0T Garstang & Knott End Railway Unclassified

Built 1908

Weight:
31 tons 10 cwt.

Driving Wheel Diameter:
3′ 9″

Boiler Pressure:
160 lbs.

Tractive Effort:
11,847 lbs.

Cylinders:
14″ × 20″

Valve Gear:
Stephenson

Number built: 1.

Loco withdrawn 1924.

No. in service (1/1/23) 1; (1/1/48) 0.

11302	Knott End	L.M.S. number never carried.

Not-numbered on G. & K.E.R., known by name only.

0-6-0ST Barton Wright Rebuilt Aspinall L. & Y.R. 2F

L. & Y.R. Class F16

Originally built 1876-87 as 0-6-0 tender engines
Rebuilt 1891-1900 as saddle tanks

Weight:
43 tons 17 cwt.

Driving Wheel Diameter:
4′ 6″

Boiler Pressure:
160 lbs.

Tractive Effort:
20,040 lbs.

Cylinders:
$17\frac{1}{2}'' \times 26''$

Valve Gear:
Stephenson

Original Number in Class:
280.

Number rebuilt:
230.

First loco withdrawn 1926; last loco withdrawn 1964.
No. in service (1/1/23) 230; (1/1/48) 101.

11303 (543)	11338 (562)	11373 (163)	11408 (148)	11443 (773)
11304 (558)	11339 (172)	11374 (207)	11409 (573)	11444 (322)
11305 (553)	11340 (180)	11375 (137)	11410 (144)	11445 (588)
11306 (565)	11341 (168)	11376 (181)	11411 (266)	11446 (596)
11307 (534)	11342 (249)	11377 (170)	11412 (598)	11447 (748)
11308 (533)	11343 (544)	11378 (132)	11413 (747)	11448 (808)
11309 (542)	11344 (314)	11379 (136)	11414 (133)	11449 (766)
11310 (567)	11345 (236)	11380 (204)	11415 (284)	11450 (779)
11311 (556)	11346 (245)	11381 (138)	11416 (313)	11451 (784)
11312 (560)	11347 (248)	11382 (176)	11417 (140)	11452 (594)
11313 (538)	11348 (165)	11383 (307)	11418 (304)	11453 (801)
11314 (554)	11349 (268)	11384 (179)	11419 (166)	11454 (758)
11315 (536)	11350 (546)	11385 (306)	11420 (171)	11455 (308)
11316 (531)	11351 (548)	11386 (222)	11421 (599)	11456 (752)
11317 (539)	11352 (128)	11387 (303)	11422 (769)	11457 (782)
11318 (535)	11353 (122)	11388 (776)	11423 (583)	11458 (292)
11319 (561)	11354 (545)	11389 (126)	11424 (584)	11459 (572)
11320 (566)	11355 (258)	11390 (783)	11425 (175)	11460 (589)
11321 (537)	11356 (277)	11391 (775)	11426 (324)	11461 (811)
11322 (530)	11357 (280)	11392 (177)	11427 (571)	11462 (580)
11323 (563)	11358 (549)	11393 (785)	11428 (615)	11463 (804)
11324 (552)	11359 (240)	11394 (173)	11429 (778)	11464 (763)
11325 (559)	11360 (250)	11395 (167)	11430 (749)	11465 (777)
11326 (550)	11361 (547)	11396 (762)	11431 (582)	11466 (581)
11327 (564)	11362 (124)	11397 (574)	11432 (597)	11467 (774)
11328 (541)	11363 (238)	11398 (575)	11433 (754)	11468 (756)
11329 (557)	11364 (143)	11399 (755)	11434 (795)	11469 (765)
11330 (532)	11365 (311)	11400 (807)	11435 (753)	11470 (592)
11331 (540)	11366 (242)	11401 (768)	11436 (767)	11471 (578)
11332 (529)	11367 (182)	11402 (770)	11437 (149)	11472 (587)
11333 (178)	11368 (131)	11403 (759)	11438 (196)	11473 (600)
11334 (174)	11369 (256)	11404 (799)	11439 (793)	11474 (194)
11335 (528)	11370 (257)	11405 (197)	11440 (621)	11475 (803)
11336 (555)	11371 (164)	11406 (309)	11441 (798)	11476 (853)
11337 (551)	11372 (153)	11407 (780)	11442 (591)	11477 (847)

11478 (577)	11489 (663)	11500 (579)	11511 (305)	11522 (850)
11479 (855)	11490 (812)	11501 (293)	11512 (781)	11523 (856)
11480 (857)	11491 (852)	11502 (854)	11513 (751)	11524 (802)
11481 (254)	11492 (772)	11503 (787)	11514 (809)	11525 (570)
11482 (843)	11493 (757)	11504 (859)	11515 (861)	11526 (761)
11483 (771)	11494 (858)	11505 (862)	11516 (860)	11527 (800)
11484 (788)	11495 (760)	11506 (848)	11517 (796)	11528 (806)
11485 (569)	11496 (846)	11507 (786)	11518 (576)	11529 (849)
11486 (585)	11497 (586)	11508 (590)	11519 (844)	11530 (595)
11487 (797)	11498 (851)	11509 (593)	11520 (750)	11531 (794)
11488 (845)	11499 (764)	11510 (810)	11521 (568)	11532 (805)

Most of the survivors at Nationalisation had 40000 added to their numbers, but five of the class which were works shunters at Horwich never did so, and retained their L.M.S. Nos. to the end. These were Nos. 11304, 11305, 11324, 11368 and 11394, of which No. 11305, withdrawn 1964, was the last survivor of the whole class.

0-6-0T Aspinall L. & Y.R. 2F
L. & Y.R. Class F20

Built 1897

Weight:
50 tons

Driving Wheel Diameter:
4′ 0″

Boiler Pressure:
160 lbs.

Tractive Effort:
17,470 lbs.

Cylinders:
17″×24″

Valve Gear:
Allan

Number built: 20.

First loco withdrawn 1917; last loco withdrawn 1961.

No. in service (1/1/23) 14; (1/1/48) 5.

11533 (1352)	11536 (1356)	11539 (1360)	11542 (496)	11545 (505)
11534 (1353)	11537 (1358)	11540 (494)	11543 (499)	11546 (506)
11535 (1355)	11538 (1359)	11541 (495)	11544 (501)	

The five survivors of 1948 had 40000 added to their numbers, becoming 51535-7, 51544 and 51546. No. 11537 which was not dealt with until September 1954, was the last engine in the whole of the L.M.S. stock to retain its pre-Nationalisation number, apart from the five saddletanks in the previous class, which as already mentioned were never renumbered.

0-6-0ST Furness (originally Whitehaven, Cleator & Egremont) 1F

Built 1871 (11547)
Built 1875 (11548)

Weight:
Details unavailable

Boiler Pressure:
125 lbs.

Cylinders:
17″×24″

Driving Wheel Diameter:
4′ 6″

Tractive Effort:
13,647 lbs.

Original Number in class:
4

No. 11547 had outside frames, and No. 11548 inside.

First loco withdrawn before 1923; last loco withdrawn 1925.
No. in service (1/1/23) 2.; (1/1/48) 0.

11547	(109A)	Originally W.C. & E.R. 13 " Springfield "
11548	(108A)	Originally W.C. & E.R. 17 " Wastwater "

Neither engine actually carried its L.M.S. number.

0-6-0T Furness 2F

Built 1871-3

Weight:
Unavailable

Boiler Pressure:
140 lbs.

Cylinders:
18″×24″

Driving Wheel Diameter:
4′ 6″

Tractive Effort:
17,136 lbs.

Valve Gear:
Stephenson

Original number in class: 6.

First loco withdrawn before 1900; last loco withdrawn 1926.
No. in class (1/1/23) 4.; (1/1/48) 0.

11549 (68)	11550 (69)	11551 (82)	11552 (83)

It is doubtful whether any of these engines carried their L.M.S. Nos.

0-6-0T Pettigrew Furness 2F

Built 1910-1916

Weight:
49 tons 10 cwt.

Driving Wheel Diameter:
4′ 7½″

Boiler Pressure:
160 lbs.

Tractive Eeffort:
18,011 lbs.

Cylinders:
17½″ × 24″

Valve Gear:
Stephenson

Number built: 10.

First loco withdrawn 1930; last loco withdrawn 1943.
No. in class (1/1/23) 10; (1/1/48) 0.

11553 (55)	11555 (57)	11557 (59)	11559 (51)	11561 (53)
11554 (56)	11556 (58)	11558 (60)	11560 (52)	11562 (54)

0-6-0T Maryport & Carlisle 1F

Built 1865 as 0-4-2T
Rebuilt 1907 as 0-6-0T

Weight:
35 tons 10 cwt.

Driving Wheel Diameter:
4′ 9½″

Boiler Pressure:
140 lbs.

Tractive Effort:
15,150 lbs.

Cylinders:
17″ × 24″

Number built: 1

Loco withdrawn 1927.
No. in class (1/1/23) 1; (1/1/48) 0.

11563 (M. & C. 17)

0-6-0ST Cleator & Workington 1F

Built 1894-1920

Engines	Weight	Boiler Pressure	Cylinders	Driving Wheels	Tractive Effort
11564 } 11565 }	50 tons 5 cwt.	160 lbs.	17″ × 24″	4′ 6″	16,360 lbs.
11566	53 tons 3 cwt.	140 lbs.	18″ × 24″	4′ 6″	17,136 lbs.
11567	53 tons 3 cwt.	135 lbs.	18″ × 24″	4′ 6″	16,489 lbs.
11568	54 tons 10 cwt.	180 lbs.	18″ × 24″	4′ 6″	22,032 lbs.

Valve Gear: Stephenson

Number built: 5.

First loco withdrawn 1926; last loco withdrawn 1932†.
No. in service (1/1/23) 5; (1/1/48) 0.

†The last engine, " Skiddaw Lodge " was sold to the Hartley Main Collieries, Northumberland, where it worked until 1956.

11564	(C. & W. 6)	Brigham Hall	11567	(C. & W. 9)	Millgrove
11565	(C. & W. 7)	Ponsonby Hall	11568	(C. & W. 10)	Skiddaw Lodge
11566	(C. & W. 8)	Hutton Hall			

0-6-2T Barton Wright L. & Y.R. 1F
L. & Y.R. Classes H2* and H3

Built 1881-3

Weight:
52 tons 4 cwt.
47 tons 17 cwt.*

Boiler Pressure:
160 lbs.
140 lbs.*

Cylinders:
$17\frac{1}{2}'' \times 26''$

Driving Wheel Diameter:
5′ 1″
4′ 6″*

Tractive Effort:
17,975 lbs.
17,540 lbs.*

Valve Gear:
Stephenson

Number built: 10*; 54.

No. 11601 fitted with steam crane for use at Horwich works.

First loco withdrawn 1906; last loco withdrawn 1932.
No. in service (1/1/23) 20, 2*; (1/1/48) 0.

11600*	(145)	11605	(264)	11610	(262)	11615	(282)	11620	(23)
11601*	(146)	11606	(273)	11611	(278)	11616	(283)	11621	(218)
11602	(244)	11607	(679)	11612	(688)	11617	(294)		
11603	(251)	11608	(639)	11613	(160)	11618	(295)		
11604	(263)	11609	(655)	11614	(203)	11619	(623)		

0-6-2T Pettigrew Furness 3F

Built 1898-1907

Weight:
58 tons 11 cwt.
55 tons*

Boiler Pressure:
150 lbs.

Cylinders:
$18'' \times 26''$

Driving Wheel Diameter:
5′ 1″
4′ 8″*

Tractive Effort:
17,781 lbs.; 19,165 lbs.*

Valve Gear:
Stephenson

Number built: 19.

First loco withdrawn 1927; last loco withdrawn 1945.
No. in service (1/1/23) 19; (1/1/48) 0.

11622*	(112)	11626	(99)	11630	(103)	11634	(107)	11638	(109)
11623*	(113)	11627	(100)	11631	(104)	11635	(96)	11639	(110)
11624*	(114)	11628	(101)	11632	(105)	11636	(97)	11640	(111)
11625	(98)	11629	(102)	11633	(106)	11637	(108)		

0-6-2T Pettigrew Furness 3F

Built 1912-4

Weight:
56 tons 18 cwt. (11641/2)
58 tons 12 cwt. (11643/4)

Driving Wheel Diameter:
4′ 7½″

Boiler Pressure:
170 lbs.

Tractive Effort:
21,933 lbs.

Cylinders:
18″×26″

Valve Gear:
Stephenson

Number built: 4.

First loco withdrawn 1929; last loco withdrawn 1934.
No. in service (1/1/23) 4; (1/1/48) 0.

11641 (94)	11642 (95)	11643 (92)	11644 (93)

2-6-0T Garstang and Knott End 1F

Built 1909

Weight:
40 tons 10 cwt.

Driving Wheel Diameter:
4′ 6″

Boiler Pressure:
160 lbs.

Tractive Effort:
14,184 lbs.

Cylinders:
16″×22″

Number built:
1

Loco withdrawn 1927.
No. in service (1/1/23) 1; (1/1/48) 0.

11680 Blackpool. Un-numbered on G. & K.E.R., known by name only.

2-6-2T

Hoy L. & Y.R. 3F
L. & Y.R. Class M1

Built 1903-4

Weight:
77 tons 10 cwt.

Driving Wheel Diameter:
5′ 8″

Boiler Pressure:
175 lbs.

Tractive Effort:
19,797 lbs.

Cylinders:
19″ × 26″

Valve Gear:
Stephenson

Number built: 20.

First loco withdrawn 1922; last loco withdrawn 1926.
No. in service (1/1/23) 17; (1/1/48) 0.

11700	(387)	11704	(712)	11708	(1442)	11711	(1445)	11714	(1448)
11701	(454)	11705	(744)	11709	(1443)	11712	(1446)	11715	(1449)
11702	(467)	11706	(837)	11710	(1444)	11713	(1447)	11716	(1450)
11703	(527)	11707	(1441)						

Only Nos. 11704 and 11711 actually carried their L.M.S. numbers.

0-8-2T

Hughes L. & Y.R. 6F
L. & Y.R. Class R1

Built 1908

Weight:
84 tons

Driving Wheel Diameter:
4′ 6″

Boiler Pressure:
180 lbs.

Tractive Effort:
34,052 lbs.

Cylinders:
$21\frac{1}{2}$″ × 26″

Valve Gear:
Stephenson

Number built: 5.

First loco withdrawn 1925; last loco withdrawn 1929.
No. in service (1/1/23) 5; (1/1/48) 0.

11800	(1501)	11801	(1502)	11802	(1503)	11803	(1504)	11804	(1505)

Only No. 11803 actually carried its L.M.S. number.

0-6-0 Sharp, Stewart Furness Unclassified

Built 1866-1882

Weight:
50 tons 10 cwt.

Boiler Pressure:
150 lbs.

Cylinders:
16″×24″

Driving Wheel Diameter:
4′ 6½″

Tractive Effort:
14,505 lbs.

Valve Gear:
Stephenson

Number built: 53*.

First loco withdrawn before 1923; last loco withdrawn 1927.
No. in service (1/1/23) 15; (1/1/48) 0.

*Some of these engines were rebuilt by Pettigrew from 1903 onwards, see 12065-12076.

12000	(48)	12003	(66)	12006	(76)	12009	(85)	12012	(75)
12001	(61)	12004	(67)	12007	(62)	12010	(86)	12013	(77)
12002	(25A)	12005	(78)	12008	(80)	12011	(87)	12014	(71)

0-6-0 Barton Wright L. & Y.R. 2F
L. & Y.R. Class F15

Built 1887

Weight:
39 tons 1 cwt.

Boiler Pressure:
160 lbs.

Cylinders:
17½″×26″

Driving Wheel Diameter:
4′ 6″

Tractive Effort:
20,040 lbs.

Valve Gear:
Stephenson

Number built: 280.

230 of this Class rebuilt by Aspinall to 0-6-0ST (see L.M.S. 11303-532).

First unrebuilt loco withdrawn 1930; last unrebuilt loco withdrawn 1959.
No. in service (1/1/23) 50; (1/1/48) 25.

12015	(928)	12025	(938)	12035	(948)	12045	(958)	12055	(968)
12016	(929)	12026	(939)	12036	(949)	12046	(959)	12056	(969)
12017	(930)	12027	(940)	12037	(950)	12047	(960)	12057	(970)
12018	(931)	12028	(941)	12038	(951)	12048	(961)	12058	(971)
12019	(932)	12029	(942)	12039	(952)	12049	(962)	12059	(972)
12020	(933)	12030	(943)	12040	(953)	12050	(963)	12060	(973)
12021	(934)	12031	(944)	12041	(954)	12051	(964)	12061	(974)
12022	(935)	12032	(945)	12042	(955)	12052	(965)	12062	(975)
12023	(936)	12033	(946)	12043	(956)	12053	(966)	12063	(976)
12024	(937)	12034	(947)	12044	(957)	12054	(967)	12064	(977)

Most of the surviving engines in 1948 had 40000 added to their numbers.
*No. 12044 has been preserved under private ownership.

0-6-0 Sharp Stewart Furness 1F Reb. Pettigrew

Rebuilt 1871-1883

Weight:
53 tons 7 cwt.

Boiler Pressure:
150 lbs.

Cylinders:
16″×24″

Driving Wheel Diameter:
4′ 6½″

Tractive Effort:
14,505 lbs.

Valve Gear:
Stephenson

Number rebuilt: 12

First loco withdrawn 1925; last loco withdrawn 1930.
No. in service (1/1/23) 12; (1/1/48) 0.

12065 (65)	12068 (88)	12071 (70)	12073 (73)	12075 (49)
12066 (63)	12069 (89)	12072 (72)	12074 (74)	12076 (50)
12067 (79)	12070 (90)			

0-6-0 Maryport & Carlisle 1F

Built 1866-1873

Weight:
33 tons 5 cwt.

Boiler Pressure:
140 lbs.

Cylinders:
17″×24″

Driving Wheel Diameter:
5′ 1½″ (12077-12080)
4′ 9″ (12081-12082)

Tractive Effort:
13,400 lbs. (12077-12080)
14,600 lbs. (12081-12082)

Valve Gear:
Stephenson

Number built: 6

First loco withdrawn 1924; last loco withdrawn 1929.
No. in service (1/1/23) 6; (1/1/48) 0.

12077 (R4)	12079 (6)	12080 (20)	12081 (21)	12082 (24)
12078 (12)				

0-6-0 Aspinall L. & Y.R. 2F L. & Y.R. Class F19

Built 1889-1917

Weight:
42 tons 3 cwt.
44 tons 5 cwt. (Belpaire rebuilds)

Boiler Pressure:
180 lbs.

Cylinders:
18″×26″

Driving Wheel Diameter:
5′ 1″

Tractive Effort:
21,129 lbs.

Valve Gear:
Stephenson

Number built: 448.

This very numerous class was turned out not only by Aspinall between 1889 and 1899, but perpetuated by his successors, Hoy and Hughes for a further period of 18 years, although the later engines appeared with slight modifications, such as the provision of Belpaire fireboxes and extended smokeboxes. Others were also superheated, and these were separated by the L.M.S. into a different series 12557-12619 (q.v.), but the unsuperheated engines, whether modified by Belpaire, etc., or not, were renumbered in one batch as 12083 to 12467.

First loco withdrawn 1931; last loco withdrawn 1961.
No. in service (1/1/23) 385; (1/1/48) 234.

12083	(130)	12132	(1113)	12181	(1195)	12230	(1235)	12279	(51)
12084	(484)	12133	(1114)	12182	(1196)	12231	(1236)	12280	(100)
12085*	(1018)	12134*	(1115)	12183	(1197)	12232	(1237)	12281	(200)
12086	(1019)	12135	(1117)	12184	(1198)	12233	(1238)	12282	(213)
12087	(1020)	12136	(1118)	12185	(1199)	12234	(1239)	12283	(214)
12088*	(1023)	12137	(1119)	12186	(1200)	12235	(1240)	12284	(228)
12089	(1024)	12138	(1120)	12187	(1202)	12236	(1241)	12285	(1276)
12090	(1025)	12139	(1121)	12188	(1203)	12237	(1242)	12286	(1277)
12091*	(1207)	12140*	(1122)	12189	(1204)	12238	(445)	12287	(1278)
12092	(1209)	12141	(1124)	12190	(1205)	12239	(469)	12288	(1279)
12093	(1030)	12142	(1125)	12191	(1206)	12240	(1243)	12289	(1280)
12094	(1031)	12143	(1126)	12192	(1207)	12241	(1244)	12290	(1281)
12095	(1032)	12144	(1127)	12193	(1208)	12242	(1245)	12291	(1282)
12096	(1054)	12145	(1128)	12194	(1209)	12243	(1246)	12292	(1284)
12097	(1056)	12146	(1129)	12195	(13)	12244	(1248)	12293	(1285)
12098	(1057)	12147	(1130)	12196	(184)	12245	(1249)	12294	(269)
12099	(1058)	12148	(1131)	12197	(186)	12246	(1250)	12295	(317)
12100	(1059)	12149	(1133)	12198	(279)	12247*	(1251)	12296	(348)
12101*	(1060)	12150	(1134)	12199	(290)	12248	(1252)	12297	(354)
12102	(1061)	12151	(1136)	12200	(336)	12249	(1253)	12298	(364)
12103	(1062)	12152	(1137)	12201*	(437)	12250*	(1254)	12299	(365)
12104	(1063)	12153	(1139)	12202	(502)	12251	(1255)	12300	(372)
12105	(1064)	12154*	(1141)	12203	(606)	12252	(1256)	12301	(417)
12106	(1065)	12155	(1142)	12204	(22)	12253*	(1257)	12302	(420)
12107	(1066)	12156	(1143)	12205	(30)	12254	(47)	12303*	(441)
12108	(1067)	12157	(1144)	12206	(42)	12255	(161)	12304	(444)
12109	(1068)	12158	(1145)	12207	(50)	12256*	(212)	12305	(450)
12110*	(1069)	12159	(1146)	12208	(78)	12257	(217)	12306	(466)
12111	(1070)	12160	(1147)	12209	(82)	12258	(410)	12307	(471)
12112	(1071)	12161	(1148)	12210	(101)	12259	(44)	12308	(472)
12113	(1072)	12162	(1149)	12211	(105)	12260	(57)	12309	(475)
12114	(1074)	12163	(1150)	12212	(106)	12261	(62)	12310*	(477)
12115	(1075)	12164	(1151)	12213	(291)	12262	(66)	12311	(478)
12116	(1076)	12165	(1152)	12214	(326)	12263	(72)	12312*	(482)
12117	(1077)	12166	(1180)	12215	(335)	12264	(73)	12313	(1291)
12118	(1078)	12167	(1181)	12216	(341)	12265	(77)	12314	(1292)
12119	(1079)	12168	(1182)	12217	(438)	12266*	(158)	12315	(1293)
12120	(1080)	12169	(1183)	12218	(607)	12267	(187)	12316	(1294)
12121	(1081)	12170	(1184)	12219	(608)	12268	(198)	12317	(1295)
12122	(1082)	12171	(1185)	12220	(53)	12269	(231)	12318	(1296)
12123	(1083)	12172	(1186)	12221	(92)	12270	(232)	12319*	(1297)
12124	(1084)	12173	(1187)	12222	(121)	12271	(270)	12320	(1298)
12125	(1085)	12174	(1188)	12223	(210)	12272	(333)	12321	(1299)
12126	(1086)	12175	(1189)	12224	(286)	12273*	(343)	12322†	(1300)
12127	(1087)	12176	(1190)	12225	(315)	12274	(355)	12323	(1301)
12128	(1088)	12177	(1191)	12226	(358)	12275	(422)	12324	(1302)
12129	(1089)	12178	(1192)	12227	(440)	12276	(427)	12325	(1303)
12130	(1090)	12179	(1193)	12228	(1233)	12277	(25)	12326	(1305)
12131*	(1091)	12180	(1194)	12229	(1234)	12278	(40)	12327	(1306)

12328	(1308)	12356	(456)	12384	(692)	12412	(401)	12440	(247)
12329	(1309)	12357	(457)	12385	(80)	12413	(424)	12441	(255)
12330*	(1310)	12358	(458)	12386	(152)	12414	(428)	12442	(824)
12331	(4)	12359	(464)	12387	(393)	12415	(432)	12443	(881)
12332	(15)	12360	(465)	12388	(397)	12416	(435)	12444*	(60)
12333	(27)	12361	(470)	12389	(409)	12417	(442)	12445	(99)
12334	(116)	12362	(479)	12390	(416)	12418	(81)	12446	(261)
12335	(127)	12363	(486)	12391	(421)	12419	(102)	12447	(604)
12336	(199)	12364	(487)	12392	(426)	12420	(220)	12448*	(834)
12337	(211)	12365	(489)	12393	(468)	12421	(225)	12449	(838)
12338	(272)	12366	(491)	12394	(473)	12422	(274)	12450	(864)
12339	(328)	12367	(508)	12395	(485)	12423	(288)	12451	(872)
12340	(331)	12368	(509)	12396	(490)	12424	(302)	12452	(874)
12341	(350)	12369	(510)	12397	(492)	12425	(385)	12453	(885)
12342	(352)	12370	(523)	12398*	(520)	12426*	(386)	12454	(888)
12343	(357)	12371	(524)	12399	(526)	12427	(400)	12455	(873)
12344	(359)	12372	(602)	12400*	(610)	12428*	(431)	12456	(892)
12345	(360)	12373	(609)	12401	(681)	12429	(452)	12457	(895)
12346	(363)	12374*	(620)	12402	(33)	12430	(497)	12458	(896)
12347	(366)	12375	(622)	12403	(103)	12431*	(605)	12459	(897)
12348	(370)	12376	(650)	12404	(135)	12432	(647)	12460	(899)
12349	(414)	12377	(662)	12405*	(193)	12433	(652)	12461	(919)
12350	(418)	12378	(677)	12406	(215)	12434	(726)	12462	(921)
12351	(419)	12379*	(682)	12407	(330)	12435	(727)	12463	(925)
12352	(425)	12380	(683)	12408	(375)	12436	(55)	12464	(926,
12353	(439)	12381	(684)	12409	(388)	12437	(115)	12465	(1600)
12354	(447)	12382	(685)	12410	(391)	12438*	(123)	12466	(1602)
12355	(451)	12383	(690)	12411	(398)	12439	(246)	12467	(1603)

*Rebuilt with Belpaire firebox and extended smokebox.

†Engine 12322 has been restored to its L. & Y.R. condition, with the number 1122 formerly carried by 12140, under private ownership.

Most of the surviving engines in 1948 had 40000 added to their numbers.

0-6-0 Pettigrew Furness 2F

Built 1899-1907

Weight:
38 tons 10 cwt. (12468-79)
40 tons 8 cwt. (12480-3)

Boiler Pressure:
150 lbs. (12468-79)
160 lbs. (12480-3)

Cylinders:
18″×26″

Driving Wheel Diameter:
4′ 8″ (12468-79)
5′ 1″ (12480-3)

Tractive Effort:
19,352 lbs.; (12468-79)
18,781 lbs. (12480-3)

Valve Gear:
Stephenson

Number built: 16.

First loco withdrawn 1929; last loco withdrawn 1936.
No. in service (1/1/23) 16; (1/1/48) 0.

12468	(7)	12472	(11)	12475	(14)	12478	(17)	12481	(4)
12469	(8)	12473	(12)	12476	(15)	12479	(18)	12482	(5)
12470	(9)	12474	(13)	12477	(16)	12480	(3)	12483	(6)
12471	(10)								

0-6-0 Maryport & Carlisle 2F

Built 1873-1908

Weight:
Varied on individual engines between 36 tons 5 cwt. and 39 tons 15 cwt.

Driving Wheel Diameter:
5′ 1½″

Boiler Pressure:
140 lbs.

Tractive Effort:
17,550 lbs. (12484/5)
16,300 lbs. (12486-93)

Cylinders:
18″×26″
(Nos. 12484/5 had 18″×28″ cylinders)

Valve Gear:
Stephenson

Number built: 10.

First loco withdrawn 1925; last loco withdrawn 1930.
No. in service (1/1/23) 10; (1/1/48) 0.

12484	(9)	12486	(25)	12488	(7)	12490	(27)	12492	(1)
12485	(14)	12487	(11)	12489	(19)	12491	(28)	12493	(18)

0-6-0 Pettigrew Furness 3F

Built 1913-20

Weight:
42 tons 13 cwt. (12494-7)
44 tons 17 cwt. (12498-512)

Driving Wheel Diameter:
4′ 7½″

Boiler Pressure:
170 lbs.

Tractive Effort:
21,935 lbs.

Cylinders:
18″×26″

Valve Gear:
Stephenson

Number built: 19.

Some of the later survivors were rebuilt with L. & Y.R. boilers embodying a Belpaire firebox.

First loco withdrawn 1930; last loco withdrawn 1957.
No. in service (1/1/23) 19; (1/1/48) 6.

12494	(1)	12498	(27)	12502	(21)	12506	(29)	12510	(33)
12495	(2)	12499	(28)	12503	(22)	12507	(30)	12511	(34)
12496	(25)	12500	(19)	12504	(23)	12508	(31)	12512	(35)
12497	(26)	12501	(20)	12505	(24)	12509	(32)		

The six survivors in 1948 became B.R. Nos. 52494, 52499, 52501, 52508, 52509 and 52510.

0-6-0 Maryport & Carlisle 3F

Built 1921

Weight:
49 tons 12 cwt.

Boiler Pressure:
170 lbs.

Cylinders:
19″×26″

Driving Wheel Diameter:
5′ 0″

Tractive Effort:
22,600 lbs.

Valve Gear:
Stephenson

Number built: 2.

First loco withdrawn 1933; last loco withdrawn 1934.
No. in service (1/1/23) 2; (1/1/48) 0.

12513 (29)	12514 (30)

0-6-0 Hughes L. & Y.R. Superheater 3F
L. & Y.R. Class F21

Built 1909

(Nos. 12515 and 12516 were rebuilds of Aspinall engines.)

Weight:
44 tons 6 cwt.

Boiler Pressure:
180 lbs.

Cylinders:
$20\frac{1}{2}$″×26″

Driving Wheel Diameter:
5′ 0″

Tractive Effort:
27,863 lbs.

Valve Gear:
Joy

Number built: 22.

First loco withdrawn 1933; last loco withdrawn 1962.
No. in service (1/1/23) 22; (1/1/48) 12.

Some engines later had the superheaters removed.

12515 (898)	12520 (94)	12525 (815)	12529 (633)	12533 (830)
12516 (900)	12521 (109)	12526 (826)	12530 (665)	12534 (901)
12517 (85)	12522 (634)	12527 (61)	12531 (818)	12535 (903)
12518 (89)	12523 (636)	12528 (625)	12532 (828)	12536 (904)
12519 (93)	12524 (642)			

Survivors in 1948 had 40000 added to their numbers.

0-6-0 Hughes L. & Y.R. Superheater 3F
L. & Y.R. Class F22

Built 1912

Weight:
46 tons 10 cwt.

Boiler Pressure:
180 lbs.

Cylinders:
$20\frac{1}{2}'' \times 26''$

Driving Wheel Diameter:
5′ 0″

Tractive Effort:
27,863 lbs.

Valve Gear:
Joy

Number built: 20.

These engines differed from class F21 in having Belpaire fireboxes, and were identical with the rebuilt Aspinall engines (12557-12619).

First loco withdrawn 1935; last loco withdrawn 1957.
No. in service (1/1/23) 20; (1/1/48) 6.

12537	(657)	12541	(907)	12545	(1364)	12549	(239)	12553	(233)
12538	(691)	12542	(917)	12546	(1366)	12550	(300)	12554	(237)
12539	(791)	12543	(918)	12547	(209)	12551	(20)	12555	(243)
12540	(883)	12544	(1363)	12548	(234)	12552	(219)	12556	(920)

Survivors in 1948 had 40000 added to their numbers.

0-6-0 Aspinall Reb. Hughes L. & Y.R. 4F
L. & Y.R. Class F22

Built 1889-1909
Rebuilt 1913-22

Weight:
46 tons 10 cwt.

Boiler Pressure:
180 lbs.

Cylinders:
$20\frac{1}{2}'' \times 26''$

Driving Wheel Diameter:
5′ 0″

Tractive Effort:
27,863 lbs.

Valve Gear:
Joy

Number rebuilt: 63.

First loco withdrawn 1935; last loco withdrawn 1957.
No. in service (1/1/23) 63; (1/1/48) 30.

12557	(1)	12563	(474)	12569	(483)	12575	(1307)	12581	(327)
12558	(1123)	12564	(52)	12570	(1304)	12576	(890)	12582	(624)
12559	(374)	12565	(11)	12571	(361)	12577	(1201)	12583	(205)
12560	(347)	12566	(1138)	12572	(376)	12578	(1073)	12584	(1247)
12561	(1053)	12567	(1092)	12573	(891)	12579	(342)	12585	(449)
12562	(1055)	12568	(893)	12574	(195)	12580	(367)	12586	(1028)

12587	(453)	12594	(886)	12601	(648)	12608	(302)	12615	(320)
12588	(252)	12595	(1601)	12602	(863)	12609	(459)	12616	(871)
12589	(1116)	12596	(1599)	12603	(875)	12610	(21)	12617	(882)
12590	(513)	12597	(619)	12504	(889)	12611	(884)	12618	(1132)
12591	(1021)	12598	(923)	12605	(1140)	12612	(1026)	12619	(887)
12592	(446)	12599	(1283)	12606	(1022)	12613	(462)		
12593	(521)	12600	(1135)	12607	(41)	12614	(829)		

Survivors in 1948 had 40000 added to their numbers.

0-8-0 Aspinall L. & Y.R. 5F
L. & Y.R. Class Q1

Built 1900-8

Weight:
Loco 53 tons 16 cwt.

Boiler Pressure:
175 lbs.

Cylinders:
20″×26″

Driving Wheel Diameter:
4′ 6″

Tractive Effort:
28,644 lbs.

Valve Gear:
Joy

Number built: 130.

70 Locomotives of this Class were rebuilt by Hughes—see 12771-12994.

First loco withdrawn 1926; last loco withdrawn 1950.
No. in service (1/1/23) 60; (1/1/48) 1.

12700	(325)	12712	(405)	12724	(1426)	12736	(835)	12748	(1483)
12701	(383)	12713	(411)	12725	(1428)	12737	(880)	12749	(1488)
12702	(407)	12714	(511)	12726	(1430)	12739	(870)	12750	(1489)
12703	(433)	12715	(710)	12727	(1433)	12739	(49)	12751	(1490)
12704	(635)	12716	(715)	12728	(1434)	12740	(83)	12752	(1492)
12705	(659)	12717	(95)	12729	(1451)	12741	(836)	12753	(1493)
12706	(676)	12718	(378)	12730	(1454)	12742	(876)	12754	(1494)
12707	(736)	12719	(656)	12731	(1455)	12743	(894)	12755	(1495)
12708	(69)	12720	(739)	12732	(1457)	12744	(108)	12756	(1496)
12709	(154)	12721	(792)	12733	(1458)	12745	(79)	12757	(1497)
12710	(159)	12722	(822)	12734	(1460)	12746	(1481)	12758	(1498)
12711	(390)	12723	(987)	12735	(820)	12747	(1482)	12759	(1499)

The sole surviving engine in 1948, No. 12727, duly became B.R. No. 52727 before withdrawal.

0-8-0 Hughes L. & Y.R. 4-cylinder Compound 5F
L. & Y.R. Class Q2

Built 1907

The first engine was a conversion from Class Q1, rebuilt in 1904.

Weight:
60 tons 16 cwt.

Driving Wheel Diameter:
4′ 6″

Wirral Railway 4-4-4T No. 14, allocated L.M.S. No. 6850, but never carried. [L.P.C.

Wirral Railway 0-6-4T No. 12 allocated L.M.S. No. 6948. but never carried. [A. W. Croughton

An early Furness 5′ 7½″ 4-4-0 No. 10134. [W. H. Whitworth

Furness 6′ 6″ 4-4-0 No. 10144, leaving Carlisle. [H. L. Salmon

Furness 4-4-2T No. 11082. [L.P.C.

Furness 4-6-4T No. 11102. [A. W. Croughton

Furness 0-6-0ST No. 109A - allocated L.M.S. No. 11547, but never carried. [W. H. Whitworth

Furness 0-6-2T No. 11633.

Maryport and Carlisle 2-4-0 No. 13 (allocated L.M.S. No. 10005 but not carried). [L.P.C.

Maryport and Carlisle 0-4-2 No. 10013. [W. H. Whitworth

Cleator and Workington 0-6-0ST No. 11566 'Hutton Hall'. [W. H. Whitworth

Garstang and Knott End Railway 0-6-0ST 'New Century' and 2-6-0T 'Blackpool' (allocated L.M.S. Nos. 11301 and 11680). [W. H. Whitworth

Caledonian 'Oban bogie' No. 14103.

Pickersgill 4-4-0 No. 86, the final development of the well known 'Dunalastair' type first introduced by McIntosh in 1896. Later L.M.S. No 14491. [L.P.C.

Caledonian single No. 14010 with Drummond boiler as running in 1924. [L.P.C.

Caledonian Railway. A later type designed by McIntosh for work over the Oban line, and in turn again known as 'Oban bogies'

Boiler Pressure:
175 lbs.

Tractive Effort:
35,652 lbs.

Cylinders:
2 H.P. 15½″×26″
2 L.P. 22″ ×26″

Valve Gear:
Stephenson

Number built: 11 (including initial rebuilds)

First loco withdrawn 1926; last loco withdrawn 1927.
No. in service (1/1/23) 11; (1/1/48) 0.

12760	(1452)	12763	(1473)	12765	(1475)	12767	(1477)	12769	(1479)
12761	(1471)	12764	(1474)	12766	(1476)	12768	(1478)	12770	(1480)
12762	(1472)								

0-8-0 Hughes L. & Y.R. 6F
L. & Y.R. Class Q3

Built 1910-8

(Nos. 12771-12800 were rebuilds of Class Q1, originally constructed 1900-1907.)

Weight:
64 tons 4 cwt.

Driving Wheel Diameter:
4′ 6″

Boiler Pressure:
180 lbs.

Tractive Effort:
29,466 lbs.

Cylinders:
20″×26″

Valve Gear:
Joy

Number built: 40 (plus 29 rebuilds from Class Q1)

First loco withdrawn 1927; last loco withdrawn 1951.
No. in service (1/1/23) 69; (1/1/48) 11.

12771	(392)	12785	(434)	12799	(1486)	12813	(906)	12827	(1586)
12772	(463)	12786	(436)	12800	(1487)	12814	(908)	12828	(1587)
12773	(745)	12787	(396)	12801	(9)	12815	(909)	12829	(1588)
12774	(443)	12788	(512)	12802	(29)	12816	(910)	12830	(1589)
12775	(666)	12789	(612)	12803	(35)	12817	(911)	12831	(1590)
12776	(695)	12790	(720)	12804	(67)	12818	(912)	12832	(1591)
12777	(704)	12791	(1435)	12805	(87)	12819	(913)	12833	(1592)
12778	(717)	12792	(1437)	12806	(96)	12820	(914)	12834	(1593)
12779	(412)	12793	(841)	12807	(616)	12821	(927)	12835	(1594)
12780	(1425)	12794	(866)	12808	(617)	12822	(1351)	12836	(1595)
12781	(1429)	12795	(877)	12809	(628)	12823	(1354)	12837	(1596)
12782	(114)	12796	(74)	12810	(713)	12824	(1357)	12838	(1597)
12783	(169)	12797	(1484)	12811	(902)	12825	(1368)	12839	(1598)
12784	(394)	12798	(1485)	12812	(905)	12826	(1369)		

Some of the 1948 survivors lasted long enough to have 40000 added to their numbers.

0-8-0 Hughes L. & Y.R. Superheater 7F
L. & Y.R. Class Q4

Built 1912-1920

(Nos. 12890-12901, 12922 12923 and 12969-12994 were rebuilds from Q1, originally constructed 1900-1904.)

Weight:
66 tons 11½ cwt.

Driving Wheel Diameter:
4′ 6″

Boiler Pressure:
180 lbs.

Tractive Effort:
34,052 lbs.

Cylinders:
21½″×26″

Valve Gear:
Joy

Number built: 115 (plus 35 rebuilds from classes Q1 and Q3)

First loco withdrawn 1926; last loco withdrawn 1951.
No. in service (1/1/23) 150; (1/1/48) 17.

Note: 12990-4 were rebuilt to this class in 1923. Their dimensions at 1/1/23 were as L.M.S. 12700-59.

12840	(1546)	12871	(1577)	12902	(216)	12933	(1613)	12964	(1644)
12841	(1547)	12872	(1578)	12903	(235)	12934	(1614)	12965	(1645)
12842	(1548)	12873	(1579)	12904	(241)	12935	(1615)	12966	(1646)
12843	(1549)	12874	(1580)	12905	(265)	12936	(1616)	12967	(1647)
12844	(1550)	12875	(1581)	12906	(312)	12937	(1617)	12968	(1648)
12845	(1551)	12876	(1582)	12907	(493)	12938	(1618)	12969	(408)
12846	(1552)	12877	(1583)	12908	(503)	12939	(1619)	12970	(706)
12847	(1553)	12878	(1584)	12909	(601)	12940	(1620)	12971	(738)
12848	(1554)	12879	(1585)	12910	(603)	12941	(1621)	12972	(381)
12849	(1555)	12880	(6)	12911	(507)	12942	(1622)	12973	(611)
12850	(1556)	12881	(7)	12912	(626)	12943	(1623)	12974	(500)
12851	(1557)	12882	(134)	12913	(631)	12944	(1624)	12975	(1500)
12852	(1558)	12883	(141)	12914	(660)	12945	(1625)	12976	(448)
12853	(1559)	12884	(142)	12915	(640)	12946	(1626)	12977	(831)
12854	(1560)	12885	(150)	12916	(673)	12947	(1627)	12978	(91)
12855	(1561)	12886	(229)	12917	(694)	12948	(1628)	12979	(1491)
12856	(1562)	12887	(259)	12918	(697)	12949	(1629)	12980	(373)
12857	(1563)	12888	(281)	12919	(698)	12950	(1630)	12981	(1440)
12858	(1564)	12889	(460)	12920	(789)	12951	(1631)	12982	(461)
12859	(1565)	12890	(522)	12921	(915)	12952	(1632)	12983	(86)
12860	(1566)	12891	(1436)	12922	(1431)	12953	(1633)	12984	(709)
12861	(1567)	12892	(423)	12923	(1459)	12954	(1634)	12985	(413)
12862	(1568)	12893	(157)	12924	(1604)	12955	(1635)	12986	(201)
12863	(1569)	12894	(1439)	12925	(1605)	12956	(1636)	12987	(1365)
12864	(1570)	12895	(59)	12926	(1606)	12957	(1637)	12988	(384)
12865	(1571)	12896	(1456)	12927	(1607)	12958	(1638)	12989	(687)
12866	(1572)	12897	(1432)	12928	(1608)	12959	(1639)	12990	(1427)
12867	(1573)	12898	(1438)	12929	(1609)	12960	(1640)	12991	(190)
12868	(1574)	12899	(395)	12930	(1610)	12961	(1641)	12992	(827)
12869	(1575)	12900	(117)	12931	(1611)	12962	(1642)	12993	(406)
12870	(1576)	12901	(65)	12932	(1612)	12963	(1643)	12994	(1453)

Most of the 1948 survivors lasted to have 40000 added to their numbers.

For 13800-13810—see 9670-9680.

2-4-0 Stirling G. & S.W.R. 1P

Built 1870-1

Weight:
32 tons 10 cwt.

Driving Wheel Diameter:
6′ 1″

Boiler Pressure:
140 lbs.

Tractive Effort:
13,638 lbs.

Cylinders:
17″×24″

Valve Gear:
Stephenson

Number built: 10.

First loco withdrawn 1898; last loco withdrawn 1923.
No. in service (1/1/23) 2; (1/1/48) 0.

14000 (727)	726 (G.S.W.R. No.—Not allocated L.M.S. Number)

No. 727 never carried its L.M.S. number.

2-4-0 Smellie G. & S.W.R. 1P

Built 1879-80

Weight:
38 tons 10 cwt.

Driving Wheel Diameter:
6′ 9½″

Boiler Pressure:
140 lbs.

Tractive Effort:
12,300 lbs.

Cylinders:
18″×26″

Valve Gear:
Stephenson

Number built: 12.

First loco withdrawn 1912; last loco withdrawn 1923.
No. in service (1/1/23) 6; (1/1/48) 0.

14001 (720)	14002 (723)	721*	722*	724*	725*

*G.S.W.R. numbers—not allocated L.M.S. numbers.
Nos. 720 and 723 never carried their L.M.S. numbers.

4-2-2 Neilson & Co. C.R. 1P

Built 1886

Weight:
41 tons 7 cwt.

Boiler Pressure:
160 lbs.

Cylinders:
18″×26″

Driving Wheel Diameter:
7′ 0″

Tractive Effort:
13,638 lbs.

Valve Gear:
Stephenson

Number built: 1.

Withdrawn 1935 and restored in C.R. colours for preservation with original number 123. Put back into working order in 1957 for running special trains.

14010 (1123) Originally C.R. No. 123; it had been placed on the "duplicate list" as 1123 in 1914.

4-4-0 Brittain C.R. 'Oban bogie' 1P

Built 1882

Weight:
40 tons 18 cwt.

Boiler Pressure:
150 lbs.

Cylinders:
18″×24″

Driving Wheel Diameter:
5′ 2″

Tractive Effort:
16,524 lbs.

Valve Gear:
Stephenson

Number built: 10.

First loco withdrawn 1922; last loco withdrawn 1930.
No. in service (1/1/23) 8; (1/1/48) 0.

14100 (1179)	14102 (1181)	14104 (1183)	14106 (1187)	14107 (1188)
14101 (1180)	14103 (1182)	14105 (1186)		

Only No. 14100/3/5 actually carried their L.M.S. numbers.

4-4-0 D. Drummond C.R. 1P

Built 1888-1891

Weight:
43 tons 10 cwt.

Driving Wheel Diameter:
5′ 9″

Boiler Pressure:
170 lbs.

Tractive Effort:
17,641 lbs.

Cylinders:
18″×26″

Valve Gear:
Stephenson

Number built: 12.

First loco withdrawn before 1923; last loco withdrawn 1930.
No. in service (1/1/23) 8; (1/1/48) 0.

14108	(1080)	14110	(1082)	14112	(1195)	14114	(1197)	14115	(1198)
14109	(1081)	14111	(1114)	14113	(1196)				

Nos. 14109, 14111 and 14112 never carried their L.M.S. numbers.

4-4-0 Smellie G. & S.W.R. 1P2/P*†

†* Built 1882-5

Originally domeless. Most later rebuilt with domed boilers (Class 2P).

Weight:
41 tons 10 cwt.*†
44 tons 10 cwt.

Driving Wheel Diameter:
6′ $1\frac{1}{4}$″

Boiler Pressure:
140 lbs. *(small domeless boiler)
†(small domed boiler)
160 lbs. (larger domed boiler)

Tractive Effort:
14,522 lbs.*†
16,020 lbs.

The two varieties of small boilered engines retained the Stirling-type round half cab, the others acquired larger all-over cabs.

Cylinders:
$18\frac{1}{4}$″×26″

Valve Gear:
Stephenson

Number built: 22.

First loco withdrawn 1913; last loco withdrawn 1934.
No. in service (1/1/23) 22; (1/1/48) 0.

14116*	(700)	14121	(706)	14126	(711)	14130	(468)	14134*	(717)
14117	(701)	14122†	(707)	14127*	(712)	14131	(714)	14135†	(705)
14118	(702)	14123	(708)	14128	(713)	14132*	(715)	14136	(718)
14119	(703)	14124*	(709)	14129	(467)	14133	(716)	14137*	(719)
14120	(704)	14125*	(710)						

4-4-0 Smellie G. & S.W.R. 1P*†

†* Built 1886-9

Originally domeless. Most later rebuilt with larger domed boilers (Class 2P).

Weight:
42 tons 10 cwt*†
46 tons 4 cwt.

Driving Wheel Diameter:
6′ 9½″

Boiler Pressure:
140 lbs. *(small domeless boiler)
†(small domed boiler)
160 lbs. (larger domed boiler)

Tractive Effort:
12,642 lbs.*†
14,447 lbs.

The same remarks regarding cabs of 14116-14137 also apply to this class.

Cylinders:
18¼″×26″

Valve Gear:
Stephenson

Number built: 20.

First loco withdrawn 1898§; last loco withdrawn 1935.
No. in service (1/1/23) 19; (1/1/48) 0.

§Collision, remainder withdrawn 1925-1935.

14138*	(448)	14142	(465)	14146	(453)	14150	(457)	14154*	(462)
14139	(449)	14143	(466)	14147*	(454)	14151*	(458)	14155*	(463)
14140*	(450)	14144	(451)	14148*	(455)	14152*	(460)	14156*	(464)
14141*	(459)	14145	(452)	14149	(456)	14153†	(461)		

4-4-0 Manson G. & S.W.R. 1P/2P

Built 1892-1904

Some later rebuilt with larger boilers (class 2P)*

Weignt:
45 tons
49 tons 16 cwt.*

Driving Wheel Diameter:
6′ 9½″

Boiler Pressure:
150 lbs. (small boiler)
170 lbs. *(large boiler)

Tractive Effort:
13,491 lbs.
15,300 lbs.*

Cylinders:
18¾″×26″

Valve Gear:
Stephenson

Number built: 57.

First loco withdrawn 1925; last loco withdrawn 1933.
No. in service (1/1/23) 57; (1/1/48) 0.

14157	(399)	14162	(415)	14167	(420)	14172	(421)	14177	(398)
14158*	(412)	14163*	(416)	14168*	(377)	14173*	(422)	14178	(400)
14159	(413)	14164	(417)	14169*	(406)	14174	(427)	14179	(401)
14160*	(446)	14165	(418)	14170*	(407)	14175*	(434)	14180	(402)
14161	(414)	14166	(419)	14171*	(408)	14176	(435)	14181	(409)

14182	(410)	14189	(405)	14196	(433)	14244*	(411)	14253	(445)
14183*	(426)	14190	(423)	14197	(396)	14245	(440)	14266*	(375)
14184	(429)	14191	(424)	14198	(397)	14249	(441)	14267*	(378)
14185*	(430)	14192*	(425)	14199	(436)	14250	(442)	14268*	(395)
14186*	(447)	14193	(428)	14200*	(437)	14251	(443)	14269*	(376)
14187	(403)	14194	(431)	14201*	(438)	14252*	(444)	14270*	(485)
14188	(404)	14195	(432)	14202	(439)				

4-4-0 Manson G. & S.W.R. 2P

Built 1895-9

Some later rebuilt with larger boilers*

Weight:
45 tons

Boiler Pressure:
165 lbs.

Cylinders:
$18\frac{1}{4}'' \times 26''$

Driving Wheel Diameter:
$6'\ 1\frac{1}{4}''$

Tractive Effort:
16,780 lbs.

Valve Gear:
Stephenson

Number built: 25.

First loco withdrawn 1926; last loco withdrawn 1932.
No. in service (1/1/23) 25; (1/1/48) 0.

14203	(350)	14208*	(355)	14213*	(360)	14218	(365)	14223*	(370)
14204*	(351)	14209	(356)	14214*	(361)	14219	(366)	14224	(371)
14205	(352)	14210	(357)	14215	(362)	14220	(367)	14225	(372)
14206	(353)	14211*	(358)	14216	(363)	14221	(368)	14226	(373)
14207	(354)	14212	(359)	14217	(364)	14222	(369)	14227	(374)

4-4-0 Stirling G. & S.W.R. 1P

Built 1873-7

Originally domeless. Some later rebuilt with domed boilers*

Weight:
40 tons

Boiler Pressure:
150 lbs.

Cylinders:
$18'' \times 26''$

Driving Wheel Diameter:
$7'\ 1''$

Tractive Effort:
12,586 lbs.

Valve Gear:
Stephenson

Number built: 22.

All of this class had received larger all-over cabs in place of the original Stirling round type.

First loco withdrawn 1895; last loco withdrawn 1930.
No. in service (1/1/23) 16; (1/1/48) 0.

14228	(469)	14232	(473)	14235	(476)	14238	(479)	14241	(482)
14229	(470)	14233*	(474)	14236	(477)	14239	(480)	14242	(483)
14230	(471)	14234*	(475)	14237	(478)	14240	(481)	14243	(484)
14231	(472)								

For locomotives 14244, 14245 see 14157-14202.

4-4-0 Manson G. & S.W.R. 2P

Built 1904-6

Weight:
50 tons 8 cwt.

Driving Wheel Diameter:
6′ 9½″

Boiler Pressure:
170 lbs.

Tractive Effort:
15,453 lbs.

Cylinders:
18¼″ × 26″

Valve Gear:
Stephenson

Number built: 15.

First loco withdrawn 1925; last loco withdrawn 1932.
No. in service (1/1/23) 15; (1/1/48) 0.

14246	(379)	14254	(382)	14257	(385)	14260	(388)	14263	(391)
14247	(380)	14255	(383)	14258	(386)	14261	(389)	14264	(392)
14248	(381)	14256	(384)	14259	(387)	14262	(390)	14265	(393)

For locomotives 14249-14253 see 14157-14202.

For locomotives 14266-14270 see 14157-14202.

4-4-0 Jones H.R. 'Strath' Class 1P

Built 1892

Weight:
45 tons

Driving Wheel Diameter:
5′ 3″

Boiler Pressure:
160 lbs.

Tractive Effort:
16,786 lbs.

Cylinders:
18″ × 24″

Valve Gear:
Stephenson

Number built: 12.

First loco withdrawn 1922; last loco withdrawn 1930.
No. in service (1/1/23) 6; (1/1/48) 0.

14271	(89)	Sir George	14274	(95)	Strathcarron
14272	(92A)	Glendean	14275	(98)	Glentruim
14273	(94)	Strathtay	14276	(100)	Glenbruar

No. 14273 never carried its L.M.S. number.

4-4-0 Jones H.R. 'Skye Bogie' Class 1P

Built 1882-1901

Weight:
43 tons

Driving Wheel Diameter:
5′ 3″

Boiler Pressure:
150 lbs.

Tractive Effort:
15,737 lbs.

Cylinders:
18″×24″

Valve Gear:
Stephenson

Number built: 9.

First loco withdrawn 1922; last loco withdrawn 1930.
No. in service (1/1/23) 9.; (1/1/48) 0.

14277*	(67)	14280	(87)	14282	(32)	14284	(34)	14285	(48)
14279	(86)	14281	(88)	14283	(33)				

*See note contained in next class regarding the numbering of this engine.
Nos. 14280 and 14281 never carried their L.M.S. numbers.

4-4-0 Jones H.R. "Bruce" Class 1P

Built 1886

Weight:
43 tons

Driving Wheel Diameter:
6′ 3″

Boiler Pressure:
160 lbs.

Tractive Effort:
14,100 lbs.

Cylinders:
18″×24″

Valve Gear:
Stephenson

Number built: 8.

First loco withdrawn before 1923; Number in service 1/1/23—1

Loco withdrawn 1930.

When the L.M.S. renumbering scheme was drawn up, No. 14277 was apparently thought in error to have belonged to the above class, whereas it was in fact a 5′ 3″ engine of the 'Skye bogie' series, which accounts for its being numbered out of order (see previous class).

The mistake probably arose owing to the fact that about 1916 engines 70 (Skye bogie) and 67 (an earlier engine of the 'Bruce' class, built in 1874) had exchanged numbers. The latter engine, which had meanwhile become No. 70A, was scrapped before 1923 and consequently did not come into L.M.S. stock. No doubt however some error in the records had shown engine No. 67 as a 6′ 3″ engine, hence the confusion.

14278 (82A)

4-4-0 Drummond C.R. 1P

Built 1884-1894

Weight:
46 tons 1 cwt.

Boiler Pressure:
160 lbs.

Cylinders:
18″×26″

Driving Wheel Diameter:
6′ 6″

Tractive Effort:
14,688 lbs.

Valve Gear:
Stephenson

Number built: 29.

First loco withdrawn before 1923; last loco withdrawn 1930.
No in service (1/1/23) 21; (1/1/48) 0.

14290	(1067)	14295	(1061)	14299	(1070)	14303	(1060)	14307	(1090)
14291	(1068)	14296	(1124)	14300	(1071)	14304	(1062)	14308	(1013)
14292	(1069)	14297	(1079)	14301	(1073)	14305	(1083)	14309	(1015)
14293	(1072)	14298	(1066)	14302	(1075)	14036	(1084)	14310	(1018)
14294	(1074)								

Some of these engines never carried their L.M.S. numbers.

4-4-0 McIntosh C.R. 2P
‘Dunalastair I’

Built 1896

Weight:
47 tons

Boiler Pressure:
160 lbs.

Cylinders:
$18\frac{1}{4}$″×26″

Driving Wheel Diameter:
6′ 6″

Tractive Effort:
15,100 lbs.

Valve Gear:
Stephenson

Number built: 15.

First loco withdrawn 1930; last loco withdrawn 1935.
No. in service (1/1/23) 15; (1/1/48) 0.

14311	(721)	14314	(724)	14317	(727)	14320	(730)	14323	(733)
14312	(722)	14315	(725)	14318	(728)	14321	(731)	14324	(734)
14313	(723)	14316	(726)	14319	(729)	14322	(732)	14325	(735)

4-4-0 McIntosh C.R. 2P
'Dunalastair II'
Built 1897

(Four engines converted to Dunalastair IV in 1914)

Weight:
49 tons

Driving Wheel Diameter:
6′ 6″

Boiler Pressure:
175 lbs.

Tractive Effort:
17,900 lbs.

Cylinders:
19″×26″

Valve Gear:
Stephenson

Number built: 15.

First loco withdrawn 1936; last loco withdrawn 1947.
No. in service (1/1/23) 11; (1/1/48) 0.

14326	(767)	14329	(773)	14332	(776)	14335	(779)	Breadalbane*
14327	(768)	14330	(774)	14333	(777)	14336	(780)	
14328	(770)	14331	(775)	14334	(778)			

*Name removed 1925 on being repainted in L.M.S. colours.

4-4-0 McIntosh C.R. 2P
'Dunalastair III'
Built 1899-1900

(Four engines converted to Dunalastair IV in 1914-1918)

Weight:
51 tons 14 cwt.

Driving Wheel Diameter:
6′ 6″

Boiler Pressure:
180 lbs.

Tractive Effort:
18,411 lbs.

Cylinders:
19″×26″

Valve Gear:
Stephenson

Number built: 16.

First loco withdrawn 1932; last loco withdrawn 1947.
No. in service (1/1/23) 12; (1/1/48) 0.

14337	(887)	14340	(890)	14343	(893)	14345	(896)	14347	(897)
14338	(888)	14341	(891)	14344	(895)	14346	(902)	14348	(899)
14339	(889)	14342	(892)						

4-4-0

McIntosh C.R. 2P
'Dunalastair IV'

Built 1904-1910

(Two engines converted to Dunalastair IV in 1915-7)

Weight:
56 tons 10 cwt.

Boiler Pressure:
180 lbs.

Cylinders:
19″ × 26″

Driving Wheel Diameter:
6′ 6″

Tractive Effort:
18,411 lbs.

Valve Gear:
Stephenson

Number built: 19.

First loco withdrawn 1937; last loco withdrawn 1948.
No. in service (1/1/23) 17; (1/1/48) 1.

14349	(140)	14353	(144)	14357	(148)	14360	(925)	14363	(137)
14350	(141)	14354	(145)	14358	(149)	14361	(926)	14364	(138)
14351	(142)	14355	(146)	14359	(150)	14362	(927)	14365	(136)
14352	(143)	14356	(147)						

4-4-0

Manson G. & S.W.R. 2P

Built 1907-12

Weight:
51 tons 14 cwt.

Boiler Pressure:
170 lbs.

Cylinders:
$18\frac{1}{4}$″ × 26″

Driving Wheel Diameter:
6′ $9\frac{1}{2}$″

Tractive Effort:
15,300 lbs.

Valve Gear:
Stephenson

Number built: 13.

First loco withdrawn 1925; last loco withdrawn 1932.
No. in service (1/1/23) 13; (1/1/48) 0.

14366	(337)	14369	(340)	14372	(343)	14375	(347)	14377	(349)
14367	(338)	14370	(341)	14373	(344)	14376	(348)	14378	(345)
14368	(339)	14371	(342)	14374	(346)				

4-4-0 Jones H.R. 'Loch' 2P

Built 1896 (14379-14393)
Built 1917 (14394:14396)

Weight:
49 tons

Driving Wheel Diameter:
6′ 3½″

Boiler Pressure:
175 lbs.

Tractive Effort:
17,070 lbs.

Cylinders:
19″×24″

Valve Gear:
Stephenson

Number built: 18.

*Some engines later rebuilt with larger C.R. type boilers. 4′ 8″ diameter in place of original 4′ 4¾″. Nos. 14384 and 14388 also lost their distinctive louvre chimneys and smokebox wing plates in the early 1930's.

First loco withdrawn 1930; last loco withdrawn 1950.
No. in service (1/1/23) 18; (1/1/48) 2.

14379*	(119)	Loch Insh	14388	(128)	Loch Luichart
14380*	(120)	Loch Ness	14389	(129)	Loch Maree
14381*	(121)	Loch Ericht	14390*	(130)	Loch Fannich
14382*	(122)	Loch Moy	14391*	(131)	Loch Shin
14383*	(123)	Loch an Dorb	14392*	(132)	Loch Naver
14384	(124)	Loch Laggan	14393	(133)	Loch Laoghal
14385*	(125)	Loch Tay	14394	(70)	Loch Ashie
14386*	(126)	Loch Tummel	14395	(71)	Loch Garve
14387	(127)	Loch Garry	14396	(72)	Loch Ruthven

Neither of the two 1948 survivors carried their allotted B.R. numbers, 54379 and 54385.

4-4-0 P. Drummond H.R. 2P 'Small Ben'

Built 1898-1906

Weight:
46 tons 17 cwt.

Driving Wheel Diameter:
6′ 0″

Boiler Pressure:
175 lbs.

Tractive Effort:
17,890 lbs.

Cylinders:
18¼″×26″

Valve Gear:
Stephenson

Number built: 20.

Nos. 14404 and 14411 still retained Drummond boilers with safety valves on dome at the grouping, later replaced by C.R. type boilers. All the class eventually lost their smokebox wingplates. No. 54399 latterly acquired a stovepipe chimney.

First loco withdrawn 1931; last loco withdrawn 1953.
No. in service (1/1/23) 20; (1/1/48) 10.

14397	(1)	Ben-y-Gloe	14407	(11)	Ben Macdhui
14398	(2)	Ben Alder	14408	(12)	Ben Hope
14399	(3)	Ben Wyvis	14409	(13)	Ben Alisky
14400	(4)	Ben More	14410	(14)	Ben Dearg
14401	(5)	Ben Vrackie	14411	(15)	Ben Loyal
14402	(6)	Ben Armin	14412	(16)	Ben Avon
14403	(7)	Ben Attow	14413	(17)	Ben Alligan
14404	(8)	Ben Clebrig	14414	(38)	Ben Udlaman
14405	(9)	Ben Rinnes	14415	(41)	Ben Bhach Ard
14406	(10)	Ben Slioch	14416	(47)	Ben a'Bhuird

Nos. 14398, 14399 and 14404, lasted long enough to have 40000 added to their numbers by B.R.

No. 54398 " Ben Alder " has been retained with a view to preservation.

4-4-0 P. Drummond H.R. ' Large Ben ' 2P

Built 1908-9

Weight:
52 tons 6 cwt. before rebuilding
53 tons 15 cwt. after rebuilding

Driving Wheel Diameter:
6′ 0″

Boiler Pressure:
175 lbs.

Tractive Effort:
17,890 lbs.

Cylinders:
$18\frac{1}{4}'' \times 26''$

Valve Gear:
Stephenson

Number built: 6.

All latterly rebuilt with extended smokebox. No. 14417 remained in original condition until 1928.

First loco withdrawn 1932; last loco withdrawn 1937.
No. in service (1/1/23) 6; (1/1/48) 0.

14417	(61)	Ben na Cailich	14420	(65)	Ben a'Chait
14418	(63)	Ben Mheadhoin	14421	(60)	Ben Bhreach Mhor
14419	(64)	Ben Mholach	14422	(62)	Ben a'Chaoruinn

4-4-0 McIntosh C.R. 3P ' Dunalastair II Rebuilt '

Built 1898
Rebuilt 1914

Weight:
52 tons

Driving Wheel Diameter:
6′ 6″

Boiler Pressure:
170 lbs.

Tractive Effort:
18,315 lbs.

Cylinders:
$19\frac{1}{2}'' \times 26''$

Valve Gear:
Stephenson

Number rebuilt: 4.

First loco withdrawn 1935; last loco withdrawn 1937.
No. in service (1/1/23) 4; (1/1/48) 0.

14430 (766)	14431 (769)	14432 (771)	14433 (772)

4-4-0 McIntosh C.R. 3P
' Dunalastair III Rebuilt '
Built 1899-1900
Rebuilt 1914-1918

Weight:
54 tons 10 cwt.

Boiler Pressure:
170 lbs.

Cylinders:
$19\frac{1}{2}'' \times 26''$

Driving Wheel Diameter:
6′ 6″

Tractive Effort:
18,315 lbs.

Valve Gear:
Stephenson

Number rebuilt: 4.

First loco withdrawn 1928; last loco withdrawn 1948.
No. in service (1/1/23) 4; (1/1/48) 1.

14434 (894)	14435 (900)	14436 (901)	14437 (898)

4-4-0 McIntosh C.R. 3P
' Dunalastair IV Rebuilt '
Built 1907
Rebuilt 1915-1917

Weight:
56 tons 10 cwt.

Boiler Pressure:
170 lbs.

Cylinders:
$20\frac{1}{4}'' \times 26''$

Driving Wheel Diameter:
6′ 6″

Tractive Effort:
19,623 lbs.

Valve Gear:
Stephenson

Number rebuilt: 2.

First loco withdrawn 1955; last loco withdrawn 1958.
No. in service (1/2/23) 2; (1/1/48) 2.

14438 (923)	14439 (924)

Latterly renumbered 54438 and 54439 by B.R.

4-4-0 McIntosh C.R. 3P
'139' Class
Built 1910-1914

Weight:
59 tons

Driving Wheel Diameter:
6′ 6″

Boiler Pressure:
165 lbs. (14440-4)
170 lbs. (14445-60)

Tractive Effort:
18,700 lbs. (14440-4)
19,751 lbs. (14445-60)

Cylinders:
20″ ×26″ (14440-4)
$20\frac{1}{4}$″×26″ (14445-60)

Valve Gear:
Stephenson

Number built: 22.

First loco withdrawn 1915†; last loco withdrawn 1957.
No. in service (1/1/23) 21; (1/1/48) 20.

†C.R. No. 121 was withdrawn after being involved in the accident at Quintinshill in 1915. This locomotive was replaced by another 4-4-0 of the next class, which also took the number 121.

14440 (139)	14445 (117)	14449 (122)	14453 (46)	14457 (40)
14441 (132)	14446 (118)	14450 (43)	14454 (47)	14458 (41)
14442 (133)	14447 (119)	14451 (44)	14455 (48)	14459 (42)
14443 (134)	14448 (120)	14452 (45)	14456 (39)	14460 (123)
14444 (135)				

All except 14442 (withdrawn 1946) survived to become 54440-54460 in B.R. stock.

4-4-0 Pickersgill C.R. 3P
Built 1916-1922

Weight:
61 tons 5 cwt.

Driving Wheel Diameter:
6′ 6″

Boiler Pressure:
175 lbs. (14461-76)
180 lbs. (14477-508)

Tractive Effort:
19,833 lbs. (14461-76)
21,435 lbs. (14477-508)

Cylinders:
20″ ×26″ (14461-76)
$20\frac{1}{2}$″×26″ (14477-508)

Valve Gear:
Stephenson

Number built: 48.

First loco withdrawn 1953; last loco withdrawn 1963.
No. in service (1/1/23) 48; (1/1/48) 48.

14461 (113) 14462 (114) 14463 (115) 14464 (116) 14465 (121) 14466 (124) 14467 (928) 14468 (929) 14469 (930) 14470 (931)	14471 (932) 14472 (933) 14473 (934) 14474 (935) 14475 (936) 14476 (937) 14477 (72) 14478 (73) 14479 (74) 14480 (75)	14481 (76) 14482 (77) 14483 (78) 14484 (79) 14485 (80) 14486 (81) 14487 (82) 14488 (83) 14489 (84) 14490 (85)	14491 (86) 14492 (87) 14493 (88) 14494 (89) 14495 (90) 14496 (91) 14497 (66) 14498 (67) 14499 (68)	14500 (69) 14501 (70) 14502 (71) 14503 (92) 14504 (93) 14505 (94) 14506 (95) 14507 (96) 14508 (97)

All carried their B.R. Numbers 54461-54508.

4-4-0 Whitelegg G. & S.W.R. 3P '394' Class

Built 1897
Rebuilt 1922

Weight:
61 tons 8 cwt.

Boiler Pressure:
180 lbs.

Cylinders:
(I) 14″×26″
(O) 14″×24″

Driving Wheel Diameter:
6′ 9½″

Tractive Effort:
18,390 lbs.

Valve Gear:
Stephenson (outside valves driven through rocking shafts)

Number built: 1.

This engine was notable as being the first 4-cylinder simple locomotive in the British Isles.

Number in service 1/1/23; 1. Withdrawn 1934.

14509 (394) Lord Glenarthur

4-4-0 Drummond G. & S.W.R. 3P '331' Class

Built 1913

Weight:
61 tons

Boiler Pressure:
180 lbs.

Cylinders:
19½″×26″

Driving Wheel Diameter:
6′ 0″

Tractive Effort:
21,008 lbs.

Valve Gear:
Walschaerts

Number built: 6.

First loco withdrawn 1934; last loco withdrawn 1937.
No. in service (1/1/23) 6; (1/1/48) 0.

14510 (331) 14511 (332)	14512 (333)	14513 (334)	14514 (335)	14515 (336)

4-4-0 Drummond G. & S.W.R. 3P '325' Class

Built 1914-5

Weight:
61 tons 17 cwt.

Driving Wheel Diameter:
6′ 0″

Boiler Pressure:
180 lbs.

Tractive Effort:
21,008 lbs.

Cylinders:
$19\frac{1}{2}'' \times 26''$

Valve Gear:
Walschaerts

Number built: 6.

First loco withdrawn 1934; last loco withdrawn 1937.

No. in service (1/1/23) 6; (1/1/48) 0.

14516 (325) 14517 (326)	14518 (327)	14519 (328)	14520 (329)	14521 (330)

4-4-0 Cummings H.R. 3P

Built 1916

Weight:
54 tons $19\frac{1}{2}$ cwt.

Driving Wheel Diameter:
6′ 3″

Boiler Pressure:
175 lbs.

Tractive Effort:
20,627 lbs.

Cylinders:
$20'' \times 26''$ (outside)

Valve Gear:
Walschearts

Number built: 2.

First loco withdrawn 1935; last loco withdrawn 1936.

No. in service (1/1/23) 2; (1/1/48) 0.

14522 (73) Snaigow	14523 (74) Durn

4-6-0 McIntosh C.R. 4P
'55' Class
Built 1902-1905

Weight:
57 tons 8 cwt.
(increased to 60 tons on engines 14606/7 after rebuilding)

Driving Wheel Diameter:
5′ 0″

Boiler Pressure:
175 lbs.

Tractive Effort:
23,269 lbs.

Cylinders:
19″×26″

Valve Gear:
Stephenson

Number built: 9.

Nos. 14606 and 14607 were rebuilt in 1930 with large boilers from engines 17901 and 17904.

First loco withdrawn 1928; last loco withdrawn 1937.
No. in service (1/1/23) 9; (1/1/48) 0.

14600 (55) 14601 (56)	14602 (57) 14603 (58)	14604 (59) 14605 (51)	14606 (52) 14607 (53)	14608 (54)

4-6-0 McIntosh C.R. 4P
'908' Class
Built 1906

Weight:
64 tons

Driving Wheel Diameter:
5′ 9″

Boiler Pressure:
180 lbs.

Tractive Effort:
20,812 lbs.

Cylinders:
19″×26″

Valve Gear:
Stephenson

Number built: 10.

No. 14618 differed from the others in being provided with a side-window cab.

First loco withdrawn 1930; last loco withdrawn 1935.
No. in service (1/1/23) 10; (1/1/48) 0.

14609 (908) 14610 (909) Sir James King* 14611 (910) 14612 (911) Barochan*	14613 (912) 14614 (913)	14615 (914) 14616 (915)	14617 (916) 14618 (917)

*Names removed on repainting in L.M.S. colours.

4-6-0 Pickersgill C.R. 3P ' 191 ' Class

Built 1922

Weight:
62 tons 15 cwt.

Driving Wheel Diameter:
5′ 6″

Boiler Pressure:
185 lbs.

Tractive Effort:
23555 lbs.

Cylinders:
19½″ × 26″

Valve Gear:
Stephenson

Number built: 8.

First loco withdrawn 1939; last loco withdrawn 1945.
No. in service (1/1/23) 8; (1/1/48) 0.

14619 (191) 14620 (192)	14621 (193) 14622 (194)	14623 (195) 14624 (196)	14625 (197)	14626 (198)

4-6-0 Pickersgill C.R. 3P ' 60 ' Class

Built 1916-7

Weight:
75 tons

Driving Wheel Diameter:
6′ 1″

Boiler Pressure:
175 lbs.

Tractive Effort:
21,155 lbs.

Cylinders:
20″ × 26″

Valve Gear:
Stephenson

Number built: 6.

First loco withdrawn 1944; last loco withdrawn 1953.
No. in service (1/1/23) 6; (1/1/48) 23.

A further 20 locomotives, of a similar design but with 20½″ × 26″ cylinders and a weight of 74 tons 15 cwt, were constructed by the L.M.S. during 1925-6. These were numbered 14630-14649.

14650 (60) 14651 (61)	14652 (62)	14653 (63)	14654 (64)	14655 (65)

Several of this class had 40000 added to their numbers by B.R.

4-6-0 Manson G. & S.W.R. 3P '495' Class

Built 1903-11

Weight:
67 tons 2 cwt.

Boiler Pressure:
175 lbs.

Cylinders:
20″×26″

Driving Wheel Diameter:
6′ 6″

Tractive Effort:
19,733 lbs.

Valve Gear:
Stephenson

Number built: 17.

First loco withdrawn 1928; last loco withdrawn 1933.
No. in service (1/1/23) 17; (1/1/48) 0.

14656 (495)	14660 (499)	14664 (503)	14667 (506)	14670 (509)
14657 (496)	14661 (500)	14665 (504)	14668 (507)	14671 (511)
14658 (497)	14662 (501)	14666 (505)	14669 (508)	14672 (510)
14659 (498)	14663 (502)			

4-6-0 Manson G. & S.W.R. 3P '512' Class

Built 1911

Weight:
69 tons 2 cwt.

Boiler Pressure:
160 lbs.

Cylinders:
21″×26″

Driving Wheel Diameter:
6′ 6″

Tractive Effort:
19,992 lbs.

Valve Gear:
Stephenson

Number built: 2.

First loco withdrawn 1933; last loco withdrawn 1934.
No. in service (1/1/23) 2; (1/1/48) 0.

14673 (512)	14674 (513)

4-6-0 — P. Drummond H.R. 3P
'Castle' Class
Built 1900-1917

Weight:
59 tons 18 cwt.
60 tons 13 cwt.*

Driving Wheel Diameter:
5′ 9″
6′ 0″*

Boiler Pressure:
175 lbs.

Tractive Effort:
21,313 lbs.
20,425 lbs.*

Cylinders:
$19\frac{1}{2}'' \times 26''$

Valve Gear:
Stephenson

Number built: 19.

First loco withdrawn 1930; last loco withdrawn 1946.
No. in service (1/1/23) 19; (1/1/48) 0.

14675 (140) Taymouth Castle
14676 (141) Ballindalloch Castle
14677 (142) Dunrobin Castle
14678 (143) Gordon Castle
14679 (144) Blair Castle
14680 (145) Murthly Castle
14681 (146) Skibo Castle
14682 (147) Beaufort Castle
14683 (148) Cawdor Castle
14684 (149) Duncraig Castle
14685 (30) Dunvegan Castle
14686 (35) Urquhart Castle
14687 (26) Brahan Castle
14688 (27) Thurso Castle
14689 (28) Cluny Castle
14690 (29) Dalcross Castle
14691* (50) Brodie Castle
14692* (58) Darnaway Castle
14693* (59) Foulis Castle

4-6-0 — McIntosh C.R. 4P
'49' Class
Built 1903

Weight:
71 tons 10 cwt.

Driving Wheel Diameter:
6′ 6″

Boiler Pressure:
175 lbs.

Tractive Effort:
21,348 lbs.

Cylinders:
$20\frac{3}{4}'' \times 26''$

Valve Gear:
Stephenson

Number built: 2.

First loco withdrawn 1933; last loco withdrawn 1933.
No. in service (1/1/23) 2; (1/1/48) 0.

14750 (49)
14751 (50) *Sir James Thompson

*Name removed on being repainted in L.M.S. colours.

4-6-0 McIntosh C.R. 4P
'903' or 'Cardean' Class

Built 1906

Weight:
74 tons 5 cwt.

Boiler Pressure:
175 lbs.

Cylinders:
$20\frac{3}{4}'' \times 26''$

Driving Wheel Diameter:
6′ 6″

Tractive Effort:
21,348 lbs.

Valve Gear:
Stephenson

Number built: 5.

First loco withdrawn 1915; last loco withdrawn 1930.
No. in service (1/1/23) 4; (1/1/48) 0.

C.R. No. 907 was withdrawn after being involved in the accident at Quintinshill in 1915.

14752 (903) *Cardean	14753 (904)	14754 (905)	14755 (906)

*Name removed on being repainted in L.M.S. colours.

4-6-0 Smith H.R. 4P
'River' Class

Built 1915

Weight:
71 tons 16 cwt.

Boiler Pressure:
160 lbs.

Cylinders:
$21'' \times 28''$

Driving Wheel Diameter:
6′ 0″

Tractive Effort:
23,324 lbs.

Valve Gear:
Walschaert

Number built: 6.

First loco withdrawn 1939; last loco withdrawn 1945.
No. in service (1/1/23) 6; (1/1/48) 0.

These locomotives were found to be too heavy for the lines of the Highland Railway and were sold to the Caledonian Railway. The running numbers in brackets are those of the Caledonian Railway.

14756* (938) 14757* (939)	14758 (940)	14759 (941)	14760 (942)	14761 (943)

*The first two engines were turned out by the makers as Highland Railway Nos. 70 River Ness and 71 River Spey, but never worked on that system in pre-grouping days.

4-6-0 Cumming H.R. 4P ' Clan ' Class

Built 1919-1921

Weight:
62 tons 5 cwt.

Driving Wheel Diameter:
6′ 0″

Boiler Pressure:
175 lbs.

Tractive Effort:
23,688 lbs.

Cylinders:
21″×26″

Valve Gear:
Walschaerts

Number built: 8.

First loco withdrawn 1944; last loco withdrawn 1950.
No. in service (1/1/23) 8; (1/1/48) 2.

14762	(49)	Clan Campbell	14766	(54)	Clan Chattan
14763	(51)	Clan Fraser	14767	(55)	Clan Mackinnon
14764	(52)	Clan Munro	14768	(56)	Clan Mackenzie
14765	(53)	Clan Stewart	14769	(57)	Clan Cameron

No. 14767 survived to receive its B.R. No. 54767.

4-6-0 Pickersgill C.R. 5P ' 956 ' Class

Built 1921

Weight:
81 tons

Driving Wheel Diameter:
6′ 1″

Boiler Pressure:
180 lbs.

Tractive Effort:
28,000 lbs.

Cylinders (3):
$18\frac{1}{2}$″×26″

Valve Gear:
Walschaerts

Number built: 4.

First loco withdrawn 1931; last loco withdrawn 1935.
No. in service (1/1/23) 4; (1/1/48) 0.

14800 (956)	14801 (957)	14802 (958)	14803 (959)

0-4-2ST D. Drummond C.R. Unclassified ' Killin Tanks '

Built 1885

Weight:
31 tons 4 cwt.

Boiler Pressure:
140 lbs.

Cylinders:
14″×20″

Driving Wheel Diameter:
3′ 8″

Tractive Effort:
10,600 lbs.

Valve Gear:
Stephenson

Number built: 2.

First loco withdrawn 1928; last loco withdrawn 1947.
No. in service (1/1/23) 2.; (1/1/48) 0.

15000 (1262)	15001 (1263)

No. 15000 never carried its L.M.S. number.

4-4-0T Jones H.R. Unclassified

Built 1878-9 as 2-4-0T
Rebuilt 1881-2 to 4-4-0T

Weight:
44 tons

Boiler Pressure:
160 lbs.

Cylinders:
16″×22″

Driving Wheel Diameter:
5′ 3″

Tractive Effort:
12,158 lbs.

Valve Gear:
Allan

Number built: 3.

First loco withdrawn 1928; last loco withdrawn 1932.
No. in service (1/1/23) 3; (1/1/48) 0.

15010 (59B)	15011 (58B)	15012 (50B)

4-4-0T Dubs & Co. H.R. Unclassified

Built 1891-3

Weight:
41 tons 12 cwt. (15013/4)
44 tons 0 cwt. (15015-7)

Driving Wheel Diameter:
5′ 3″

Boiler Pressure:
140 lbs.

Tractive Effort:
10,638 lbs.

Cylinders:
16″×22″

Valve Gear:
Stephenson

Number built: 5.

First loco withdrawn 1924; last loco withdrawn 1934.
No. in service (1/1/23) 5; (1/1/48) 0.

15013 (101)	15014 (102)	15015 (51B)	15016 (52B)	15017 (54B)

No. 15015 never carried its allocated L.M.S. number.

4-4-0T Lambie C.R. 1P

Built 1893

Weight:
50 tons 7 cwt.

Driving Wheel Diameter:
5′ 0″

Boiler Pressure:
150 lbs.

Tractive Effort:
14,739 lbs.

Cylinders:
17″×24″

Valve Gear:
Stephenson

Number built: 12.

First loco withdrawn 1927; last loco withdrawn 1938.
No. in service (1/1/23) 12; (1/1/48) 0.

15020	(1)	15022	(3)	15024	(5)	15026	(7)	15028	(9)	15030	(11)
15021	(2)	15023	(4)	15025	(6)	15027	(8)	15029	(10)	15031	(12)

No. 15031 never carried its L.M.S. number.

0-4-4T Jones H.R. Unclassified

Built 1890 as saddle tank
Rebuilt 1901 with side tanks

Weight:
34 tons

Boiler Pressure:
150 lbs.

Cylinders:
14″×20″

Driving Wheel Diameter:
4′ 3″

Tractive Effort:
9,800 lbs.

Valve Gear:
Stephenson

Number built: 1.

Withdrawn 1929.

15050 (53A)

0-4-4T P. Drummond H.R. Unclassified

Built 1905-6

Weight:
35 tons 15 cwt.

Boiler Pressure:
150 lbs.

Cylinders:
14″×20″

Driving Wheel Diameter:
4′ 6″

Tractive Effort:
9,255 lbs.

Valve Gear:
Stephenson

Number built: 4.

First loco withdrawn 1930; last loco withdrawn 1957.
No. in service (1/1/23) 4; (1/1/48) 2.

15051 (25)	15052 (40)	15053 (45)	15054 (46)

Nos. 15051 and 15053 survived as B.R. 55051 and 55053 until 1956 working the Dornoch branch. The last H.R. engines to remain in ordinary service.

0-4-4T D. Drummond C.R. 1P

Built 1884-1891

Weight:
37 tons 15 cwt.

Boiler Pressure:
150 lbs.

Cylinders:
16″×22″

Driving Wheel Diameter:
5′ 0″

Tractive Effort:
11,968 lbs.

Valve Gear:
Stephenson

Number built: 24.

First loco withdrawn before 1923; last loco withdrawn 1944.
No. in service (1/1/23) 15; (1/1/48) 0.

15100 (1172)	15103 (1177)	15106 (1222)	15109 (1227)	15112 (1192)
15101 (1174)	15104 (1178)	15107 (1223)	15110 (190)	15113 (1193)
15102 (1175)	15105 (1229)	15108 (1224)	15111 (1191)	15114 (1194)

Some never carried their L.M.S. numbers.

0-4-4T McIntosh C.R. 2P

Built 1895

Weight:
53 tons 16 cwt.

Driving Wheel Diameter:
5′ 9″

Boiler Pressure:
150 lbs.

Tractive Effort:
15,566 lbs.

Cylinders:
18″×26″

Valve Gear:
Stephenson

Number built: 10.

First loco withdrawn 1946; last loco withdrawn 1961.
No. in service (1/1/23) 10; (1/1/48) 7.

15115 (19)	15117 (21)	15119 (23)	15121 (25)	15123 (27)
15116 (20)	15118 (22)	15120 (24)	15122 (26)	15124 (28)

Several engines survived to have 40000 added to their numbers by B.R.

0-4-4T McIntosh C.R. 2P

Built 1897-1900

Weight:
55 tons 15 cwt. (15125-15136)
56 tons 10¾ cwt. (15137-15146)

Driving Wheel Diameter:
5′ 9″

Boiler Pressure:
150 lbs.

Tractive Effort:
15,566 lbs.

Cylinders:
18″×26″

Valve Gear:
Stephenson

Number built: 22.

A number of these engines latterly carried stove-pipe chimneys.

First loco withdrawn 1946; last loco withdrawn 1961.
No. in service (1/1/23) 22; (1/1/48) 19.

15125 (13) 15126 (14) 15127 (15) 15128 (16) 15129 (17)	15130 (18) 15131 (98) 15132 (99) 15133 (100) 15134 (101)	15135 (102) 15136 (103) 15137 (879) 15138 (880)	15139 (881) 15140 (882) 15141 (883) 15142 (884)	15143 (885) 15144 (886) 15145 (437) 15146 (438)

Most of the class survived to have 40000 added to their numbers by B.R.

0-4-4T McIntosh C.R. 1P 'Balerno' Class

Built 1899

Weight:
51 tons 2½ cwt.

Boiler Pressure:
150 lbs.

Cylinders:
17″×24″

Driving Wheel Diameter:
4′ 6″

Tractive Effort:
16,376 lbs.

Valve Gear:
Stephenson

Number built: 12.

First loco withdrawn 1929; last loco withdrawn 1938.
No. in service (1/1/23) 12; (1/1/48) 0.

15147 (104) 15148 (105) 15149 (106)	15150 (107) 15151 (108) 15152 (109)	15153 (110) 15154 (111)	15155 (167) 15156 (168)	15157 (169) 15158 (170)

0-4-4T McIntosh C.R. 2P

Built 1900-14

Weight:
53 tons 19 cwt.

Boiler Pressure:
160 lbs.

Cylinders:
18″×26″

Driving Wheel Diameter:
5′ 9″

Tractive Effort:
16,603 lbs.

Valve Gear:
Stephenson

Number built: 68.

A number of these engines latterly carried stove pipe chimneys.

First loco withdrawn 1946; last loco withdrawn 1962.
No. in service (1/1/23) 68; (1/1/48) 66.

15159 (439)	15173 (453)	15187 (666)	15201 (468)	15215 (457)
15160 (440)	15174 (454)	15188 (158)	15202 (469)	15216 (458)
15161 (441)	15175 (455)	15189 (419)	15203 (155)	15217 (228)
15162 (442)	15176 (151)	15190 (422)	15204 (160)	15218 (229)
15163 (443)	15177 (423)	15191 (429)	15205 (459)	15219 (230)
15164 (444)	15178 (473)	15192 (470)	15206 (461)	15220 (231)
15165 (445)	15179 (112)	15193 (126)	15207 (152)	15221 (222)
15166 (446)	15180 (125)	15194 (127)	15208 (153)	15222 (223)
15167 (447)	15181 (424)	15195 (420)	15209 (154)	15223 (224)
15168 (448)	15182 (463)	15196 (421)	15210 (156)	15224 (225)
15169 (449)	15183 (464)	15197 (427)	15211 (460)	15225 (226)
15170 (450)	15184 (465)	15198 (428)	15212 (462)	15226 (227)
15171 (451)	15185 (466)	15199 (456)	15213 (157)	
15172 (452)	15186 (660)	15200 (467)	15214 (164)	

All but a few of these engines survived to have 40000 added to their numbers by B.R. No. 15189 has been acquired by the Scottish Locomotive Preservation Society and restored with its C.R. blue livery as No. 419.

0-4-4T McIntosh/Pickersgill C.R. 2P

Built 1915–22

Weight:
57 tons 12 cwt.

Driving Wheel Diameter:
5′ 9″

Boiler Pressure:
180 lbs.

Tractive Effort:
16,603 lbs.

Cylinders:
18″×26″

Valve Gear:
Stephenson

Number built: 10.

First loco withdrawn 1961; last loco withdrawn 1962.
No. in service (1/1/23) 10; (1/1/48) 10.

Some of these engines latterly carried stove-pipe chimneys.

15227 (159)	15229 (162)	15231 (418)	15233 (426)	15235 (435)
15228 (161)	15230 (163)	15232 (425)	15234 (430)	15236 (436)

All carried their B.R. Nos. 55227-55236.

0-4-4T McIntosh/Pickersgill C.R. 2P

Built 1922

Weight:
57 tons 17½ cwt.

Driving Wheel Diameter:
5′ 9″

Boiler Pressure:
180 lbs.

Tractive Effort:
19,200 lbs.

Cylinders:
18¼″×26″

Valve Gear:
Stephenson

Number built: 4.

These were a slightly modified version of the original design built for banking purposes. No. 55237 latterly carried a stove-pipe chimney.

First loco withdrawn 1961; last loco withdrawn 1961.
No. in service (1/1/23) 4; (1/1/48) 4.

15237 (431)	15238 (432)	15239 (433)	15240 (434)

Ten additional engines were built by the L.M.S. in 1925, Nos. 15260-15269. All of these series survived to become B.R. 55237-55240 and 55260-55269.

0-4-4T J. Stirling G. & S.W.R. 1P

Built 1879

Weight:
49 tons 6 cwt.

Boiler Pressure:
140 lbs. (domeless boilers)

Cylinders:
18″×26″

Driving Wheel Diameter:
5′ 7″

Tractive Effort:
13,744 lbs.

Valve Gear:
Stephenson

Number built: 4.

First loco withdrawn 1925; last loco withdrawn 1926.
No. in service (1/1/23) 4; (1/1/48) 0.

15241 (728)	15242 (729)	15243 (730)	15244 (731)

None survived to carry its L.M.S. number.

0-4-4T Manson G. & S.W.R. 1P

Built 1893

Weight:
51 tons 8 cwt.*
54 tons 4 cwt.†

Boiler Pressure:
150 lbs.

Cylinders:
17¼″×24″

Driving Wheel Diameter:
5′ 2″

Tractive Effort:
14,686 lbs.

Valve Gear:
Stephenson

Number built: 10.

First loco withdrawn 1930; last loco withdrawn 1932.
No. in service (1/1/23) 10; (1/1/48) 0.

15245† (520) 15246* (521)	14257* (522) 15248† (523)	15249* (524) 15250* (525)	15251* (526) 15252* (527)	15253† (528) 15254† (529)

For 15260-15269 see footnote with class 15237-15240.

0-6-4T Drummond H.R. 4P

Built 1909-1911

Weight:
69 tons 10 cwt.

Boiler Pressure:
175 lbs.

Cylinders:
$18\frac{1}{4}'' \times 26''$

Driving Wheel Diameter:
5′ 0″

Tractive Effort:
21,464 lbs.

Valve Gear:
Stephenson

Number built: 8.

First loco withdrawn 1932; last loco withdrawn 1936.
No. in service (1/1/23) 8; (1/1/48) 0.

15300 (39) 15301 (66)	15302 (68) 15303 (69)	15304 (43) 15305 (31)	15306 (42)	15307 (44)

4-6-2T Pickersgill C.R. 4P

Built 1917

Weight:
91 tons 13 cwt.

Boiler Pressure:
170 lbs.

Cylinders:
$19\frac{1}{2}'' \times 26''$

Driving Wheel Diameter:
5′ 9″

Tractive Effort:
20,804 lbs.

Valve Gear:
Stephenson

Number built: 12.

First loco withdrawn 1946; last loco withdrawn 1953.
No. in service (1/1/23) 12; (1/1/48) 10.

15350 (944) 15351 (945) 15352 (946)	15353 (947) 15354 (948) 15355 (949)	15356 (950) 15357 (951)	15358 (952) 15359 (953)	15360 (954) 15361 (955)

Most of these engines survived to have 40000 added to their numbers by B.R.

. Kirtley 2-4-0 No. 4 at Inverness in 1928, when it spent a few months working on the Highland
way. The engine in the background is No. 14271 'Sir George'.

.. Johnson 2-4-0, one of the 7′ 0″ series, rebuilt with Belpaire, as were many of the class in later days.
Peterboro' East in 1937.

atford-on-Avon and Midland Junction 2-4-0 No. 13, allocated L.M.S. No. 290, but never carried.

[*L.P.C*

One of the original Johnson 7′ 0″ 4-4-0's of 1877. Unlike the many later series, these early engines were never rebuilt and remained practically in their original state to the end.

One of the various styles of rebuilding by Deeley, in this case with extended smokebox but round topped boiler (others had Belpaire boilers with or without extended smokeboxes). This series had seperate splashers.

Another style of Deeley rebuild, with combined sweeping splashers. [L.P.C.

The final stage of rebuild, as introduced by Fowler, and later adopted as standard for new construction by the L.M.S. This photograph, taken at Bourne in 1937, showed the temporary style of block lettering and figures adopted about that time.

One of the five 4-4-0's acquired from the North Stafford Railway, later renumbered 5413. [W. H. Whitworth

North Stafford 2-4-0T No. 1447 [L.P.C.

North Stafford 2-4-2T No. 1454 [W. Leslie Good

North Stafford 0-6-0T No. 1579

M.R. No. 1604, an ancient 0-6-0WT of 1862. A sister engine, No. 1601, was even older, dating back to 1848. The brass cabside figures were of a style in vogue before 1907, but the view was taken in 1920 and shows also one of the small saddle tanks used in docks, Brewery yards, etc.

0-6-0T No. 1831, rebuilt in 1932 as a diesel shunter, and as such the direct forerunner of the standart type later adopted by all four groups and eventually constructed in large numbers by B.R.

Two of Johnson's standard 0-6-0T's introduced in 1874, of which 380 were built, followed by a further 60 of an enlarged design, which with slight modification was adopted as a standard L.M.S. type, and of which a number still remain in 1966. The two engines shown depict the original Johnson boiler with safety valve on the dome, and the later Belpaire rebuild. Some engines of both varieties had all-over cabs.

One of the old Fox Walker saddle tanks taken over from the S. & D.J.R., and given numbers rendered vacant by the scrapping of 0-4-0ST's.

4-6-4T Whitelegg G. & S.W.R. 5P

Built 1922

Weight:
99 tons

Boiler Pressure:
180 lbs.

Cylinders:
22″×26″

Driving Wheel Diameter:
6′ 0″

Tractive Effort:
26,741 lbs.

Valve Gear:
Stephenson

Number built: 6.

First loco withdrawn 1934; last loco withdrawn 1935.
No. in service (1/1/23) 6; (1/1/48) 0.

15400 (540) 15401 (541)	15402 (542)	15403 (543)	15404 (544)	15405 (545)

0-4-0ST A. Barclay C.R. Unclassified

Built 1896

Weight:
(figure unavailable)

Boiler Pressure:
140 lbs.

Cylinders:
13″×20″ (outside)

Driving Wheel Diameter:
3′ 2″

Tractive Effort:
9,141 lbs.

Valve Gear:
Stephenson

Number built: 1.

Loco withdrawn 1924.
No. in service (1/1/23) 1; (1/1/48) 0.

16000 (1781) It is unlikely that this engine ever carried its L.M.S. number.

0-4-0ST Drummond/McIntosh C.R. Unclassified

Built 1878-1908

Weight:
27 tons 7½ cwt.

Boiler Pressure:
140 lbs.

Cylinders:
14″×20″ (outside)

Driving Wheel Diameter:
3′ 8″

Tractive Effort:
10,601 lbs.

Valve Gear:
Stephenson

Number built: 39.

One or two of these engines latterly carried stove-pipe chimneys.

First loco withdrawn 1923; last loco withdrawn 1962.

No. in service (1/1/23) 39; (1/1/48) 14.

16001	(1162)	16009	(267)	16017	(617)	16025	(1515)	16033	(624)
16002	(1163)	16010	(268)	16018	(618)	16026	(611)	16034	(625)
16003	(1503)	16011	(270)	16019	(620)	16027	(612)	16035	(626)
16004	(1505)	16012	(1264)	16020	(1510)	16028	(613)	16036	(627)
16005	(1529)	16013	(1265)	16021	(1511)	16029	(614)	16037	(628)
16006	(1532)	16014	(1271)	16022	(1512)	16030	(621)	16038	(265)
16007	(1534)	16015	(615)	16023	(1513)	16031	(622)	16039	(269)
16008	(266)	16016	(616)	16024	(1514)	16032	(623)		

Nos. 16002 and 16023 never carried their allocated L.M.S. numbers.

0-4-0ST Contractors' Locos. for G. & S.W.R. Unclassified

*** Built by Andrews, Barr in 1881**

† Built by Andrew Barclay in 1883

§Built by Peckett & Sons in 1904, aquired by the G. & S.W.R 1918

Weight:
28 tons 14 cwt.*
20 tons 2 cwt.†
24 tons 10 cwt.§

Driving Wheel Diameter:
3′ 6″*
3′ 6″†
3′ $2\frac{1}{2}$″§

Boiler Pressure:
120 lbs.*
120 lbs.†
150 lbs.§

Tractive Effort:
10,472 lbs.*
8,208 lbs.†
12,981 lbs.§

Cylinders: (outside)
14″×22″*
13″×20″†
14″×20″§

Valve Gear:
Stephenson

Number built: 2*; 1†; 1§.

Locos withdrawn, 1932, 1928, 1924 and 1930 respectively.

No. in service (1/1/23) 2*, 1†, 1§; (1/1/48) 0.

16040* (659)	16041* (658)	16042† (734)	16043§ (735)

No. 16042 never carried its L.M.S. number.

0-4-0T Manson G. & S.W.R. Unclassified

Built 1907-9

Weight:
39 tons 6 cwt.

Boiler Pressure:
140 lbs.

Cylinders:
16″×24″

Driving Wheel Diameter:
4′ 7½″

Tractive Effort:
13,174 lbs.

Valve Gear:
Stephenson

Number built: 6.

First loco withdrawn 1930; last loco withdrawn 1931.
No. in service (1/1/23) 6; (1/1/48) 0.

16044 (316) 16045 (317)	16046 (318)	16047 (319)	16048 (320)	16049 (321)

0-4-0ST Glasgow & Paisley Joint Railway

Weight:
27 tons

Boiler Pressure:
140 lbs.

Cylinders:
14″×22″ (outside)

Driving Wheel Diameter:
3′ 6″

Tractive Effort:
12,214 lbs.

Number built:
2

First loco withdrawn 1924; last loco withdrawn 1924.
No. in service (1/1/23) 2; (1/1/48) 0.

16050 (G. & P. 1)	16051 (G. & P. 2)

It is unlikely that either of these engines ever carried its L.M.S. number.

0-4-4T Manson G. & S.W.R. Unclassified '305' Class

Built 1906

Weight:
42 tons 8 cwt.

Boiler Pressure:
140 lbs.

Cylinders:
16″×22″

Driving Wheel Diameter:
4′ 7½″

Tractive Effort:
12,078 lbs.

Valve Gear:
Stephenson

Number built: 6.

First loco withdrawn 1925; last loco withdrawn 1932.
No. in service (1/1/23) 6; (1/1/48) 0.

16080 (305) 16081 (306)	16082 (307)	16083 (308)	16084 (309)	16085 (310)

0-6-0ST Drummond C.R. Unclassified 'Dock Saddletanks' Class

Built 1888

Weight:
31 tons

Boiler Pressure:
140 lbs.

Cylinders:
14″×20″ (outside)

Driving Wheel Diameter:
3′ 8″

Tractive Effort:
10,601 lbs.

Valve Gear:
Stephenson

Number built: 3.

First loco withdrawn 1928; last loco withdrawn 1929.
No. in service (1/1/23) 3; (1/1/48) 0.

16100 (1273)	16101 (1274)	16102 (1509)

No. 16102 never carried its L.M.S. number.

0-6-0T Manson G. & S.W.R. Unclassified '275' Class

Built 1896-1914

Weight:
40 tons 2 cwt.*
43 tons 13 cwt.†

Boiler Pressure:
140 lbs.

Cylinders:
16″×22″

Driving Wheel Diameter:
4′ 7½″

Tractive Effort:
12,078 lbs.

Valve Gear:
Stephenson

Number built: 15.

First loco withdrawn 1928; last loco withdrawn 1932.
No. in service (1/1/23) 15; (1/1/48) 0.

16103* (277) 16104* (278) 16105† (280)	16106* (282) 16107* (284) 16108* (285)	16109† (286) 16110* (287) 16111* (288)	16112* (289) 16113† (275) 16114* (276)	16115* (279) 16116* (281) 16117* (283)

0-6-0T Stroudley H.R. Unclassified

Built 1869-1874

Weight:
26 tons

Driving Wheel Diameter:
3′ 8″

Boiler Pressure:
120 lbs.

Tractive Effort:
9,087 lbs.

Cylinders:
14″×20″

Valve Gear:
Stephenson

Number built: 3.

First loco withdrawn 1927; last loco withdrawn 1932.
No. in service (1/1/23) 3; (1/1/48) 0.

16118	(56B)	Dornoch	16383	(49A)	St. Martins
16119	(57B)	Lochgorm			

The names were removed when the engines were repainted in L.M.S. livery, which in the case of No. 57B Lochgorm did not take place until 1929, this being the last H.R. engine to retain its pregrouping colours.

When the renumbering scheme was drawn up some confusion apparently arose with regard to No. 49A St. Martins, which was quite erroneously thought to be of the same class as the quite dissimilar engines 16380-16382. The mistake could have been easily corrected by renumbering it 16120 in its rightful place, but this was never done.

0-6-0ST Brittain C.R. 1F

Built 1881

Weight:
41 tons 17 cwt.

Driving Wheel Diameter:
4′ 0″

Boiler Pressure:
140 lbs.

Tractive Effort:
17,671 lbs.

Cylinders:
18″×22″ (outside)

Valve Gear:
Stephenson

Number built: 1.

Loco withdrawn 1928.
No. in service (1/1/23) 1; (1/1/48) 0.

16150 (1489) L.M.S. number never carried.

0-6-0T McIntosh C.R. 2F

Built 1911-1921

Weight:
47 tons 15 cwt.

Boiler Pressure:
160 lbs.

Cylinders:
17″×22″ (outside)

Driving Wheel Diameter:
4′ 0″

Tractive Effort:
18,014 lbs.

Valve Gear:
Stephenson

Number built: 23.

Several engines latterly carried stove-pipe chimneys.

First loco withdrawn 1958; last loco withdrawn 1962.
No. in service (1/1/23) 23; (1/1/48) 23.

16151 (498)	16156 (530)	16161 (535)	16166 (503)	16170 (512)
16152 (499)	16157 (531)	16162 (536)	16167 (504)	16171 (513)
16153 (527)	16158 (532)	16163 (537)	16168 (510)	16172 (514)
16154 (528)	16159 (533)	16164 (538)	16169 (511)	16173 (515)
16155 (529)	16160 (534)	16165 (502)		

All survived to have 40000 added to their numbers by B.R.

0-6-0ST Drummond C.R. 3F

Built 1887-1890

Weight:
43 tons 16 cwt.

Boiler Pressure:
150 lbs.

Cylinders:
18″×26″

Driving Wheel Diameter:
4′ 6″

Tractive Effort:
19,890 lbs.

Valve Gear:
Stephenson

Number built: 30.

First loco withdrawn before 1923; last loco withdrawn 1930.
No. in service (1/1/23) 27; (1/1/48) 0.

16200 (216)	16205 (505)	16210 (220)	16215 (388)	16220 (399)
16201 (217)	16206 (506)	16211 (221)	16216 (389)	16221 (400)
16202 (383)	16207 (507)	16212 (1232)	16217 (391)	16222 (401)
16203 (384)	16208 (218)	16213 (1233)	16218 (392)	16223 (402)
16204 (385)	16209 (219)	16214 (1235)	16219 (398)	16224 (1395)

0-6-0ST Lambie C.R. 3F

Built 1895

Weight:
46 tons 5 cwt.

Boiler Pressure:
150 lbs.

Cylinders:
18″×26″

Driving Wheel Diameter:
4′ 6″

Tractive Effort:
19,890 lbs.

Valve Gear:
Stephenson

Number built: 5.

First loco withdrawn 1926; last loco withdrawn 1929.
No. in service (1/1/23) 5; (1/1/48) 0.

16225 (211)	16226 (212)	16227 (213)	16228 (214)	16229 (215)

0-6-0T McIntosh C.R. 3F
'29' and '782' Classes

Built 1895-1922

Weight:
47 tons 15¼ cwt.

Boiler Pressure:
150 lbs.

Cylinders:
18″×26″

Driving Wheel Diameter:
4′ 6″

Tractive Effort:
19,890 lbs.

Valve Gear:
Stephenson

Number built: 147.

Many engines were latterly fitted with stove-pipe chimneys.

First loco withdrawn 1952; last loco withdrawn 1962.
No. in service (1/1/23) 147; (1/1/48) 147.

16230 (650)	16244 (240)	16258 (786)	16272 (800)	16286 (632)
16231 (29)	16245 (241)	16259 (787)	16273 (801)	16287 (633)
16232 (203)	16246 (242)	16260 (788)	16274 (802)	16288 (634)
16233 (204)	16247 (243)	16261 (789)	16275 (803)	16289 (635)
16234 (205)	16248 (244)	16262 (790)	16276 (804)	16290 (636)
16235 (206)	16249 (245)	16263 (791)	16277 (805)	16291 (637)
16236 (207)	16250 (246)	16264 (792)	16278 (806)	16292 (638)
16237 (208)	16251 (247)	16265 (793)	16279 (807)	16293 (639)
16238 (209)	16252 (485)	16266 (794)	16280 (808)	16294 (640)
16239 (210)	16253 (516)	16267 (795)	16281 (809)	16295 (641)
16240 (236)	16254 (782)	16268 (796)	16282 (810)	16296 (642)
16241 (237)	16255 (783)	16269 (797)	16283 (811)	16297 (643)
16242 (238)	16256 (784)	16270 (798)	16284 (488)	16298 (644)
16243 (239)	16257 (785)	16271 (799)	16285 (631)	16299 (645)

16300 (646)	16316 (667)	16332 (483)	16347 (171)	16362 (235)
16301 (647)	16317 (668)	16333 (484)	16448 (172)	16363 (272)
16302 (648)	16318 (669)	16334 (500)	16349 (173)	16364 (273)
16303 (649)	16319 (475)	16335 (608)	16350 (174)	16365 (274)
16304 (128)	16320 (476)	16336 (609)	16351 (651)	16366 (248)
16305 (129)	16321 (477)	16337 (610)	16352 (781)	16367 (249)
16306 (166)	16322 (478)	16338 (277)	16353 (175)	16368 (250)
16307 (271)	16323 (479)	16339 (393)	16354 (176)	16369 (251)
16308 (275)	16324 (480)	16340 (397)	16355 (177)	16370 (252)
16309 (276)	16325 (487)	16341 (405)	16356 (178)	16371 (253)
16310 (417)	16326 (490)	16342 (471)	16357 (508)	16372 (254)
16311 (472)	16327 (491)	16343 (486)	16358 (509)	16373 (255)
16312 (489)	16328 (416)	16344 (390)	16359 (232)	16374 (394)
16313 (501)	16329 (474)	16345 (130)	16360 (233)	16375 (395)
16314 (629)	16330 (481)	16346 (131)	16361 (234)	16376 (396)
16315 (630)	16331 (482)			

All survived to carry their B.R. numbers 56230-56376.

0-6-0T Drummond G. & S.W.R. 2F ' 322 ' Class

Built 1917

Weight:
40 tons

Boiler Pressure:
160 lbs.

Cylinders:
17″×22″ (outside)

Driving Wheel Diameter:
4′ 2″

Tractive Effort:
17,294 lbs.

Valve Gear:
Walschaerts

Number built: 3.

First loco withdrawn 1932; last loco withdrawn 1934.
No. in service (1/1/23) 3; (1/1/48) 0.

16377 (322)	16378 (323)	16379 (324)

Two of these engines, Nos. 16378 and 16379, were sold out of service in 1934, No. 16378 to the Hatfield Main Colliery, Yorks., and No. 16379 to the Hafod Colliery, Denbigh. In 1964 it was discovered that the last mentioned engine was the only G. & S.W.R. locomotive still in existence, and it has now been acquired by B.R. with a view to preservation.

0-6-0T H.R. 2F

Built 1903-4

Weight:
47 tons 18 cwt.

Boiler Pressure:
160 lbs.

Cylinders (outside):
18″×24″

Driving Wheel Diameter:
5′ 2½″

Tractive Effort:
16,920 lbs.

Valve Gear:
Stephenson

Number built: 3.

First loco withdrawn 1930; last loco withdrawn 1932.
Number in service (1/1/23) 3; (1/1/48) 0.

16380 (22)	16381 (23)	16382 (24)

For engine 16383, see class 16118, 16119.

0-6-2T Drummond G. & S.W.R. 3F

Built 1915-1919

Weight:
66 tons 4 cwt.

Boiler Pressure:
180 lbs.

Cylinders:
$18\frac{1}{4}'' \times 26''$

Driving Wheel Diameter:
5′ 0″

Tractive Effort:
22,078 lbs.

Valve Gear:
Stephenson

Number built: 28.

First loco withdrawn 1936; last loco withdrawn 1948.
No. in service (1/1/23) 28; (1/1/48) 1.

16400 (1)	16406 (7)	16412 (13)	16418 (19)	16423 (24)
16401 (2)	16407 (8)	16413 (14)	16419 (20)	16424 (25)
16402 (3)	16408 (9)	16414 (15)	16420 (21)	16425 (26)
16403 (4)	16409 (10)	16415 (16)	16421 (22)	16426 (27)
16404 (5)	16410 (11)	16416 (17)	16422 (23)	16427 (28)
16405 (6)	16411 (12)	16417 (18)		

All renumbered 16900-16927 in consequence of the construction of new standard 0-6-0T's (see 7317 onwards).

16405, then 16905, was the only G. & S.W.R. to survive to pass into the hands of British Railways at 1/1/48. It never carried its allocated B.R. No. 56905.

0-8-0T McIntosh C.R. 4F
'492' Class

Built 1903

Weight:
62 tons 15 cwt.

Boiler Pressure:
175 lbs.

Cylinders:
$19'' \times 26''$

Driving Wheel Diameter:
4′ 6″

Tractive Effort:
25,855 lbs.

Valve Gear:
Stephenson

Number built: 6.

First loco withdrawn 1932; last loco withdrawn 1939.
No. in service (1/1/23) 6; (1/1/48) 0.

16500 (492) 16501 (493)	16502 (494)	16503 (495)	16504 (496)	16505 (497)

All renumbered 16950-16955 in 1926.

0-4-2 Brittain C.R. Unclassified

Built 1878-1881

Weight:
34 tons 12 cwt. (17000-6)
36 tons 19 cwt. (17007-20)

Driving Wheel Diameter:
5′ 0″

Boiler Pressure:
140 lbs. (17000-6)
150 lbs. (17007-20)

Tractive Effort:
13,756 lbs. (17000-6)
14,739 lbs. (17007-20)

Cylinders:
17″×24″ (outside)

Valve Gear:
Stephenson

Number built: 30.

First loco withdrawn before 1923; last loco withdrawn 1923.
No. in service (1/1/23) 21; (1/1/48) 0.

17000	(1672)	17005	(1718)	17009	(1677)	17013	(279)	17017	(1251)
17001	(1673)	17006	(1716)	17010	(1679)	17014	(1164)	17018	(1275)
17002	(1676)	17007	(1674)	17011	(165)	17015	(1248)	17019	(1280)
17003	(1253)	17008	(1675)	17012	(278)	17016	(1250)	17020	(1717)
17004	(1255)								

0-4-2 P. Stirling G. & S.W.R. Unclassified

Built 1866

Weight:
30 tons 8 cwt.

Driving Wheel Diameter:
5′ 1″

Boiler Pressure (domeless boiler):
120 lbs.

Tractive Effort:
9,942 lbs.

Cylinders:
17″×24″

Valve Gear:
Stephenson

Number built: 10.

First loco withdrawn 1902; last loco withdrawn 1924.
No. in service (1/1/23) 2; (1/1/48) 0.

17021 (656)	17022 (657)

Neither engine carried its allocated L.M.S. number.

0-4-2 J. Stirling G. & S.W.R. Unclassified

Built 1873

Weight:
30 tons 16 cwt.

Driving Wheel Diameter:
5′ 7″

Boiler Pressure (domeless boiler):
130 lbs.

Tractive Effort:
14,408 lbs.

Cylinders:
18″ × 24″

Valve Gear:
Stephenson

Number built: 9.

First loco withdrawn 1904; last loco withdrawn 1923.
No. in service (1/1/23) 5; (1/1/48) 0.

17023 (651)	17024 (652)	17025 (653)	17026 (654)	17027 (655)

None of these engines carried their allocated L.M.S. numbers.

0-4-2 J. Stirling G. & S.W.R. Unclassified

Built 1870-1
Rebuilt 1900

Weight:
32 tons 2 cwt.

Driving Wheel Diameter:
5′ 7″

Boiler Pressure (domeless boiler):
140 lbs.

Tractive Effort:
12,248 lbs.

Cylinders:
17″ × 24″

Valve Gear:
Stephenson

Number built: 20.

Rebuilt with all-over cabs.

First loco withdrawn before 1923; last loco withdrawn 1930.
No. in service (1/1/23) 7; (1/1/48) 0.

17028 (268) 17029 (269)	17030 (270) 17031 (271)	17032 (272)	17033 (273)	17034 (274)

0-4-2 J. Stirling G. & S.W.R. Unclassified '635' Class

Built 1874-8

Weight:
31 tons 4 cwt.

Driving Wheel Diameter:
5′ 7½″

Boiler Pressure (domeless boiler):
130 lbs.

Tractive Effort:
14,321 lbs.

Cylinders:
18″×26″

Valve Gear:
Stephenson

Number built: 60.

Retaining Stirling round topped half cab.

First loco withdrawn 1911; last loco withdrawn 1930.
No. in service (1/1/23) 16; (1/1/48) 0.

17035 (635) 17036 (636) 17037 (637)	17038 (639) 17039 (641)	17040 (644) 17041 (645)	17042 (646) 17043 (647)	17044 (648) 17045 (649)
638*	640*	*642	*643	*650

*(G.S.W.R. Numbers—not allocated L.M.S.R. numbers.)
None of the others actually carried their L.M.S. numbers.
Thirty of this class rebuilt to class below, Nos. 17046-17075.

0-4-2 Stirling G. & S.W.R. Unclassified '238' Class, rebuilds of '635' Class

Built 1874-6
Rebuilt Manson 1901-3

Weight:
34 tons 16 cwt.

Driving Wheel Diameter:
5′ 7½″

Boiler Pressure:
140 lbs.
(rebuilt with domed boiler and all-over cab)

Tractive Effort:
15,428 lbs.

Cylinders:
18″×26″

Valve Gear:
Stephenson

Number built: 30.

First loco withdrawn 1925; last loco withdrawn 1931.
No. in service (1/1/23) 30; (1/1/48) 0.

17046 (241)	17052 (257)	17058 (245)	17064 (260)	17070 (248)
17047 (243)	17053 (262)	17059 (253)	17065 (261)	17071 (250)
17048 (244)	17054 (266)	17060 (254)	17066 (263)	17072 (264)
17049 (249)	17055 (267)	17061 (256)	17067 (265)	17073 (240)
17050 (251)	17056 (238)	17062 (258)	17068 (242)	17074 (247)
17051 (255)	17057 (239)	17063 (259)	17069 (246)	17075 (252)

Some engines never carried their allotted L.M.S. numbers.

0-6-0 P. Stirling G. & S.W.R. Unclassified

Built 1866-9

Weight:
31 tons 10 cwt.

Boiler Pressure:
120 lbs.

Cylinders:
17″×24″

Driving Wheel Diameter:
5′ 1″

Tractive Effort:
9,942 lbs.

Valve Gear:
Stephenson

Number built: 26.

First loco withdrawn 1896; last loco withdrawn 1923.
No. in service (1/1/23) 8; (1/1/48) 0.

17100 (619)	617*	618*	620*	621*	622*	623*	624*

*(G.S.W.R. Nos.—not allocated L.M.S. Nos.)

The other engine did not carry its L.M.S. number.

0-6-0 Solway Junction Railway Locos. Unclassified

Built 1868

Taken over by Caledonian Railway in 1869.

Weight:
34 tons

Boiler Pressure:
140 lbs.

Cylinders:
17″×24″

Driving Wheel Diameter:
5′ 0″

Tractive Effort:
13,756 lbs.

Valve Gear:
Stephenson

Number built: 2.

First loco withdrawn 1927; last loco withdrawn 1928.
No. in service (1/1/23) 2; (1/1/48) 0.

17101 (381)	17102 (382)

0-6-0 J. Stirling G. & S.W.R. 1F
'563' Class
Built 1877-8

Weight:
35 tons 10 cwt.

Driving Wheel Diameter:
5′ 1″

Boiler Pressure:
130 lbs.

Tractive Effort:
15,538 lbs.

Cylinders:
18″×26″

Valve Gear:
Stephenson

Number built: 12.

First loco withdrawn 1898; last loco withdrawn 1928.
No. in service (1/1/23) 9; (1/1/48) 0.

17103 (563)	17105 (565)	17107 (575)	17109 (577)	17111 (584)
17104 (573)	17106 (572)	17108 (576)	17110 (578)	

Few, if any, of these engines carried their L.M.S. numbers.

0-6-0 Smellie G. & S.W.R. 1F/2F†
† Built 1881-90

*Some rebuilt with small boilers with round cabs.
†Others rebuilt with larger boilers and all-over cabs.
Remainder with Stirling type domeless boilers and round cabs.

Weight:
37 tons 10 cwt.
39 tons 10 cwt.*
40 tons 10 cwt.†

Driving Wheel Diameter:
5′ 1½″

Boiler Pressure:
140 lbs.
150 lbs.*†

Tractive Effort:
16,707 lbs.
17,464 lbs.*†

Cylinders:
18″×26″

Valve Gear:
Stephenson

Number built: 64.

First loco withdrawn 1913: last loco withdrawn 1935.
No. in service (1/1/23) 63; (1/1/48) 0.

17112	(566)	17119	(606)	17126	(574)	17133†	(569)	17140	(610)
17113	(567)	17120	(564)	17127	(580)	17134	(138)	17141†	(611)
17114	(570)	17121	(579)	17128	(135)	17135	(581)	17142	(612)
17115	(571)	17122*	(590)	17129	(560)	17136†	(582)	17143	(613)
17116	(592)	17123	(591)	17130	(561)	17137	(607)	17144†	(614)
17117*	(139)	17124	(593)	17131†	(562)	17138†	(608)	17145	(615)
17118†	(605)	17125	(594)	17132	(568)	17139	(609)	17146	(616)

17147	(136)	17151	(597)	17155†	(137)	17159	(598)	17162	(604)
17148	(583)	17152	(599)	17156†	(587)	17160	(600)	17163†	(588)
17149	(585)	17153	(601)	17157†	(595)	17161	(603)	17164	(589)
17150	(586)	17154†*	(602)	17158	(596)				
17203*	(140)	17205*	(143)	17207*	(142)	17209*	(146)	17211*	(148)
17204*	(141)	17206*	(144)	17208*	(145)	17210*	(147)	17212*	(149)

0-6-0 Smellie G. & S.W.R. 1F

Built 1892

Weight:
39 tons 10 cwt., small boiler
40 tons 10 cwt, large boiler†

Boiler Pressure:
150 lbs.

Cylinders:
18″×26″

Driving Wheel Diameter:
5′ 1½″

Tractive Effort:
17,464 lbs.

Valve Gear:
Stephenson

Number built: 20.

First loco withdrawn 1925; last loco withdrawn 1932.

No. in service (1/1/23) 20; (1/1/48) 0.

Small boiler engines, Stirling-type round cab. Large boiler, all-over cab.

17165	(178)	17169	(182)	17173†	(186)	17177	(190)	17181	(194)
17166	(179)	17170	(183)	17174	(187)	17178	(191)	17182	(195)
17167	(180)	17171	(184)	17175	(188)	17179	(192)	17183	(196)
17168	(181)	17172	(185)	17176†	(189)	17180	(193)	17184	(197)

0-6-0 Manson G. & S.W.R. 1F

Built 1897-9

Weight:
39 tons 10 cwt. (small boiler)
40 tons 10 cwt. (large boiler)†

Boiler Pressure:
150 lbs.

Cylinders:
18″×26″

Driving Wheel Diameter:
5′ 1½″

Tractive Effort:
17,464 lbs.

Valve Gear:
Stephenson

Number built: 18.

All of this class, small and large boiler, had all-over cabs.

First loco withdrawn 1925; last loco withdrawn 1933.

No. in service (1/1/23) 18; (1/1/48) 0.

17185	(160)	17189	(164)	17193	(168)	17197	(172)	17200	(175)
17186	(161)	17190	(165)	17194	(169)	17198	(173)	17201†	(176)
17187	(162)	17191	(166)	17195†	(170)	17199	(174)	17202	(177)
17188	(163)	17192	(167)	17196	(171)				

For locomotives 17203-17212, see 17112-17164 above.

0-6-0

Drummond C.R. 2F
'Jumbo' Class

Built 1883-97

(Class perpetuated by Smellie, Lambie and McIntosh)

Weight:
41 tons 6 cwt.
42 tons 4 cwt.

Driving Wheel Diameter:
5′ 0″

(Engines fitted with condensing apparatus for working through Glasgow low level lines, including 17469-17473 and others.)

Boiler Pressure:
150 lbs.

Tractive Effort:
17,901 lbs.

Cylinders:
18″×26″

Valve Gear:
Stephenson

Number built: 244.

Many engines fitted with Westinghouse brakes for working passenger trains. A large number of engines received stove-pipe chimneys in more recent years.

First loco withdrawn 1946; last loco withdrawn 1962.
No. in service (1/1/23) 244; (1/1/48) 238.

17230	(259)	17251	(354)	17272	(361)	17293	(1319)	17314	(404)
17231	(260)	17252	(518)	17273	(362)	17294	(1365)	17315	(406)
17232	(262)	17253	(519)	17274	(363)	17295	(340)	17316	(407)
17233	(263)	17254	(520)	17275	(364)	17296	(341)	17317	(408)
17234	(264)	17255	(521)	17276	(690)	17297	(342)	17318	(409)
17235	(335)	17256	(522)	17277	(355)	17298	(343)	17319	(410)
17236	(337)	17257	(523)	17278	(356)	17299	(344)	17320	(411)
17237	(349)	17258	(524)	17279	(357)	17300	(345)	17321	(412)
17238	(350)	17259	(525)	17280	(358)	17301	(346)	17322	(413)
17239	(351)	17260	(526)	17281	(359)	17302	(347)	17323	(414)
17240	(352)	17261	(681)	17282	(360)	17303	(348)	17324	(415)
17241	(365)	17262	(683)	17283	(553)	17304	(366)	17325	(372)
17242	(367)	17263	(684)	17284	(558)	17305	(368)	17326	(373)
17243	(374)	17264	(685)	17285	(680)	17306	(369)	17327	(375)
17244	(403)	17265	(686)	17286	(682)	17307	(370)	17328	(376)
17245	(517)	17266	(687)	17287	(703)	17308	(371)	17329	(377)
17246	(539)	17267	(688)	17288	(705)	17309	(380)	17330	(378)
17247	(548)	17268	(689)	17289	(707)	17310	(708)	17331	(379)
17248	(549)	17269	(1517)	17290	(1310)	17311	(1323)	17332	(540)
17249	(1294)	17270	(1680)	17291	(1315)	17312	(1367)	17333	(541)
17250	(353)	17271	(1682)	17292	(1318)	17313	(1403)	17334	(542)

One of the original series of L.T. & S.R. 4-4-2T's. [L.P.C.

Two further stages in the development of the 4-4-2T's on the L.T. & S.R. 'Intermediate' No. 2109 (this one somewhat unusually carrying two domes) and the larger class No. 2144.

L.T. & S.R. 0-6-2T. fourteen of which were built for freight work.

Amongst the smallest and largest tank engines at the Grouping. M.R. 0-4-0ST No. 1507 and one of Whitelegg's L.T. & S.R. 4-6-4-T's which did not appear until after absorbtion by the Midland and never ran in L.T. & S.R. colours. [W. H. Whitworth

One of the varieties of 0-6-2T taken over from the North Stafford Railway.

Deeley designs of 0-6-4T for express passenger work. They were found to be somewhat unsteady at speed and were relegated to freight duties before being withdrawn.

North Stafford 0-6-4T No. 2044.

The famous 0-10-0 banking engine for the Lickey Incline, as originally built in 1919. The only one of its class, it spent its entire working life on this duty until withdrawn in 1956. It eventually became B.R. No. 58100.

One of the earlier Somerset and Dorset 4-4-0's, taken into L.M.S. stock and numbered in the gap created by the scrapping of the original Johnson engines.

Two of the surviving Johnson single wheelers, Nos. 665 and 663. The new initials on the cabside were of a short lived style introduced immediately at the amalgamation.

The second No. 320, another S. & D.J.R. 4-4-0, still carrying the blue livery of that railway.

Johnson's final design cf simple 4-4-0, the large Belpaires of 1900, as later rebuilt withe suprheater.

Deeley's large 4-4-0 simple of 1907. Ten of these engines were built for comparison against the compounds. [L. R. Tomsett

One of Kirtley's long lived double framed well tanks, which were a familiar feature in St. Pancras on empty stock workings until their final disappearance in the 1930's.

One of the earlier well known Deeley Compounds, Including the original five Johnson engines, later modified to conform, 45 were built by the M.R. and a furthur 195 by the L.M.S.

The second 1207, acquired from the S. & D.J.R. in 1930 ,the older Kirtley engine having by that time been broken up.

17335	(543)	17363	(560)	17391	(1335)	17419	(752)	17447	(578)
17336	(544)	17364	(561)	17392	(1337)	17420	(753)	17448	(579)
17337	(545)	17365	(562)	17393	(711)	17421	(754)	17449	(580)
17338	(546)	17366	(563)	17394	(712)	17422	(755)	17450	(581)
17339	(547)	17367	(697)	17395	(713)	17423	(756)	17451	(582)
17340	(551)	17368	(698)	17396	(714)	17424	(757)	17452	(588)
17341	(552)	17369	(699)	17397	(715)	17425	(758)	17453	(589)
17342	(691)	17370	(700)	17398	(716)	17426	(759)	17454	(590)
17343	(692)	17371	(701)	17399	(717)	17427	(760)	17455	(591)
17344	(693)	17372	(702)	17400	(718)	17428	(329)	17456	(592)
17345	(694)	17373	(199)	17401	(719)	17429	(330)	17457	(593)
17346	(695)	17374	(200)	17402	(720)	17430	(331)	17458	(594)
17347	(696)	17375	(201)	17403	(736)	17431	(332)	17459	(595)
17348	(1374)	17376	(202)	17404	(737)	17432	(333)	17460	(596)
17349	(1548)	17377	(256)	17405	(738)	17433	(564)	17461	(597)
17350	(1549)	17378	(257)	17406	(739)	17434	(565)	17462	(598)
17351	(1553)	17379	(258)	17407	(740)	17435	(566)	17463	(599)
17352	(1558)	17380	(261)	17408	(741)	17436	(567)	17464	(761)
17353	(1704)	17381	(334)	17409	(742)	17437	(568)	17465	(762)
17354	(1706)	17382	(336)	17410	(743)	17438	(569)	17466	(763)
17355	(1707)	17383	(338)	17411	(744)	17439	(570)	17467	(764)
17356	(1708)	17384	(339)	17412	(745)	17440	(571)	17468	(765)
17357	(550)	17385	(704)	17413	(746)	17441	(572)	17469	(583)
17358	(554)	17386	(706)	17414	(747)	17442	(573)	17470	(584)
17359	(555)	17387	(709)	17415	(748)	17443	(574)	17471	(585)
17360	(556)	17388	(710)	17416	(749)	17444	(575)	17472	(586)
17361	(557)	17389	(1259)	17417	(750)	17445	(576)	17473	(587)
17362	(559)	17390	(1260)	17418	(751)	17446	(577)		

The 25 locomotives on the duplicate list, i.e., with running numbers over 1000, had been on war service with the R.O.D. and their original numbers had been taken by Pickersgill 0-6-0s or by displaced Jumbo locomotives.

Nearly all of the class survived to have 40000 added to their numbers by B.R.

0-6-0 Manson G. & S.W.R. 2F/3F* '115' Class

Built 1900-10

(Nos. 17523/4 built 1921 new with large boilers)

Some later rebuilt with large boilers*.

Weight:
44 tons
47 tons 14 cwt.*

Boiler Pressure:
165 lbs.; 170 lbs.*

Cylinders:
18″×26″

Driving Wheel Diameter:
5′ 1½″

Tractive Effort:
19,210 lbs.; 19,795 lbs.*

Valve Gear:
Stephenson

Number built: 36.

First loco withdrawn 1928; last loco withdrawn 1937.
No. in service (1/1/23) 36; (1/1/48) 0.

17474	(115)	17482*	(129)	17489*	(116)	17496	(112)	17503*	(111)
17475	(117)	17483*	(131)	17490*	(120)	17497*	(103)	17504*	(113)
17476	(118)	17484	(133)	17491*	(123)	17498*	(104)	17505*	(114)
17477	(119)	17485*	(134)	17492*	(128)	17499*	(106)	17506	(101)
17478	(121)	17486*	(122)	17493*	(132)	17500*	(107)	17507	(102)
17479*	(124)	17487*	(125)	17494	(105)	17501*	(108)	17523*	(150)
17480	(126)	17488*	(130)	17495	(110)	17502*	(109)	17524*	(151)
17481	(127)								

0-6-0 Manson G. & S.W.R. 3F '86' Class

Built 1910

One engine (17509) rebuilt 1920 with larger boiler.

Weight:
46 tons 14 cwt.
47 tons 14 cwt.*

Driving Wheel Diameter:
5′ 1½″

Boiler Pressure:
170 lbs.

Tractive Effort:
19,795 lbs.

Cylinders:
18″×26″

Valve Gear:
Stephenson

Number built: 15.

First loco withdrawn 1930; last loco withdrawn 1936.
No. in service (1/1/23) 15; (1/1/48) 0.

17508	(86)	17511	(89)	17514	(92)	17517	(95)	17520	(98)
17509*	(87)	17512	(90)	17515	(93)	17518	(96)	17521	(99)
17510	(88)	17513	(91)	17516	(94)	17519	(97)	17522	(100)

For locomotives 17523, 17524 see 17474-17507 above.

0-6-0 McIntosh C.R. 3F '812' Class

Built 1899-1909

Weight:
45 tons 13 cwt.

Driving Wheel Diameter:
5′ 0″

Boiler Pressure:
160 lbs.

Tractive Effort:
20,169 lbs.

Cylinders:
18½″×26″

Valve Gear:
Stephenson

Number built: 96.

First loco withdrawn 1948; last loco withdrawn 1963.
No. in service (1/1/23) 96; (1/1/48) 93.

17550 (812)	17570 (832)	17589 (851)	17608 (870)	17627 (292)
17551 (813)	17571 (833)	17590 (852)	17609 (871)	17628 (293)
17552 (814)	17572 (834)	17591 (853)	17610 (872)	17629 (652)
17553 (815)	17573 (835)	17592 (854)	17611 (873)	17630 (653)
17554 (816)	17574 (836)	17593 (855)	17612 (874)	17631 (654)
17555 (817)	17575 (837)	17594 (856)	17613 (875)	17632 (655)
17556 (818)	17576 (838)	17595 (857)	17614 (876)	17633 (656)
17557 (819)	17577 (839)	17596 (858)	17615 (877)	17634 (657)
17558 (820)	17578 (840)	17597 (859)	17616 (878)	17635 (658)
17559 (821)	17579 (841)	17598 (860)	17617 (282)	17636 (659)
17560 (822)	17580 (842)	17599 (861)	17618 (283)	17637 (662)
17561 (823)	17581 (843)	17600 (862)	17619 (284)	17638 (663)
17562 (824)	17582 (844)	17601 (863)	17620 (285)	17639 (664)
17563 (825)	17583 (845)	17602 (864)	17621 (286)	17640 (665)
17564 (826)	17584 (846)	17603 (865)	17622 (287)	17641 (325)
17565 (827)	17585 (847)	17604 (866)	17623 (288)	17642 (326)
17566 (828)	17586 (848)	17605 (867)	17624 (289)	17643 (327)
17567 (829)	17587 (849)	17606 (868)	17625 (290)	17644 (328)
17568 (830)	17588 (850)	17607 (869)	17626 (291)	17645 (661)
17569 (831)				

Nearly all of the class survived to have 40000 added to their numbers by B.R.

0-6-0 McIntosh C.R. 3F
'30' Class

Built 1912

Weight:
51 tons $2\frac{1}{2}$ cwt.

Driving Wheel Diameter:
5′ 0″

Boiler Pressure:
160 lbs.

Tractive Effort:
22,409 lbs.

Cylinders:
$19\frac{1}{2}'' \times 26''$

Valve Gear:
Stephenson

Number built: 4.

First loco withdrawn 1935; last loco withdrawn 1946.
No. in service (1/1/23) 4; (1/1/48) 0.

17646 (30)	17647 (31)	17648 (32)	17649 (33)

0-6-0 Pickersgill C.R. 3F

Built 1918-1920

Weight:
49 tons 5 cwt.

Boiler Pressure:
170 lbs.

Cylinders:
$18\frac{1}{2}'' \times 26''$

Driving Wheel Diameter:
5′ 0″

Tractive Effort:
21,437 lbs.

Valve Gear:
Stephenson

Number built: 43.

First loco withdrawn 1934; last loco withdrawn 1963.
No. in service (1/1/23) 43; (1/1/48) 29.

17650 (294)	17659 (303)	17668 (312)	17677 (321)	17686 (673)
17651 (295)	17660 (304)	17669 (313)	17678 (322)	17687 (674)
17652 (296)	17661 (305)	17670 (314)	17679 (323)	17688 (675)
17653 (297)	17662 (306)	17671 (315)	17680 (324)	17689 (676)
17654 (298)	17663 (307)	17672 (316)	17681 (280)	17690 (677)
17655 (299)	17664 (308)	17673 (317)	17682 (281)	17691 (678)
17656 (300)	17665 (309)	17674 (318)	17683 (670)	17692 (679)
17657 (301)	17666 (310)	17675 (319)	17684 (671)	
17658 (302)	17667 (311)	17676 (320)	17685 (672)	

All twenty-nine survivors at Nationalisation had 40000 added to their numbers.

0-6-0 P. Drummond H.R. 3F

Built 1900-1907

Weight:
43 tons 10 cwt.

Driving Wheel Diameter:
5′ 0″

Boiler Pressure:
160 lbs.

Tractive Effort:
21,454 lbs.

Several engines still carried Drummond boilers, with Pop safety valves on the dome, for some years after the grouping and No. 17702 in addition retained the firebox water tubes. C.R. type boilers were eventually fitted in most cases.

Cylinders:
$18\frac{1}{4}'' \times 26''$

Valve Gear:
Stephenson

Number built: 12.

Some of the engines finally acquired stove-pipe chimneys.

First loco withdrawn 1936; last loco withdrawn 1952.
No. in service (1/1/23) 12; (1/1/48) 7.

17693 (134)	17696 (137)	17699 (18)	17701 (20)	17703 (36)
17694 (135)	17697 (138)	17700 (19)	17702 (21)	17704 (37)
17695 (136)	17698 (139)			

Nos. 57695, 57697 and 57698 lasted to receive their B.R. numbers.

0-6-0 Drummond G. & S.W.R. 4F '71' Class

Built 1913

Weight:
57 tons 14 cwt.

Driving Wheel Diameter:
5′ 0″

Boiler Pressure:
180 lbs.

Tractive Effort:
25,211 lbs.

Cylinders:
$19\frac{1}{2}'' \times 26''$

Valve Gear:
Stephenson

Number built: 15.

First loco withdrawn 1930; last loco withdrawn 1933.

No. in service (1/1/23) 15; (1/1/48) 0.

17750 (71)	17753 (74)	17756 (77)	17759 (80)	17762 (83)
17751 (72)	17754 (75)	17757 (78)	17760 (81)	17763 (84)
17752 (73)	17755 (76)	17758 (79)	17761 (82)	17764 (85)

2-6-0 McIntosh C.R. 3F '34' Class

Built 1912

Weight:
54 tons 5 cwt.

Driving Wheel Diameter:
5′ 0″

Boiler Pressure:
160 lbs.

Tractive Effort:
22,409 lbs.

Cylinders:
$19\frac{1}{2}'' \times 26''$

Valve Gear:
Stephenson

Number built: 5.

First loco withdrawn 1935; last loco withdrawn 1937.

No. in service (1/1/23) 5; (1/1/48) 0.

17800 (34)	17801 (35)	17802 (36)	17803 (37)	17804 (38)

2-6-0 Drummond G. & S.W.R. 4F '51' Class

Built 1915

Weight:
62 tons

Driving Wheel Diameter:
5′ 0″

Boiler Pressure:
180 lbs.

Tractive Effort:
25,209 lbs.

Cylinders:
$19\frac{1}{2}'' \times 26''$

Valve Gear:
Stephenson

Number built: 11.

First loco withdrawn 1935; last loco withdrawn 1947.

No. in service (1/1/23) 11; (1/1/48) 0.

17820 (51)	17823 (54)	17825 (56)	17827 (58)	17829 (60)
17821 (52)	17824 (55)	17826 (57)	17828 (59)	17830 (61)
17822 (53)				

4-6-0 McIntosh C.R. 3F '918' Class

Built 1906

Weight:
60 tons 8 cwt.

Driving Wheel Diameter:
5′ 0″

Boiler Pressure:
175 lbs.

Tractive Effort:
23,269 lbs.

Cylinders:
$19'' \times 26''$

Valve Gear:
Stephenson

Number built: 5.

First loco withdrawn 1929; last loco withdrawn 1930.

No. in service (1/1/23) 5; (1/1/48) 0.

17900 (918)	17901 (919)	17902 (920)	17903 (921)	17904 (922)

4-6-0 McIntosh C.R. 3F ' 179 ' Class

Built 1913-1914

Weight:
68 tons 10 cwt.

Boiler Pressure:
170 lbs.

Cylinders:
$19\frac{1}{2}'' \times 26''$

Driving Wheel Diameter:
5′ 9″

Tractive Effort:
20,704 lbs.

Valve Gear:
Stephenson

Number built: 11.

First loco withdrawn 1935; last loco withdrawn 1946.
No. in service (1/1/23) 11; (1/1/48) 0.

17905 (179)	17908 (182)	17910 (184)	17912 (186)	17914 (188)
17906 (180)	17909 (183)	17911 (185)	17913 (187)	17915 (189)
17907 (181)				

4-6-0 Jones H.R. 4F

Built 1894

This class is notable as being the first 4-6-0 tender engine design in the British Isles.

Weight:
56 tons

Boiler Pressure:
175 lbs.

Cylinders:
$20'' \times 26''$

Driving Wheel Diameter:
5′ 3″

Tractive Effort:
24,555 lbs.

Valve Gear:
Stephenson

Number built: 15.

Some engines lost their smokebox wingplates in later years and had their distinctive louvre type chimney replaced by C.R. pattern. Otherwise the engines remained largely unaltered.

First loco withdrawn 1929; last loco withdrawn 1940.
No. in service (1/1/23) 15; (1/1/48) 0.

No. 17916 was preserved on withdrawal in 1934 as H.R. 103 in green livery. In 1959 it was restored to working order and repainted in Stroudley yellow livery.

17916 (103)	17919 (106)	17922 (109)	17925 (112)	17928 (115)
17917 (104)	17920 (107)	17923 (110)	17926 (113)	17929 (116)
17918 (105)	17921 (108)	17924 (111)	17927 (114)	17930 (117)

4-6-0 C. Cumming H.R. 5F

Built 1917-1919

Weight:
56 tons 9 cwt.

Boiler Pressure:
175 lbs.

Cylinders:
$20\frac{1}{2}'' \times 26''$

Driving Wheel Diameter:
5′ 3″

Tractive Effort:
25,800 lbs.

Valve Gear:
Walschaerts

Number built: 8.

First loco withdrawn 1946; last loco withdrawn 1952.
No. in service (1/1/23) 8; (1/1/48) 6.

17950 (75) 17951 (76)	17952 (77) 17953 (78)	17954 (79) 17955 (80)	17956 (81)	17957 (82)

Nos. 57950/1/4/5/6 survived to carry their B.R. numbers.

0-8-0 McIntosh C.R. 4F ' 600 ' Class

Built 1901-1903

Weight:
60 tons 12 cwt.

Boiler Pressure:
175 lbs.

Cylinders:
$21'' \times 26''$

Driving Wheel Diameter:
4′ 6″

Tractive Effort:
31,584 lbs.

Valve Gear:
Stephenson

Number built: 8.

First loco withdrawn 1927; last loco withdrawn 1929.
No. in service (1/1/23) 8; (1/1/48) 0.

17990 (600) 17991 (601)	17992 (602) 17993 (603)	17994 (604) 17995 (605)	17996 (606)	17997 (607)

The last engine to be scrapped, No. 605, retained its C.R. livery to the end, the others had all meanwhile acquired their L.M.S. numbers.

Steam Rail Motors

The combined engine and coach enjoyed a considerable—but in most cases brief—vogue during the early 1900's as a more economical working of branch lines. Its chief disadvantage was that usually the engine was not powerful enough to propel an additional coach at busy times when traffic was heavier, and these vehicles had a comparatively short life on most lines which adopted them.

Of the L.M.S. constituents, the L.N.W.R. had seven, the M.R. two, the North Stafford three, the Furness one (normally used with a 4 wheel trailer) the G. & S.W.R. three, the largest user of all, the L. & Y.R., eighteen. These last were different from the usual design, in that the engine and coach were detachable and interchangeable. They all lasted into L.M.S. days, but of the others, only the three N.S.R. and the seven L.N.W.R. units, survived into the grouping period. One L. & Y.R. and one L.N.W.R. even managed to last into B.R. days at Nationalisation, albeit only for a short time.

0-2-2T North Stafford Railmotor

Built 1905-6

Weight:
32 tons 10 cwt.

Driving Wheel Diameter:
3′ 8″

Boiler Pressure:
180 lbs.

Tractive Effort:
4,020 lbs.

Cylinders:
8½″ × 16″

Valve Gear:
Walschaerts

Number built: 3.

All withdrawn 1927.
No. in service (1/1/23) 3.

1	2	3	(Railmotor number series)

0-4-0T L.N.W.R. Railmotor

Built 1905-1910

Weight:
44 tons 6 cwt.

Driving Wheel Diameter:
3′ 9″

Boiler Pressure:
175 lbs.

Tractive Effort:
4,479 lbs.

Cylinders:
9½″ × 15″

Number built:
7

First unit withdrawn 1927; last unit withdrawn 1948.
No. in service (1/1/23) 7; (1/1/48) 1.

These units were numbered by both the L.N.W.R. and the L.M.S. in the coaching stock list. Former L.N.W. Nos. in brackets.

10694 (5501) 10695 (5502)	10696 (5503) 10697 (5504)	10698 (5505)	10699 (5506)	10700 (5507)

No. 10698, then the only surviving unit became 29988 in 1933 and as such ran for a further 15 years.

0-4-0T Hughes Lancs. & Yorks. Unclassified

Built 1906-11

Weight:
(Engine) 32 tons 14 cwt.
(Coach) 14 tons 16 cwt.

Boiler Pressure:
160 lbs.

Cylinders:
12″×16″

Driving Wheel Diameter:
3′ 7½″

Tractive Effort:
7,200 lbs.

Valve Gear:
Walschaerts

Number built: 18.

First unit withdrawn 1927; last unit withdrawn 1948.
No. in service (1/1/23) 18; (1/1/48) 1.

The numbers in brackets are the special series used by the L. & Y.R. for their railmotor stock. The L.M.S. numbers are in the ordinary loco series.

10600 (3) 10601 (4) 10602 (5) 10603 (6)	10604 (7) 10605 (8) 10606 (9) 10607 (10)	10608 (11) 10609 (12) 10610 (13) 10611 (14)	10612 (15) 10613 (1) 10614 (2)	10615 (16) 10616 (17) 10617* (18)

*The last survivor was allocated B.R. No. 50617, but never carried it.

Narrow Gauge Lines

The L.M.S. on its formation acquired seven miscellaneous narrow gauge systems of varying sizes and importance, two of which were passenger carrying lines.

The larger of these two was the Leek and Manifold Valley Light Railway, actually an independent Company worked by the North Stafford, and which was absorbed into the L.M.S. at the grouping. This was a line of some eight miles in length which ran through the picturesque Manifold Valley on the borders of Staffordshire and Derbyshire through delightful scenery but very sparsely populated. It closed down in 1934.

The other passenger system was the Wolverton and Stony Stratford, previously owned by the L.N.W.R., and one of the last steam operated roadside tramways in the country (excluding Ireland) at the time of its demise in 1926. (The

Glyn Valley lasted until 1935, and the latterly freight-only Wantage until 1945, and last of all was the Wisbech and Upwell, which became part of the L.N.E.R. also freight only in its later years, but steam operated until 1951, when it was taken over by diesels, and since closed entirely.)

Two small mineral lines were the 4′ 0″ gauge, Nantlle Tramway, formerly L.N.W.R., in North Wales, but as it was worked by horses and never had any locomotives it is outside the scope of this book. The other was the Caldon Low Quarries, in Staffordshire, again a subsidiary of the N.S.R., which had three small saddle tanks of 3′ 6″ gauge.

Then there were the narrow gauge systems at the Crewe and Horwich locomotive works of the L.N.W.R. and L. & Y.R., each of which had a considerable mileage of track around the yards over which heavy items of equipment, such as boilers, could be transported on suitable conveyors hauled by diminutive locomotives. The Crewe system was abandoned in 1929, but a small portion of that at Horwich was still recently in use, although worked latterly by a diesel loco.

Finally, there was another system, practically unknown, belonging to the Permanent Way Department at Crewe, which possessed three engines of 2′ 6″ gauge, which were apparently sent out ' on location ' at various times to operate over temporarily laid track. The first engine ' Jim Crow ' appears to have been purchased by the L.N.W.R. from Messrs. Hudswell Clark & Co., for work at the Diggle Tunnel, and the others came later from Bagnall for similar operations, but apart from this very little is known about these obscure engines, which when not in use were stored at Crewe. But for the fact that they were discovered and photographed by the late W. H. Whitworth and later by Messrs. W. A. Camwell and L. W. Perkins, they would probably have remained unknown. No apology is therefore made of illustrating all three of these quite different engines, it is believed for the first time, apart from one illustration in ' Locomotive Names of the Twentieth Century ' (*H. C. Casserley, published by Ian Allan*).

A further point of interest lies in the fact that they were the only engines possessed by the L.N.W.R. which were not built by the Company itself, at Crewe from very early times right down to 1916, when a large order for ' Prince of Wales ' class 4-6-0's was placed with Messrs. Beardmore and Co.

2-6-4T

Leek & Manifold

Built 1904

(Worked by N.S.R.)

Gauge 2′ 6″

Weight:
26 tons 16 cwt.

Driving Wheel Diameter:
2′ 6″

Boiler Pressure:
150 lbs.

Tractive Effort:
8,963 lbs.

Cylinders:
$11\frac{1}{2}'' \times 16''$

Valve Gear:
Walschaerts

Number built: 2.

First loco withdrawn 1935; last loco withdrawn 1936.
No. in service (1/1/23) 2; (1/1/48) 0.

L.M.V.L.R.	1 E. R. Calthrop	2 J. B. Earle

The engines were never numbered in with the ordinary N.S.R. or L.M.S.R. stock.

0-4-0T Tram Loco — Wolverton & Stony Stratford (L.N.W.R.)

Built 1900

Gauge 4′ 0″

Boiler Pressure:
175 lbs.

Driving Wheel Diameter:
2′ 6″

Cylinders:
$7\frac{1}{2}'' \times 12''$

Tractive Effort:
3,347 lbs.

Number built: 3.

First loco withdrawn before 1923; last loco withdrawn 1926.
No. in service (1/1/23) 1.

W. & S.S. No. 2

0-4-0ST — Wolverton & Stony Stratford (L.N.W.R.)

Built 1921

Gauge 3′ 6″

Weight:
16 tons

Driving Wheel Diameter:
2′ 9″

Boiler Pressure:
150 lbs.

Tractive Effort:
5,795 lbs.

Cylinders:
10″ × 15″

Number built:
1

No. in service (1/1/23) 1. Withdrawn 1926.

W. & S.S. No. 1

0-4-0ST — Caldon Low Quarries

Built 1887-1900

(Worked by N.S.R.)

Gauge 3′ 6″

Cylinders:
7″ × 12″

Driving Wheel Diameter:
2′ 3″

Boiler Pressure:
140 lbs.

Tractive Effort:
2,592 lbs.

Number built: 3.

" Bobs " of 1900 was a somewhat larger engine than the two originals of 1887.

The quarries closed in the early 1930's and the locos presumably scrapped, although whether taken away or cut up on the spot is not known.

Frog	Toad	Bobs

Unnumbered by either N.S.R. or L.M.S.R.

0-4-0T L.N.W.R. works shunter

Built 1862-1875

Gauge 18″

Cylinders:
5½″×6″

Driving Wheel Diameter:
1′ 4″

Number built: 7.

No. in service (1/1/23) 7.
System abandoned 1929 and locos scrapped with the exception of " Pet ".

Tiny Pet*	Nipper Topsy	Midge	Billie	Dickie

*Preserved at Crewe.

0-4-0ST L. & Y.R. works shunter

Built 1887-1901

Gauge 18″

Weight:
3 tons 11½ cwt.

Driving Wheel Diameter:
1′ 4¼″

Boiler Pressure:
180 lbs.

Tractive Effort:
1,434 lbs.

Cylinders:
5″×6″

Valve Gear:
Allan

Number built: 8.

Most of system latterly abandoned, but " Wren " was retained for some years to work the remaining portion. Latterly operated by a diesel loco.

First loco withdrawn 1930; last loco withdrawn 1962.
No. in service (1/1/23) 8; (1/1/48) 1.

Dot Robin	Wren* Fly	Wasp Midget	Mouse	Bee

*Preserved in Clapham Museum.

0-4-2ST L.N.W.R. Permanent Way Dept.

Built 1894

(Hudswell Clarke No. 340)

Gauge 2′ 6″

Cylinders:
6″ × 10″

Driving Wheel Diameter:
1′ 8″

No other dimensions available.

The engine was fitted with a hinged chimney for low tunnel working.

No. in service (1/1/23) 1. Ultimate disposal unknown.

Still in existence 1938 but presumed scrapped during the war period.

Jim Crow

0-4-0ST L.N.W.R. Permanent Way Dept.

Built 1895 and 1914

(Bagnall Nos. 1410 and 1999)

Gauge 2′ 6″

No dimensional particulars available.

The engines differed considerably (see illustrations).

No. in service (1/1/23) 2. Still in existence 1938 but ultimate disposal unknown. Presume scrapped during the war period.

Platelayer	Kitchener

CHIEF MECHANICAL ENGINEERS

L.M.S.

George Hughes	1923–1925
Sir Henry Fowler ...	1925–1931
E. H. J. Lemon (Sir Ernest Lemon)	1931–1932
Sir William Stanier ...	1932–1944
Charles E. Fairburn ...	1944–1945
H. G. Ivatt...	1945–1947

LOCOMOTIVE SUPERINTENDENTS AND C.M.E.'S—L.M.S. CONSTITUENT COMPANIES

CALEDONIAN RAILWAY

Robert Sinclair (First loco. engineer)*	1847–1856
Benjamin Connor... ...	1856–1876
George Brittain	1876–1882
Dugald Drummond ...	1882–1890
Hugh Smellie	1890
J. Lambie	1890–1895
J. F. McIntosh	1895–1914
William Pickersgill ...	1914–1923

FURNESS RAILWAY

R. Mason	1890–1897
W. F. Pettigrew	1897–1918
D. J. Rutherford	1918–1923

GLASGOW AND SOUTH WESTERN RAILWAY

Patrick Stirling	1853–1866
James Stirling	1866–1878
Hugh Smellie	1878–1890
James Manson	1890–1912
Peter Drummond ...	1912–1918
R. H. Whitelegg	1918–1923

HIGHLAND RAILWAY

William Stroudley (First loco. engineer) ...	1866–1869
David Jones	1869–1896
Peter Drummond ...	1896–1911
F. G. Smith	1912–1915
C. Cumming	1915–1923

L. & Y.R.

Sir John Hawkshaw (Consultant),* Hurst and Jenkins successively to 1868

W. Hurst	1868–1876
W. Barton Wright ...	1876–1886
John A. F. Aspinall ...	1886–1899
H. A. Hoy	1899–1904
George Hughes	1904–1921

The L. & Y. amalgamated with L.N.W.R. as from January 1st, 1922.

L.N.W.R.

Francis Trevithick and J. E. McConnell, first loco. engineers, 1846, with Alexander Allan largely responsible for design at Crewe.*

John Ramsbottom ...	1857–1871
Francis William Webb ...	1871–1903
George Whale	1903–1909
Charles John Bowen-Cooke	1909–1920
Capt. Hewitt Pearson Montague Beames ...	1920–1921
George Hughes	1922

L.T. & S.R.

Thomas Whitelegg ...	1880–1910
Robert Harben Whitelegg	1910–1912

(L.T. & S.R. absorbed by M.R., control of locos. transferred to Derby as from August, 1912.)

---

* Exclusive of previous service with constituent company.

LOCOMOTIVE SUPERINTENDENTS AND C.M.E.'S *(continued)*

MARYPORT & CARLISLE

Hugh Smellie	1870–1878
J. Campbell	1878–
William Coulthard ...	* –1904
J. B. Adamson	1904–1923

MIDLAND RAILWAY

Matthew Kirtley (First loco. engineer) ...	1844–1873
Samuel Waite Johnson ...	1873–1903
Richard Mountford Deeley	1903–1909
Henry Fowler	1909–1923

SOMERSET AND DORSET JOINT RAILWAY

Until leased by Mid. and L. & S.W. (as from 1st November, 1875) locomotives were bought from outside builders, principally George England of Hatcham Iron Works, S.E. After the above date, Derby and its various Loco. Supts. and C.M.E.'s have acted for S. & D.J. aided by a resident Loco. Supt. stationed at Highbridge Works.

NORTH STAFFORDSHIRE RAILWAY

L. Clare	1876–1882
L. Longbottom	1882–1902
J. H. Adams	1902–1915
J. A. Hookham	1915–1923

W. Angus was Loco. Supt. at Stoke prior to 1876. No earlier records can be traced.

WIRRAL

Eric G. Barker	1892–1902
T. B. Hunter	1903–1923

Barker of the Wirral Railway is noteworthy for originating the 4-4-4 tank type in this country (1896).

NORTH LONDON RAILWAY

(Worked by L. & N.W. by agreement dated December, 1908.)

William Adams	1853–1873
J. C. Park	1873–1893
Henry J. Pryce	1893–1908

* Date of actual entry into office not known.